Late, Lost, and Unprepared

Does your child have difficulty meeting deadlines, staying organized, or keeping track of important information? Do they tend to forget details? Are they prone to emotional meltdowns? This book will become your go-to, all-inclusive guide to helping children manage issues with these executive functions.

Late, Lost, and Unprepared is packed with encouragement, strategies, overviews, case studies, tips, and more, explained in accessible, everyday language. In this updated and expanded edition of the highly regarded book for parents, you will find valuable new insights, fresh examples, and an all-new chapter on emotional regulation. Featuring down-to-earth examples and a flexible framework that allows you to think on your feet, the strategies within this book can be adapted to any child or situation.

In addition to providing approaches for helping your child to manage demands in the short run, this book offers strategies for building independent skills for long-term self-management. *Late, Lost, and Unprepared* gives parents the support they need to help their child become productive and independent – today and in the future.

Joyce Cooper-Kahn, Ph.D., is a clinical child psychologist who specializes in the treatment of children and adolescents with ADHD, executive functioning challenges, and other learning disabilities.

Laurie Dietzel, Ph.D. (1962–2015), was a clinical psychologist who specialized in the neuropsychological assessment of ADHD, learning disabilities, and other neurodevelopmental disorders. She was a co-author of the first edition of this book. Her work lives on in this edition.

Late, Lost, and Unprepared

A Parents' Guide to Helping Children with Executive Functioning

Second Edition

Joyce Cooper-Kahn, Ph.D. and
Laurie Dietzel, Ph.D.

Routledge
Taylor & Francis Group

NEW YORK AND LONDON

Designed cover image: © Carol Yepes / Getty Images

Second edition published 2024
by Routledge
605 Third Avenue, New York, NY 10158

and by Routledge
4 Park Square, Milton Park, Abingdon, Oxon, OX14 4RN

Routledge is an imprint of the Taylor & Francis Group, an informa business

First edition published by Woodbine House 2008

Library of Congress Cataloging-in-Publication Data
Names: Cooper-Kahn, Joyce, author. | Dietzel, Laurie C., author.
Title: Late, lost, and unprepared: a parents' guide to helping children with
executive functioning / Joyce Cooper-Kahn and Laurie Dietzel.
Description: Second edition. | New York, NY: Routledge, 2024. |
Includes bibliographical references and index.
Identifiers: LCCN 2023050289 (print) | LCCN 2023050290 (ebook) |
ISBN 9781032507835 (paperback) | ISBN 9781003403517 (ebook)
Subjects: LCSH: Executive ability in adolescence. | Executive ability in children. |
Self-management (Psychology) for teenagers. | Self-management (Psychology)
for children. | Self-control in adolescence. | Self-control in children. |
Attention in adolescence. | Attention in children.
Classification: LCC BF723.E93 C66 2024 (print) | LCC BF723.E93 (ebook) |
DDC 155.4/13–dc23/eng/20240208
LC record available at https://lccn.loc.gov/2023050289
LC ebook record available at https://lccn.loc.gov/2023050290

ISBN: 978-1-032-50783-5 (pbk)
ISBN: 978-1-003-40351-7 (ebk)

DOI: 10.4324/9781003403517

Typeset in Bembo
by Deanta Global Publishing Services, Chennai, India

This book is dedicated to the memory of Dr. Laurie Dietzel (1962–2015), my colleague, friend, and co-author of the first edition of this book. Her expertise and compassion brought hope to the lives of countless families. Her insights and sense of humor enriched mine.

Contents

Acknowledgments

I am fortunate to have the support, camaraderie, and friendship of many people in my professional and personal lives.

I treasure the lasting friendships I've made through my work with CHADD, Proyectodah, and through Camp Dendy. Conversations with these and other colleagues have helped me to sharpen my thinking and gain new perspectives on the work we all do.

I want to thank Dr. Janice Lepore for her collaboration on the chapter on assessment. She is an expert psychologist, a legislative policy wonk extraordinaire, a skilled writer, and a fierce advocate for kids.

I also want to thank my friend and colleague, Margaret Foster, M.A.ed., who responds with enthusiasm to my texts (at least most of the time) asking for a "quick" conversation about some aspect of executive functioning or educational practices, though we both know it will more likely be a long call that veers into a discussion about the state of the world.

My family buoys me, inspires me, and brings me joy.

My husband, Michael, is a silent partner in all of my professional and personal strivings. What a gift it is to share my life with someone who totally gets me.

Finally, the children, parents, and teachers I've worked with over the years make my efforts worthwhile. Thank you for trusting me and letting me into your lives.

Joyce Cooper-Kahn

I

What You Need to Know

1

Introduction

> Matthew does all his homework, but half the time he still gets
> zeroes because he doesn't turn it in to the teacher.

> Nikki seems so irresponsible in her work habits even though
> she wants to do well. How will she ever make it in the world?
> Help!

> Every morning we have a major battle in our house. Alan's
> alarm goes off at quarter to seven. I have to remind him to get
> out of bed at least five times, and then I have to keep nagging
> just to get him to brush his teeth and get dressed before the
> bus comes. And he still misses the bus! I'm so tired of going
> through this every morning.

> You should see Mary's backpack! Old papers, gum wrappers,
> homework assignments … what a mess! Her locker looks the
> same way. How can I help her get organized?

Sound familiar? All of these kids have problems with what
professionals call "executive functioning." Think of executive
functioning as the administrator and manager of a complex and busy
system – the system of the human brain. (For more on how executive
function is defined, read on to the next chapter.)

DOI: 10.4324/9781003403517-2

Some of the children in our examples may also have some specific disorder. If your child has an attention disorder, then these scenarios probably sound all too familiar. However, individuals with attention disorders are by no means the only ones who experience executive functioning problems. Problems with executive functioning are generic. Like a rash, executive dysfunction is a symptom that sometimes appears alone and sometimes is part of a larger problem. This broader diagnosis might be a learning disability (L.D.), autism spectrum disorder (A.S.D.), or other condition, such as a range of neurodevelopmental, psychiatric, and medical disorders (more on this in Chapter 7).

Are there kids with no diagnosed disability who struggle with organization, planning, self-control, and time management? Absolutely! We see them in our offices all the time.

We have good news and bad news for you. Here's the good news: There are things you can do – interventions – that help. The interventions in this book are not specific to any disorder. They are designed to be helpful whether or not your child has been diagnosed with ADHD, a learning disability, another developmental condition, or has no formal or specific diagnosis at all. Among those who work with kids with executive dysfunction, there is much accumulated wisdom and experience that can guide you as you work at your job of parenting a disorganized child.

Now the bad news: We do not have all the answers for you. We can make the job easier but we cannot make it easy.

Why Another Book?

If you are reading this book, chances are you are a parent or a teacher or other professional who works with kids. And there is also a good chance that you are frustrated and weary with the effort of trying to help your disorganized kid meet the demands of the world. You may also be confused about how to help.

This book offers practical information about the executive functions, a set of related yet distinct skills that serve as our organizers. These executive functions are complex, but with the proper information you can become the expert that you need to be.

While the number of books on executive functioning has grown in recent years, there is still a great need for straightforward information that speaks directly to parents and professionals. This book is designed to bring science-based information to those who need it most. Our goal is to offer practical strategies that are flexible enough to adapt to many children and situations, and to do so using everyday language.

Further, much of what is out there focuses on what you can do in the short term to help your child through the day. But if all you are doing is getting your child through the day, then you are only doing half your job! You also need strategies that help kids to be successful and independent in the long run.

Perhaps most importantly, we want to offer information that helps you understand the *process* of helping a child with executive dysfunction. Many books on topics related to executive functioning, such as those on study skills, seem to assume that simply giving the child information on how to organize leads to improved daily performance. But it's important to know that building better executive functioning occurs over time, and it requires practice and ongoing support.

Finally, so much of what is out there is so focused on the challenges faced by children with weak executive functioning that there is little attention paid to placing the weaknesses into the context of the whole child. That doesn't do your child justice. You already know that your child or teen has positive qualities that exist side by side with executive weaknesses. Executive functions – whether a strength or weakness – are not the total of a person! So we decided to write a basic guide that would provide:

- Down-to-earth information;
- Practical examples;
- Perspective and a sense of humor;
- A framework of understanding that allows you to think on your feet; and
- Strategies that address both short-term and long-term goals for your child.

Who Are We?

When the first edition of this book was published, we were both clinical psychologists in private practice. In our daily work we provided evaluations of children and adolescents with attention and learning problems, guidance for their parents, and school consultation regarding how to help facilitate these kids' development. (Laurie Dietzel has since passed away, but because much of the collaborative work we originally did on the first edition remains in this new edition, the plural "we" has been preserved throughout the book when referring to our joint experiences and recommendations.)

Through our work with children and adolescents, parents, and teachers, we came to appreciate the importance of the executive functions in academic performance, social interactions, and coping with daily life. As professionals and parents, we learned to value maintaining a sense of humor and reasonable perspective when dealing with these weaknesses, but we also found that executive function weaknesses can be a source of tremendous frustration and stress for kids, parents, and teachers.

These are not just abstract issues. These are issues that parents and kids struggle with every day. We hope that this guide helps you put your efforts where they will do the most good. We understand how much patience and flexibility is required to raise a child with executive weaknesses, and we applaud you for educating yourself and rising to the challenge.

The Plan for This Book

We have organized this book in short chapters so that you can use it as a reference, one topic at a time. Parents are busy people and need practical information to help them feel more comfortable trusting their judgment when making parenting decisions.

Some of you reading these words now are going to read every single word in this book. For others (you know who you are) if you have read this whole introduction, it is likely the longest stretch of reading you are going to do! You are more likely to pick up this book when you are feeling desperate and look for a paragraph, a sentence, anything that helps you at that moment. We know all kinds of parents, and we appreciate all your different styles.

The book is divided into two main parts; the first contains *what you need to know* about executive functions – that is: what they are; how you know if your child has weaknesses in these areas and why; the impact they have on daily life, family, and emotions; and the assessment process. The second part of this book details *what you can do* to help your child with executive weakness, including how to get in the right mind-set to best support your child now and in the future, and specific interventions for day-to-day struggles.

We hope that this book is useful to everyone and invite you to use the book however it makes sense to you. We're rooting for you all!

What Is Executive Functioning?

THE BASICS

> ➤ The executive functions all serve a "command and control" function. Like a GPS, our executive functions work together to help us reach a goal by figuring out the steps needed to get there, monitoring our progress, adjusting our course or speed as needed, and bringing us back from side trips to focus on our destination.
>
> ➤ Executive functions are the foundation for managing life tasks of all types. For example, executive functions are critical for organizing a trip, a research project, or a paper for school.
>
> ➤ Often, when we think of problems with executive functioning, we think of disorganization. However, organization is only one of these important skills.

The term "executive functioning" has become a common buzz-word in schools and psychology offices. This is more than just a passing fad. In fact, neuropsychologists have been studying these skills for many years. We believe that the focus on executive functioning represents a significant advancement in our understanding of children (and adults!) and their unique profiles of strengths and weaknesses.

DOI: 10.4324/9781003403517-3

A Formal Definition of Executive Functioning

The executive functions are a set of processes that all have to do with managing ourselves and our internal resources in order to achieve a goal. It is an umbrella term for the neurologically based skills involving mental control and self-regulation.

What mental processes are covered under this umbrella? Different researchers and practitioners have their own favorite lists, although the overall concept is similar. We use the list proposed by Dr. Gerard A. Gioia et al. (2000), incorporating changes based on their later research. These psychologists developed their understanding of executive functions through sound research. They created a rating scale that helps parents, teachers, and professionals understand the executive profile of individual children and teens, allowing us to think more specifically about how to help. More on this is discussed later in this chapter.

Before looking at the list of specific characteristics encompassed by the broad category of executive functions, we'd like to provide an example that makes the concepts more concrete.

Understanding Executive Functions by Looking at Life without Them

Thinking about what life is like for someone with weak executive functioning gives us a better understanding of the way these core skills affect our ability to manage life tasks. In the interest of making the concepts immediately relevant and meaningful, our example focuses on an adult, since we assume that most people reading this book are adults, too. In the rest of the book, we focus on examples of executive functioning in younger people.

The Road Trip without a Map

We'd like to tell you a story about our friend, Robin, who lives life without the benefit of strong executive functioning. Robin is a composite of many individuals we have known, and she struggles with weaknesses in executive skills, despite her well-intentioned efforts to reform herself.

One day in May, Robin gets a phone call from her Aunt Sue in Merryville, Missouri. Aunt Sue is planning a family reunion in July, and she wants to know if Robin and her family can come. All of the extended family will be there. The little town will be overrun with relatives, and it's going to be a great corralling of the family from all across the United States. Robin is excited at the prospect and eagerly says, "Of course we'll be there! We wouldn't miss it!"

Aunt Sue gives Robin all the particulars, including the dates of the reunion and places to stay. Robin rummages around in the kitchen junk drawer for a pencil while her aunt talks, but she never does find one with a point on it. She promises herself to find a pencil and write down all the details just as soon as she gets off the phone. But by the time she hangs up, she can't remember the specifics. She makes a mental note to call back soon to get the dates.

That evening, Robin excitedly tells her husband, Dan, and their two children about the reunion. Dan asks when it will take place. "Sometime in July. I don't remember exactly."

He says, "Well, please find out this week because I have to request vacation time at work."

Their 15-year-old son exclaims, "Hey, I thought July was when I was supposed to go to Band Camp!"

"Didn't you remember?" Robin's daughter practically shouts, "I'm going to Ocean City with Julie and her family sometime in July."

Robin blows up at them all, yelling, "Why are you all being so negative? This is supposed to be fun!" Robin's irritation with her family leads her to be short-tempered with them for the rest of the evening.

About once a week, Robin's husband reminds her to get the information about the reunion. She promises to do so. (And she really means to get around to it!) Finally, in June, Dan gets very annoyed and says, "Do it now! I'm going to stay right here in the kitchen until you call!" Robin makes the call and gets the dates as well as the other particulars. Her husband harrumphs around the house the rest of the evening because now he has only three weeks left before the requested time off. Luck is on their side, though, because he manages to arrange the vacation around work, and the reunion dates don't conflict with the kids' activities.

Over the next three weeks, thoughts about the trip float through Robin's head from time to time. She thinks about how the kids will need to have things to do in the car since it's a long trip. She thinks about taking food and snacks for the ride. She thinks about getting her work at the office cleared up in advance so she can be free of commitments for the vacation. She thinks, "I really should take care of that stuff."

A few days before it's time to leave for the two-day drive to Missouri, she starts piling stuff into their new van, including clothes and other supplies. (You can only imagine what the inside of this van looks like!)

Finally, it's time to pile the people into the van, too. On the way out of the house, one of the kids asks, "Who will be taking care of the cats while we're gone?" Robin moans, "Oh no! I forgot about that. We can't just leave them here to die, and there's no one to take care of them! Now we can't go. What will we tell Aunt Sue?" Dan takes over and starts calling around the neighborhood until he finds a teenager who can do the pet sitting. The crisis passes. The cats will be fine.

So, they're off. Dan drives the first shift. He pulls out of the neighborhood, gets onto the main highway, and then asks, "So, what's the game plan? What's the route?"

Robin answers, "Missouri is west, so I know we have to go west."

He looks at Robin incredulously and says, "You don't know any more details than *that*? What's the plan? Didn't you figure out a route? Pull up the hotel reservations and we can put the address into the GPS to map out our first day of driving." And, of course, Robin says, "Reservations? I thought we could just watch for places to stay along the highway. Anyway, I still haven't figured out how to use the GPS in this car."

Robin's husband sighs and shakes his head. "Oh no! Another road trip without a map!" He hands his phone to his daughter and asks her to use the navigation app to plan a route to Merryville." Turning to his wife, he says, "Why didn't you tell me you were having trouble getting it all organized? I could have helped."

Robin replies, "I didn't have any trouble. Everything is fine. We're in the car, aren't we? We'll get there. What are you so upset about?"

A List of Executive Functions

With this example as a base, let's turn back to the question of what specific abilities are covered under the umbrella term of executive functioning. Below is the list of executive functions described by Dr. Gioia and his colleagues. We've included a specific illustration of each executive function from our case study of Robin in parentheses after each definition.

1. **Inhibition:** The ability to stop ourselves from acting on impulse, including sometimes stopping ourselves from immediate actions or re-directing our thoughts. Inhibition gives us a cushion of thought between our immediate urges and our actions. The flipside of inhibition is impulsivity; if you have weak ability to stop yourself from acting on your impulses, then you are "impulsive." (When Aunt Sue called, it would have made sense for Robin to tell her, "Let me check the calendar first. It sounds great, but I just need to look at everybody's schedules before I commit the whole family.")

2. **Shift:** The ability to move freely from one situation to another and to think flexibly in order to respond to changing circumstances or expectations. (When the question emerged regarding who would watch the cats, Robin was stymied. Her husband, on the other hand, began generating possible solutions and was able to solve the problem easily.)

3. **Emotional Control:** The ability to bring thought to bear on our feelings, allowing us to influence our own emotions. (The example here is Robin's outburst of anger and frustration when confronted with her own impulsive behavior in committing the family before checking out the dates. She didn't consider that she had jeopardized the plans of other family members.)

4. **Initiation:** The ability to start a task in a timely manner and to independently generate ideas, responses, or problem-solving strategies. (Robin thought about calling to check on the date of the reunion, but she just didn't get around to it until her husband initiated the process.)

5. **Working Memory:** The capacity to hold information in our minds for the purpose of completing a task. (Robin could not keep the dates of the reunion in her head long enough to put them on the calendar after her initial phone call from Aunt Sue. While this is an example of a straightforward working memory task, this

process applies to much more complex tasks as well. For more on this, see Chapter 14.)

6. **Planning/Organization:** The ability to manage tasks by breaking them down into a step-by-step series of actions needed to achieve the desired result. (In this case, Robin lacked the ability to systematically think about what the family would need to be ready for the trip and to get to the intended place at the intended time with their needs cared for along the way.)

7. **Task Monitoring:** The ability to assess our own progress toward a goal and to adjust our plan or pace so that we remain on target to achieve the desired result. (Robin does not see a problem with her management of the trip, either during the planning process or once Dan points out the holes in her planning.)

8. **Organization of Materials:** The ability to manage our "stuff" in an orderly way, including organizing work, play, and storage spaces. (It was Robin's job to organize the things needed for the trip. Her approach? She just piled things into the car. Someone who was better at organizing might have approached the task more systematically, creating a checklist of what they needed, and organizing things so important items would be easily accessible and so that the space would be used efficiently.)

9. **Self-Monitoring:** The ability to monitor our own emotions and behavior and to measure them against a standard of what is needed or expected. (When discussing the timing of the trip, Robin does not see that her own behavior is the cause of her family's concerns. She blames them instead, so she gets stuck in her own short-tempered response.)

The executive functions are a diverse, but related and overlapping, set of processes. To understand your child's executive challenges, it is important to look at what areas of executive functioning are problematic and to what degree. There are formal rating scales that can be used to collect the observations of your child's strengths and weaknesses. You will learn more about these and about the assessment process in Chapter 6. For an informal assessment of your child, complete the Core Executive Skills worksheet (Table 2.1).

Table 2.1 Core Executive Skills Worksheet

EXECUTIVE SKILL	DEFINITION	IMPACT
Planning and Organization	The ability to create a structure that brings order to information, materials and tasks, including determining the action steps needed to reach a goal.	Individuals with poor planning and organizational skills have difficulty breaking down a task into smaller steps to reach a goal. They also have trouble creating a cognitive schema to organize information. Rather than organizing new information into a hierarchy or categories in their mind, they tend to hold on to a collection of facts. It is as if they have a file cabinet, but they just open the drawers and throw things in rather than creating files and placing information into an appropriate file folder. They may take the same haphazard approach to organizing materials as they do to organizing information in their heads.
What I see in my child:		
Working Memory	The cognitive process that allows us to hold information in mind while we work toward a goal; it is a dynamic process that involves capturing new information and retrieving previously stored information, all while we manipulate and update the data on our mental scratch pads.	Individuals with weak working memory may have difficulty holding on to multiple bits of information long enough to complete a task, such as remembering a short grocery list long enough to buy what they need or completing all the steps in multistep directions. Working memory is also critical for more complex tasks that require students to hold information over time until a goal is reached, such as completing a long-term assignment. Students may forget to do parts of the assignment or may not remember from one day to the next what they were going to include in a paper.
What I see in my child:		
Initiation	The ability to begin a task independently and in a timely manner.	Without good ability to initiate, children and teens may seem to procrastinate about starting tasks or may appear non-compliant with demands.
What I see in my child:		
Task Monitoring	The ability to monitor one's own performance and to measure it against a standard of what is needed for any given task.	Task monitoring allows someone to consider their own progress toward a goal and to adjust their plans if they are going off course. In the absence of effective task monitoring, students may not adjust the content or the pace of their work in keeping with changing conditions or feedback from the environment.

(Continued)

14

Table 2.1 (Continued)

EXECUTIVE SKILL	DEFINITION	IMPACT
What I see in my child:		
Self-Monitoring	The ability to observe one's own behavior and determine whether it conforms to explicit behavioral expectations and unwritten social rules.	Good self-monitoring allows someone to fluidly adjust their behavior in response to overt environmental feedback and more subtle social cues, such as facial reactions or the modeling of peers. Without good self-monitoring, children and teens will miss the signs that what they are doing is inappropriate or irritating to others, so they are prone to behavioral problems and social isolation.
What I see in my child:		
Inhibition	The ability to "put on the brakes" or to stop and think before acting.	Without good ability to inhibit behaviors and thoughts, individuals are impulsive and unfocused, and they tend to act before thinking about the consequences.
What I see in my child:		
Emotional Control	The ability to be thoughtful, flexible, and intentional about how we respond to our own feelings.	Individuals with weak emotional control tend to have strong, immediate, poorly controlled emotional and behavioral reactions.
What I see in my child:		
Shifting	The ability to "change gears," also described as cognitive flexibility, allows us to adapt to new or unexpected situations and to generate a variety of ways to view a situation or solve a problem.	People with weak ability to shift tend to get stuck in rigid patterns of thinking and behavior. They also have trouble transitioning from one activity to another.
What I see in my child:		

Executive skills framework adapted from G. Gioia et al., 2000; An earlier version of this table appeared in *Boosting Executive Skills in the Classroom: A Practical Guide for Educators*, by Joyce Cooper-Kahn and Margaret Foster. Copyright © 2013 by John Wiley & Sons, Inc.

How This Book Is Organized

This book addresses all of the executive functions listed by Dr. Gioia and his colleagues. For the sake of simplicity, we've combined functions that have similar interventions into single chapters in Part II of this book. For example, we merged three functions above – *Planning/Organization*, *Task Monitoring*, and *Organization of Materials* – into one in Chapter 15: Helping Children to Plan and Organize.

The strategies detailed in the second half of this book will help children with the following functions:

- Impulse control;
- Cognitive flexibility (shifting gears);
- Initiating (getting started);
- Working memory;
- Planning and organization;
- Self-monitoring;
- Emotional regulation.

Final Thoughts

Understanding your child's executive functioning abilities gives you insights into one important aspect of their profile. However, knowing about an individual's executive skills does not tell us how smart or charming or verbally expressive that person is. Nor does it teach us about the person's musical and athletic abilities, temperament, or a host of other important factors. While people with executive dysfunction share a weakness in the command-and-control system, they are as unique as the proverbial snowflake.

3

Development of the Executive Functions

- ➤ Like other skills, the executive functions follow a developmental course.
- ➤ Development of these important mental control skills is related to both brain maturation and experience (nature and nurture).
- ➤ Executive processes unfold over a long developmental period. Cognitive control is not fully developed until the mid-20s while the development of emotional control continues into the early 30s.
- ➤ There is considerable variability in the rate at which children develop executive control.
- ➤ Intellectual ability is different from executive capacity; very bright children may have weak executive functioning.
- ➤ At younger ages, development of basic impulse control and rudimentary planning begins. As children age, maturation and learning bring more refined skills, including the ability to think and problem-solve more flexibly and to work more efficiently.

DOI: 10.4324/9781003403517-4

To set realistic expectations for our children, it is important to understand the typical, or expected, development of the executive functions. Just as we expect children to walk and talk by certain ages, we expect them to learn to plan, organize, and manage tasks more efficiently and independently as they get older.

The development of executive skills is related both to the biological process of brain maturation (nature) and experience (nurture). This development moves kids from dependence on adult-provided structure and support to more independent, flexible ways of thinking and acting. There is considerable variability in the rate at which children develop executive control. Some children experience delays in the development of these important skills. Some may catch up, while others continue to experience some executive weaknesses as adults.

Simply put, we know that successful executive functioning depends upon sound development of brain structures, brain circuits, and communication systems within the brain. The brain's frontal lobes play a crucial role in executive functioning. However, executive functioning is achieved through the engagement of networks and processes in the brain that are more complex and widespread than was once thought.

The brain development supporting good executive functioning also takes longer than we once believed. Development of the executive functions associated with cognitive regulation is typically accomplished at about 25 years of age. Emotional and behavioral regulation takes even longer to develop, not achieving full maturity until the early 30s. (See Denckla 2019, for an overview.) Think about what that means for people with delays in these areas!

The good news about the extended timeline of development of executive networks in the brain is that there is a large window of time for input. In Part II of this book, you will learn about how to offer that critically important input.

There are many good books that lay out the complexities of neuroanatomy and brain development. Because this discussion is not within the scope of this book, our bibliography at the end of the book includes resources that do a great job of explaining the intricate balance between nature and nurture in this process.

Why Is My Child Having Problems with Executive Skill Development?

When parents first come to see us, they are often worried about what is causing their child's executive weaknesses and whether they are to blame. Here are examples of the questions we are frequently asked: "My wife is very disorganized; does this run in families?" "Does it mean my child is brain damaged if he has been diagnosed with executive dysfunction?" "When I was pregnant with Sara, I had an occasional glass of wine. Could that have caused her problems?"

In keeping with our very brief overview of the development of executive functioning, above, it's important to remember that executive functions follow a complex and extended path to full maturation. For many children with executive weaknesses, there is no identifiable cause. The delay becomes evident during the course of typical unfolding of the developmental process, but most often we cannot trace it back to a single event or factor that interfered with brain development. For most kids who experience executive function delays, these weaknesses are likely due to inefficient communication among brain regions rather than any overt, localized problems, such as damage in one specific area.

We *do* know that exposure to alcohol, certain drugs, or toxins during pregnancy, as well as premature birth, are all risk factors for delays in cognitive development. Kids who experienced early abuse, neglect, or other traumatic experiences are also vulnerable to delays in development. Additionally, we know that executive weaknesses (related to ADHD and learning disabilities) run in families, although we do not yet understand exactly how this genetic transmission works (except for some genetic syndromes such as Turner syndrome, velocardiofacial syndrome, and fragile X syndrome). Finally, we know that a disease process or injury to the brain may result in *acquired* executive dysfunction in kids who were previously developing typically.

The science of epigenetics focuses on how genetics and environmental input (ranging from environmental toxins to social-emotional relationships) work together to determine the expression of individual characteristics. However, we are still a long way from understanding the various contributing factors and how they operate in concert in regard to executive functioning abilities. (To learn more about the field of epigenetics and how it operates in the specific case of ADHD, see Nigg 2017.)

The bottom line is clear: parents can do a fine job of providing what a child needs, and that child can still experience delays in the development of executive functioning.

I.Q. and Executive Functioning

Many people assume that children with strong intelligence naturally have good executive skills. We expect smart kids to also have excellent work habits and the ability to easily manage daily demands at home and school. However, intelligence and executive skills are only moderately correlated. That means that a highly gifted student may experience below average impulse control, planning, and organizational skills. After all, the ability to intellectually analyze and understand a task does not mean that a child can efficiently get started on and complete the task. On the other end of the spectrum, although most people with significant intellectual disabilities also have weak executive skills, we have met many kids who perform below average on I.Q. tests yet have good ability to learn routines and manage daily tasks.

Typical Development

The Preschool Years

Infants and very young children "live in the moment" and push for immediate gratification of their needs and wants. Although one-year-olds begin to develop the ability to work toward a goal (e.g., "I want that toy"), they can often be distracted with the offer of something else that is appealing to them. They become more persistent as they begin to be better able to hold an idea in mind and to think beyond the distractions in their way. Toddlers usually remain quite impulsive, gradually increasing their abilities to make simple plans and organize their behavior and their play. To a great extent, this development mirrors the development of language, as words serve as the internal symbols that let the young child begin to think and plan. Most two- and three-year-olds are able to delay gratification for a few minutes to attain a goal.

Jimmy is a three-year-old who loves playing with his train set. However, he has learned that he has to get dressed and brush his teeth before playtime. Jimmy still needs to have a parent close by who reminds him to follow the routine, which is age appropriate. In contrast to most one-year-olds and some two-year-olds, he can often stay in control of his impulses long enough to complete the less desirable tasks in order to get to what he most wants to do.

Elementary School

O nce a child enters school, they encounter increasing demands to finish tasks and control their impulses. Children whose executive skills are developing as expected begin to think more flexibly about solving problems, although they continue to be quite focused on the "here and now." As kids proceed through elementary school, they show steady development of their planning, organizational, and self-monitoring skills and become more efficient when completing work. Working memory (the ability to hold information and directions in mind and to update that information, as needed, in order to perform a task) also continues to develop. It is reasonable to expect most second- and third-graders to be able to easily follow two- to three-step directions and to remain focused in class for relatively long periods of time. Many fourth and fifth graders are able to do a pretty good job organizing their notebooks, desks, and lockers on their own, although they may still need reminders and "check-ins" from their parents and teachers.

Lance is a typical third-grader. Although his ability to accurately record his homework assignments, complete in-class work independently, and get ready for school and bed is improving, he still needs reminders. Lance needs help a few times a week with organizing his backpack and cleaning his room and classroom cubby. While he is becoming more independent with his daily homework, he still needs considerable assistance completing long-term projects and editing his written work.

Middle School

B y about age 11 or 12, most kids are able to independently manage the daily routine at home and at school. From about age ten on, the more complex executive skills play an increasing role and build upon the impulse control and basic task management skills that were developed at earlier ages. These include time management, sequencing more complex tasks, keeping track of several bits of information at the same time, setting goals, and organizing tasks. Older children and pre-teens begin to be more effective at monitoring their own behavior and adjusting their approach when their first attempts to complete tasks are not successful.

Jenny is a seventh grader whose parents have noticed a big jump in her ability to manage her homework. She usually gets started on her own, does a good job completing the work accurately (and without rushing to finish), and has started to use an agenda book and calendar app to plan for tests and long-term projects.

In conjunction with the natural unfolding of development, even kids with age-typical executive functioning may need some help learning how to manage the increased demands of middle/junior high school. The change from one primary teacher to multiple teachers that generally occurs as children enter middle school requires increased organizational skills. Most students benefit from preparation before this transition and explicit instruction in how to keep track of assignments, effectively use a locker, and coordinate daily schedules. When students must check several different websites to monitor their homework assignments and grades from different teachers, it is particularly difficult to master the challenge of staying on top of their work. Many students benefit from some assistance and support to build the routine of a daily check of information posted by teachers online.

High School

During the high school years, growth occurs in the form of fine-tuning skills in independent planning and organization. For most students, work that once took considerable effort becomes more automatic and faster. Teens whose executive skill development is on track will show more flexible thinking and the ability to independently manage more demanding academic work.

Rick is a 15-year-old who no longer needs reminders to complete his weekly chores or to pack up his equipment and be ready to leave for soccer practice on time. He has internalized the daily and weekly schedule, and although he is not consciously aware of it, he now plans and organizes his days to include all that he needs and wants to do. The only times that he needs reminders and parental support are when he is overtired or at the end of the school semester during "crunch" time.

Research shows that during adolescence, most kids are able to work more efficiently and to handle more complex demands and tasks. The demands increase accordingly. Because of the increased expectations, students with executive weaknesses often need more external structure and support than they did in earlier grades. Of course, this needs to be provided in a sensitive way that does not lead to overdependence or compromise a student's self-esteem.

Forming social relationships and fitting in are so important for many adolescents that they may show better impulse control and planning in the social arena than in the academic domain.

Jeana is a disorganized 16-year-old who was able to plan an amazing party when her parents were away. This does not mean that she has strong planning ability across the board; rather, she was able to rise to the occasion to reach a specific short-term goal that was intrinsically motivating to her.

Teens who cannot keep up with the rapid-fire rate of communication and have a hard time reading between the lines often face increasing social difficulties.

Rowan is a very bright 14-year-old who tends to blurt things out and interrupt others (due to a delay in the development of inhibition). Although he was popular in elementary school, he now has trouble keeping friends and doesn't understand why.

Young Adulthood

During the late teens and early twenties, an individual's neurological systems continue to mature, with corresponding development of executive functioning. With experience and continued brain development come better judgment, planning, and flexibility, all of which serve young adults well as they pursue further education, enter the workplace, develop intimate relationships, or assume family responsibilities.

Carlos is a 19-year-old who made a fairly smooth transition from high school to college. After missing a few too many 8:00 a.m. classes as a college freshman, he figured out what he needed to do to successfully manage his courses while also enjoying a good amount of socializing. Now, in his sophomore year, he is applying for summer jobs and planning for his junior year abroad. Although Carlos enjoys age-appropriate executive skills, he still needs some financial, emotional, and practical support from his parents.

Some young adults are late bloomers who may have difficulty in college or in their first work experiences but are then able to manage much better with continued maturation and experience. If your child fits into this category, you may need to provide more practical and emotional support for a longer time than you had planned or than was needed for your other children. Although some kids catch up, others need to develop ways of managing executive weaknesses as adults.

Special Transition Considerations

For some young adults with executive delays, the transition from high school to college is a difficult one. Although a college education has great value, it is important to be creative and to keep an open mind when considering post-secondary options. Many different roads lead to independence and success in life. And sometimes the road winds quite a bit along the way.

For many students with executive weaknesses, a traditional college works well if the student has sufficient accommodations. (An accommodation is a change that is made to help level the playing field for a student who learns differently. Accommodations do not change the content of what the student is learning but instead may involve differences in how academic material is presented or in how the student is asked to show what they have learned.)

Olivia is a very bright 18-year-old who entered her freshman year with great hope and enthusiasm. However, she quickly became overwhelmed by the need to manage her time effectively and plan ahead. By midterm exams, she was behind in her reading and was also having lots of trouble getting started on papers. By the end of the semester, no amount of cramming was sufficient to help her pass all of her courses, and she was placed on academic probation. With her parents' support, she decided to take a reduced course load (an accommodation) the following semester and to work with an academic coach to help her build her executive skills. Her grades improved, and she began to feel more confident and hopeful again. She continues to take one less course each semester than the typical course load. She will graduate one year later than the students with whom she started.

For students with severe executive weaknesses who plan to attend college, it sometimes works best to seek a school with a specific program for students with learning disabilities.

Sometimes, the path that leads directly from high school graduation to college in the Fall is not the best one. Time off between high school and college may be spent in an organized gap year program or may be used for working. The time may extend over many years. The most important point here is that some young adults who will eventually seek formal higher education need time and life experience for further maturation and to develop the determination that comes with clearer goals.

Some people have strengths that lend themselves to careers for which college is not needed. Mentorships, apprentice positions, and other types of job opportunities that feature hands-on learning may provide the best education and job connections for these individuals.

How Do I Know If My Child's Executive Skills Are Developing Normally?

Most parents know to seek help if their child is not walking by age two or talking by age three. But when should a child be able to organize their notebook or keep track of their soccer clothes? Development varies widely and it is probably most useful to keep an eye on how peers are doing with these tasks. Teachers can also help you determine if your child seems to be on target with executive skills needed for school success.

Unlike skills such as sitting up without support, stringing two words together, or recognizing primary colors, executive skills are never demonstrated in isolation; they overlap with motor, language, memory, and other cognitive skills. In their book entitled *Executive Skills in Children and Adolescents*, Drs. Peg Dawson and Richard Guare present a list of grade-typical developmental tasks requiring executive skills. (See Table 3.1.) This table provides an overview of behaviors that are expected at various stages when a child is developing executive functions at a typical pace. If you have questions about whether your child's development is on target, you may find that a consultation with a professional, such as a psychologist or pediatrician, may be helpful. For more information regarding the evaluation process, refer to Chapter 6.

Table 3.1 Developmental Tasks Requiring Executive Skills

AGE RANGE	DEVELOPMENTAL TASK
Preschool	Run simple errands (e.g., "Get your shoes from the bedroom"). Tidy bedroom or playroom with assistance. Perform simple chores and self-help tasks with reminders (e.g., clear dishes from table, brush teeth, get dressed). Inhibit behaviors: don't touch a hot stove, run into the street, grab a toy from another child, hit, bite, push, etc.
Kindergarten – Grade 2	Run errands (two to three step directions). Tidy bedroom or playroom. Perform simple chores, self-help tasks; may need reminders (e.g., make bed). Bring papers to and from school. Complete homework assignments (20 minutes maximum). Decide how to spend money (allowance). Inhibit behaviors: follow safety rules, don't swear, raise hand before speaking in class, keep hands to self.
Grades 3–5	Run errands (may involve time delay or greater distance, such as going to a nearby store or remembering to do something after school). Tidy bedroom or playroom (may include vacuuming, dusting, etc.). Perform chores that take 15–30 minutes (e.g., clean up after dinner, rake leaves) Bring books, papers, assignments to and from school. Keep track of belongings when away from home. Complete homework assignments (one hour maximum). Plan simple school projects such as book reports (select book, read book, write report). Keep track of changing daily schedule (i.e., different activities after school). Save money for desired objects; plan how to earn money. Inhibit/self-regulate: behave when teacher is out of the classroom; refrain from rude comments, temper tantrums, bad manners.
Grades 6–8	Help out with chores around the home, including both daily responsibilities and occasional tasks (e.g., emptying dishwasher, raking leaves, shoveling snow); tasks may take 60–90 minutes to complete. Babysit younger siblings or for pay. Use system for organizing schoolwork, including assignment book, notebooks, etc. Follow complex school schedule involving changing teachers and changing schedules. Plan and carry out long-term projects, including tasks to be accomplished and reasonable timeline to follow; may require planning multiple large projects simultaneously. Plan time, including after school activities, homework, family responsibilities; estimate how long it takes to complete individual tasks and adjust schedule to fit. Inhibit rule breaking in the absence of visible authority.

(Continued)

Table 3.1 (Continued)

AGE RANGE	DEVELOPMENTAL TASK
High School	Manage schoolwork effectively on a day-to-day basis, including completing and handing in assignments on time, studying for tests, creating and following timelines for long-term projects, and making adjustments in effort and quality of work in response to feedback from teachers and others (e.g., grades on tests, papers).
	Establish and refine a long-term goal and make plans for meeting that goal. If the goal beyond high school is college, the youngster selects appropriate courses and maintains G.P.A. to ensure acceptance into college. The youngster also participates in extracurricular activities, signs up for and takes S.A.T.s or A.C.T.s at the appropriate time and carries out the college application process. If the youngster does not plan to go to college, they pursue vocational courses and, if applicable, employment outside of school to ensure the training and experience necessary to obtain employment after graduation.
	Make good use of leisure time, including obtaining employment or pursuing recreational activities during the summer.
	Inhibit reckless and dangerous behaviors (e.g., use of illegal substances, sexual acting out, shoplifting, or vandalism).

From Dawson, P. & Guare, R. *Executive Skills in Children and Adolescents: A Practical Guide to Assessment and Intervention.* New York, NY: Guilford Press, 2018. (Reprinted with permission.)

4

The Child's Experience of Executive Weaknesses

THE BASICS

> Efficient executive functioning is important for managing the practical demands of daily life.

> Executive weaknesses affect a child both in and out of school, so the impact of weak executive functioning can be quite profound.

> Executive skills, such as impulse control and cognitive flexibility, also play a crucial role in managing social situations and dealing with stress.

> Some effects of executive weaknesses are direct, in that the child or teen has trouble meeting expectations. Other effects are indirect, affecting a person's self-esteem and attitude.

> As parents, it is important to put ourselves in our child's place to understand their experience and to maintain a compassionate, helpful approach.

As frustrating and worrisome as it can be to raise a youngster with executive skill weaknesses, it is all the more frustrating for the child. Whether a child expresses this frustration openly or presents an "I don't care" façade, their emotional development is intricately

DOI: 10.4324/9781003403517-5

interwoven with their acquisition of executive skills. Sometimes, we need to step back and consider how these executive weaknesses affect the child's experience. How can we maintain a helpful, supportive approach without empathy for the child?

After all, executive skills must be considered in the context of a developing human being. At the same time that executive skills are progressing, kids are also developing emotionally, and their experiences of themselves and their environment are coalescing into a self-image. The feedback that they get from the world around them, including from adults and peers, contributes positively or negatively to self-esteem and to the child's developing identity.

Weak executive skills do not just affect a youngster's school perfor-mance, although this is often the impetus for seeking help. Kids receive feedback from people and from their environment in numerous ways over the course of a single day. So, let's look at a typical day and con-sider the child's experience of the daily routine. In the second half of the book, we offer suggestions for how you can help your child to meet these expectations. For now, though, let's focus on understanding how struggles with the daily routine might affect your child.

Daily Life

Getting Started

The sun comes up and it's another new day! Full of hope and enthusiasm, you head into your daughter's room. Her alarm is beeping, but she is still lying in bed and has the covers pulled up to shut out the light and the sound. In your most cheerful voice you say, "Time to get up, sweetheart. The bus will be here in 45 minutes." That may be the last positive thing she hears from you that morning!

Think about what we ask of a child every morning: get up on time, shift from sleep mode into action mode, keep track of time, complete a sequence of tasks that culminates in being dressed, fed, presentable, and ready to head out the door with all that they need for the day.

Disorganized kids may become distracted or lose track of what they are supposed to be doing. Since many of them have problems keeping track of time, they only realize they are not ready at the very last minute (when they hear an irritated parent call out their name). Children with initiation difficulties need considerable help "getting going" and "keeping going." We have talked to many parents who have discovered their child half-dressed and playing in their room when it is time to leave for school. We have also talked to many children who report that they just lose track of time. Often children promise to do better, because they feel bad about their lapses and really want to do what their parents are asking of them. Despite their promises, they have no clue how to change the situation.

Off to School

Schoolwork demands increasing levels of organization as the child progresses from one grade to the next. Kids with executive weaknesses typically have more difficulty with each passing year. The most critical changes in school demands occur in mid–elementary school and at the transitions to middle and high school.

At all levels, though, adequate executive functions are generally taken for granted. Here are just some of the behaviors that we expect of children at school:

- Pay attention to the teacher;
- Remember and follow instructions;
- Refrain from socializing with friends during class;
- Remember their locker combination;
- Bring the appropriate books and materials to class;
- Work efficiently and rapidly on timed tasks;
- Work slowly and carefully on more complex assignments;
- Use a tablet or laptop computer for school tasks while resisting gaming, checking email, or other activities online that compete for their attention;
- Move easily from room to room and subject to subject.

For students with executive weaknesses, a school day is filled with challenges to their performance and self-esteem. A child with weak working memory may struggle to follow directions and to hold on to prior learning while simultaneously integrating it with new information. A child with weak task monitoring skills may miss important details of the assignment and not notice that the work is not up to standard. When a student has trouble with cognitive flexibility, changes or transitions throughout the school day may result in anxiety. These changes may be as common or seemingly benign as a substitute teacher, an assembly, or an assignment that is novel and unstructured. To an inflexible child, these can cause considerable discomfort or even meltdowns. Each of these experiences can result in negative feedback from school staff and personal concern as the child perceives a difference between their own performance and that of their classmates.

After School

Finally, the students are let loose. Home again, the child now needs to face the after-school routine. Yes, that means homework.

Many students (and parents) have described homework time as the worst part of their day because of the level of tension within the family. Children may associate home with unstructured time and resist parental efforts to set routines around studying and homework completion. Worn out by the efforts of the day, students are ready to be free of demands. (Parents could use some downtime, too!) The content of the homework may be frustrating if the work is difficult. Often, though, the homework itself takes relatively little time and effort (particularly in the early grades) compared to the time and energy it takes to gear up to actually *do* the homework, which can be a struggle that is quite draining.

As students move along in school, homework and studying demands increase. As they get older, students understandably want more independence and may resist parental involvement in homework. At the same time, the students may actually need more supervision and support due to the increasing complexity and volume of work and the need to juggle the demands of a full schedule of classes. In addition, some students who were able to do quite well on tests in earlier grades simply by listening in class may have trouble adjusting to the need to take notes, study, and prepare for tests in later grades.

Homework requires a child to:

- Record or check online for homework assignments and due dates, often monitoring different websites or platforms for different classes;
- Plan ahead to have all the necessary materials on hand;

- Properly estimate and budget the amount of time necessary to finish assignments;

- Work efficiently on simple assignments and work more carefully on more complex tasks;

- Break down multi-step tasks into component parts, and consider what each step requires and when it needs to be done in order to complete projects on time;

- Determine when and what to study for tests;

- Check work for errors and completeness;

- Assemble all that is needed to be ready for class the next day; and

- Remember to turn in assignments in class or online.

Is it any wonder that many children with executive weaknesses (and their parents) dread homework? Although executive function weaknesses are not an excuse for insufficient effort, we do understand why so many students engage in avoidance, procrastination, and even lying when it comes to homework.

Winding Down (the Evening Routine)

Just as important as the morning routine, the evening routine provides a structure that includes preparing for the next day and getting ready for bed. Some disorganized kids take an exceedingly long time to transition to bedtime. They may need reminders or physical supervision to brush their teeth, bathe/shower, plan for the next day, and settle into bed. We all know that it can be helpful to select clothes, check the planner or calendar app for the next day, and pack lunches and backpacks the night before so that the morning routine runs more smoothly; however, to build these routines, many kids (even adolescents) need adult supervision and prompting.

Stressed and frustrated at the end of a long day, patience and understanding may be in short supply for both you and your child. Many kids who have held it together during the school day express their stress verbally or behaviorally in the evening. Without tolerating unacceptable or unsafe behavior, parents need to appreciate that children who must invest more effort than their peers to meet demands and stay in control need to be able to vent frustration and blow off steam. Many kids with poor self-monitoring have limited awareness of their fatigue and need help figuring out how best to manage stress. Note that some children and adolescents have good insight into the types of activities and routines that help them transition from the day to sleep.

Nighttime rituals and a slow progression toward bed and sleep help children to develop the sense of calm and soothing that allows them to give up the day with a feeling of well-being. Rituals construct a foundation of consistency and security that buffers against some of the challenges to your child's positive self-esteem. While younger kids may be comforted by listening to music, reading books, or snuggling with a parent before bed, adolescents should be supported in identifying how to wind down so that they get adequate rest before beginning the new day.

You and your child may have to give up some extracurricular activities to make evenings more relaxing. You may also have to start the routine much earlier than you would with another child to allow for your child's pace. However, both you and your child benefit from time to connect in a relaxed manner each evening. Depending upon temperament, some kids need a good amount of alone time while others crave interaction and personal contact.

Be mindful of your child's or teen's bedtime screen use, particularly if you suspect problems with sleep. It is not at all unusual for teens to share with us that they were texting friends in their bedrooms long after their parents assumed they were asleep. They usually follow that revelation with: "Please don't tell my parents!"

There is a great deal of research that shows widespread need for more sleep among children and teens, connecting this to a variety of cognitive and behavioral problems and suggesting that bedtime screen time should be avoided (see Hale et al. 2018 for a review). The research is complex, and the data is mixed, however there is enough consistency to lead to some specific recommendations. These include avoiding screen time for 30–60 minutes before bed and keeping screen devices out of the bedroom. We know some families who have set up a central, nighttime charging station in the kitchen or in the parent's bedroom; the children's evening routine includes turning in screen devices to be charged overnight. This can be particularly hard to implement with teens who are used to keeping their phones or other devices in their bedrooms at night. It's easiest to initiate this routine when children are young. However, some sleep intervention programs have found success in reducing nighttime screen use by teaching teens about the importance of sleep, helping them to identify their own goals (such as better test scores or sports performance), then creating routines that include building better sleep habits. Our advice: if you are modeling excessive use of media, then you might want to make better sleep hygiene a shared family goal.

Chores

In addition to homework, kids are expected (we hope!) to help around the house. This means that they need to follow through with daily expectations, track chores done only on specific days (e.g., taking out the trash), and monitor their work to ensure that they have done the job completely. For many children, chores are simply a part of the day, easily folded into the flow of the daily routine with only occasional reminders. However, chores can be a challenge for those with weak executive skills. Like homework time, chores can be seen as another demand by children who wish to be free of demands at the end of the school day.

We hear the same concerns about kids completing their chores around the house as we do about homework. Many parents we know have given up on requiring that their children do household chores in favor of putting all the emphasis on school-related work. Yet, chores can be an important way to help kids build their executive skills in a nonacademic setting. Just as important, there are great developmental benefits to learning to be a contributing member of the family group, with the self-esteem that follows from a sense of competence as additional payoff. The intervention chapters in the second half of this book will arm you with strategies for teaching your child to do homework *and* chores without all the nagging.

Friends and Social Life

Managing social situations is also challenging for some kids with weak executive control. The same impulsive responding, inflexibility, and poor self-monitoring that can get in the way of classroom performance can interfere with peer relationships. Just as academic demands increase as students progress through school, social situations also become more complex. For example, the kid who "doesn't know when to stop" may not be that different from the other kids, except that the other kids don't get caught because they are watching for the teacher and are paying good enough attention to others' reactions to stop shy of irritating them.

Kids with weak impulse control are at risk for social difficulties because they tend to interrupt others' conversations, have trouble with turn-taking, and can be insensitive to others' feelings or reactions. Many impulsive children and adolescents desperately want to have friends and a social life but alienate peers without understanding why peers don't want to spend time with them. It can be a painful process for kids who long to be included and accepted, and for their parents too.

Facilitating Better Social Interactions

Parents can help their children in the social realm by discreetly figuring out what is going wrong and helping to coordinate more successful social interactions.

Jamal's mom sought a consultation with a psychologist because her son was becoming depressed, stating that nobody liked him. An energetic, "over the top" 12-year-old, he felt sad at never being invited to friends' houses and at being frequently ignored at school.

At the suggestion of the psychologist, Jamal's mom called the parents of one of his friends and learned that other kids enjoyed his sense of humor but became irritated because he always needed to control what they would do. With the cooperation of another parent, she invited a peer of Jamal's to accompany their family on a tour of a hands-on science museum. Before the activity, Jamal's mom reminded Jamal that he would receive extra video game time for allowing his friend to decide which exhibits they visited and for thinking before acting. She told him that she would help by reminding him briefly if he started getting too bossy. With some verbal prompting and the help of a secret sign they had previously agreed upon, the outing was a success and Jamal began to consider that he could have more satisfactory peer interactions when he worked at controlling himself. Jamal and his mother made this a target behavior for a weekly reward, and they continued to work on the goal of letting his friends choose activities. Later, they will need to work on building a collaborative approach to decision-making.

Children with cognitive rigidity may appear blunt, insensitive, and overly literal; they often have trouble reading social cues. They tend to rely heavily on rules and have trouble determining when the situation requires a more diplomatic response. When children are quite young, it is the parents' job to teach the basic rules. "Always tell the truth." "Never break the rules." However, as kids get older, they begin to understand the shades of gray, and that rules are not absolute. Fortunately, most typically developing kids figure out that there are exceptions to all rules. However, children with cognitive rigidity have trouble with the exceptions to the rules. For example, a general rule may be "Use an inside voice; don't scream." Although this is usually the case, it may be appropriate to scream at a basketball game or if someone is in danger. Since it is impossible to actually teach a child all of the possible exceptions to rules of conduct, cognitively inflexible kids may be quite confused by these situations.

Characterized by "black-or-white" thinking, kids with this profile tend to adhere rigidly to rules and expect others to do the same. When a middle school student points their finger at a peer and says, "Bus driver, she is chewing gum and that is not allowed," there are liable to be social consequences. That child, who is just trying to do what they think is right, may earn the reputation of a tattletale. Their compulsion to strictly follow rules makes them easily misunderstood, leading to unfair treatment from peers. In more severe cases, they may become a victim of teasing, bullying, and other social cruelty.

In addition to ensuring that vulnerable children and adolescents have adequate supervision, parents, teachers, and other important adults can help inflexible kids develop increased social competence and coping skills that may buffer them from secondary emotional distress. We discuss some of these approaches in Chapter 12: Helping Children Shift Gears.

Emotions

As noted above, executive skills do not develop in a vacuum. We need to remember that a child's temperament, or personality, also plays a big role in their attitude, perceptions, and responses to executive weaknesses.

Temperament

You probably already appreciate that your child came into the world with some characteristics and features that are not in any way related to experience. A child's temperament encompasses some clear preferences and characteristics. This is particularly apparent if you have more than one child.

Take sisters Carol and Kayla. Carol has always had a "glass half full" perspective. When she spills her juice, she pops up, gets a paper towel, tells her dad, "Don't worry, I'll take care of it," cleans up the spill, and quickly returns to what she was doing. When Kayla spills her juice, on the other hand, she automatically apologizes multiple times, begins to worry that her parents will be mad at her, and can't stop thinking about her mistake. Her "wiring" results in a tendency to take a more pessimistic view of herself and the world.

How you respond to your child, as well as how your child responds to you and to life experiences, is interactive. For those who seek to please adults, meet expectations, and perform well, there is rarely the need to question motivation. It is clear that Kayla, from our example above, cares about how she is doing, as she is the first one to call attention to her shortcomings and to vow to work harder when she experiences failure or inconsistency. However, many children and adolescents with executive dysfunction or delays react to frustration and failure with decreased effort, avoidance, and declarations that they "don't care." Although both groups of kids are at risk for social, emotional, and daily living difficulties, those who deny their difficulties and who adopt an "I could not care less" attitude pose notable challenges for their parents and teachers. We encourage these important adults to look beyond the surface presentation to see the underlying weaknesses and frustration.

Self-Understanding and Self-Esteem

One of our most important jobs as parents is to help our kids develop a realistically positive self-image. Good self-esteem is built on a levelheaded appraisal of one's own strengths and weaknesses and a sense of competence in the world. People who view themselves as helpless, ineffective, or inferior are at risk for lifelong problems in social, emotional, and vocational functioning. On the other hand, people who deny their own weaknesses and fail to realistically appraise themselves will have an inflated view of their abilities and will be unprepared for the real world.

Given that children and adolescents with executive weaknesses may experience more disappointment and frustration than their peers, they are at risk of developing negative self-esteem. We have talked with many kids who have come to believe that they are just not smart enough or not trying hard enough. Like many of their parents and teachers, they are frustrated by the fact that they can sometimes excel but often fall short of expectations. How do we help children to feel good about themselves in the face of their weaknesses?

In addition to acknowledging and encouraging kids in their areas of strength, it is important to help them understand their own weaknesses and put them into context. Even in the most supportive of environments, negative feedback arises when a person with executive weaknesses is out of sync with expectations. Such experiences play a powerful role in self-assessment. You cannot (and should not!) convince a child that everything is fine when that child's experiences confirm a weakness. What parents can do is help the child to express their feelings about the experiences, develop a straightforward approach to the problems, and work on problem-solving. In the second half of the book, these principles are put into action. Although it is important to help kids understand their weaknesses, it is also important to convey that these alone do not define them as a person.

In addition to parents' input on these issues, professionals can play a strong role in the process. Teachers and guidance counselors can have a positive influence here when they understand executive functioning well and can see the child's intention and wish to succeed, even when their abilities lag behind. In the case of children who have formal psycho-educational evaluations, evaluators can offer the child an explanation of the results geared to their level of understanding and emotional development. (For information on the assessment process, refer to Chapter 6.) Sometimes, parents worry about how we will summarize evaluation results when we meet with their kids. They express concerns about the possible negative effects to self-esteem and worry that talking about problems will make the child feel different from peers. In reality, many kids view their problems and differences as more severe than they actually are. They also often underestimate their true strengths.

Our goal is to help kids understand their difficulties without defining themselves by them or becoming overwhelmed. We don't like to hear someone say, "It's hopeless. I have ADHD." In fact, although they may have attentional and executive weaknesses, they are so much more than the sum of these issues and it does them a disservice to focus exclusively on these characteristics.

Children and teens have hope when they feel that their weaknesses are balanced out by personal strengths, and when they feel understood. It is this strong foundation of support and self-awareness that allows kids with executive challenges to envision a path to success. Research clearly indicates that students with disabilities are most successful in postsecondary education when they are good self-advocates, able to discuss their strengths and needs clearly and comfortably. Working toward this level of self-understanding and confidence requires beginning much earlier than the late teens, by supporting honest self-appraisal and acknowledgment of strengths and weaknesses. As parents, you have the power to play the biggest role in this process.

Impact on the Family

➤ Living with a child who has executive weaknesses affects the whole family. Many families incorporate the challenges and thrive, but some struggle to maintain a positive environment.

➤ The complexity of setting realistic expectations for a disorganized, impulsive child typically causes parental stress and may lead to burnout. For some families, this is a source of chronic stress.

➤ Parents sometimes feel isolated from family and friends who do not understand the nature of their struggles. You may benefit from other sources of support, such as online or in-person support groups offered by organizations that advocate for children with special needs.

➤ Siblings may feel irritated, resentful, or forgotten because so much parental attention and energy is directed at their disorganized brother or sister.

➤ Some parents experience executive function weaknesses themselves, which makes it even more challenging to provide the external consistency and support that their kids need.

DOI: 10.4324/9781003403517-6

All parents experience times of frustration and fatigue. The physical demands of the job and the emotional strain of meeting others' needs are an ongoing source of stress.

Another stressful facet of the task is the angst of uncertainty and worry. Am I doing what is right for my child? Will my child turn out okay? If parents had a crystal ball that showed them that their children would, in time, grow into happy and productive adults, then they could relax. Of course, there is no such way to see into the future, and the worry may contribute to an undercurrent that can add to the routine stress of parenting.

For parents of children who have developmental delays or disabilities, the worries can be larger. Their strain is magnified by the fact that their children are out of sync with their peers and with the demands of the world. They often have worries like these: Will my child ever find a niche? Will they ever learn to compensate well enough to manage the demands of life? Will they find friends and partners who will love and accept them? Can they succeed at a job and support themselves? Parents of children with disabilities also have the added demands of providing extra supervision, monitoring, and direct help for a longer period of time than is required for their peers and siblings.

Dr. Russell Barkley, an international expert on both ADHD and executive functioning, recommends that parents of children with these challenges think about their children as having a *true* disability. Since your child's weaknesses are essentially invisible, we're not always as charitable about dealing with ongoing problems as we might be if they had a physical disability. Maintaining a "disability perspective" means that we keep in mind that the child has a weakness that is no less real for being less overt. This does not mean that we focus only on the child's disability. Nor does it mean that children with executive delays will be unsuccessful. Rather, we accept that their delays are not willful or the result of character flaws, so that we can deal with disappointments (ours and theirs) without adding negative judgments to the mix.

In the same way, it may help to think of your job as the parent of a young child or adolescent with executive weaknesses as a source of chronic stress. This does not mean that the job is not satisfying or that you never have wonderful, surprising, joyful moments with your child. It *does* mean that you are at higher risk for burnout, and you should be aware of some of the common pitfalls among families of kids with disabilities.

Impact on Parents

Your level of stress depends on a variety of factors, including the severity of your child's difficulties, your own temperament, and your network of support. The severity and nature of your child's difficulties may affect such important things as whether you are able to take your child along for routine outings or special events. Is your child difficult to handle in public places? Do they have difficulty getting along with other children? Does your teenager ask questions that embarrass peers and adults? Is your adolescent able to competently care for younger siblings? These variables affect how easily you can go about your life and how much stress you experience.

Your own temperament affects how you handle and how you interpret the demands of your job as a parent, as well. Are you a person who easily takes charge of situations? Someone who can think clearly in the midst of chaos? Or do you get overwhelmed by the action swirling around you? Do you, yourself, struggle with executive weaknesses? Do you tend to get bogged down by worries about what others think? Or can you act based on your own knowledge of your child without taking the looks or comments of others too much to heart?

The more informed you are about your child's needs, and the more comfortable you are with your own expertise, the less prone to burnout you will be. So, educating yourself is a healthy move. Learn what you can about your child and about executive weaknesses in general. If you are having trouble staying on an even keel, consider a consultation with a mental health professional to air your concerns and get back on track.

Adding to the stress of parenting a child with executive weaknesses is the isolation that can occur. Parents often feel that their friends and relatives do not understand their situation. The symptoms of executive skills problems are generic enough that it is sometimes hard for other adults to see them as other than just bad behavior or signs of poor parenting. Parents of kids with poor executive functioning often hear comments like the following:

- "Memory problems? He just remembers what he wants to remember."
- "Joey is just manipulating you. What do you mean he can't organize his room on his own?"
- "You are enabling her. How do you expect her to learn to be more responsible if you keep helping?"

We have found over the years that sometimes the "helicopter parent" who is accused of hovering is, in fact, providing the appropriate level of support for the child. Of course, some parents really do need a bit of a push to move out of the "protector" role. If you have questions about the level of support your child needs, we hope that this book helps you answer some of those questions.

It's important to recognize that individuals who feel part of a larger community tend to experience less stress. Do you have a strong circle of friends? Is your extended family a source of support? Are you grounded by a church, synagogue, or other religious community? Do you belong to other groups or organizations? All of these provide a buffer against feelings of isolation.

You may need to push yourself to stay connected with others, particularly when you are feeling weary and stretched thin from the demands of daily life. If you have difficulty finding other parents who understand your concerns, look for local chapters of organizations or online forums designed to educate and advocate for children with specific disabilities. These can be a great resource for information and support. Many offer online or in-person parent support groups free of charge, and often parents find the opportunity to connect with others managing similar challenges to be as important as the specific information and strategies that they learn.

Impact on Siblings

By definition, having a sibling means that your parents' time, effort, and energy are divided among you. That is both the beauty and the challenge of learning to live with siblings. Each of the children learns that their own needs do not always come first. Over time, children learn that the good of the family or of a specific family member sometimes trumps their own needs or wishes.

"It's not fair!" is the universal battle cry of siblings. Typical sibling conflicts can be magnified if a child with special needs requires more support and guidance than their siblings do. Siblings of disorganized kids may resent the one with special needs, at times, and may be worried and confused about their sibling's difficulties. Siblings may feel jealous of the amount of attention directed to the child with special needs.

Educating kids about their brother's or sister's weaknesses (and their strengths!) helps to create a supportive family. Sometimes, siblings can be big supporters of a child with special needs. Do not expect this to cure sibling rivalry which, at its best, is a healthy and normal striving to capture parents' attention. What you are looking for is a balance of feelings, so that your children's irritation with each other is punctuated with moments of connection and genuine concern.

Setting aside separate time for each child goes a long way toward meeting each child's need to feel appreciated. During this time, focus on your special bond with that one child. Create a ritual for the two of you, such as Monday evenings with Mom or Saturday breakfast at the local diner with Dad. Enlist a family member or sitter to stay with the other children every now and then and have a playdate with only one child. It will do you both good!

And of course, you need to keep the golden rule of raising siblings in mind. That is, fair does not mean equal or the same treatment for all. Being fair means offering each child what they need.

Impact on Couples

Raising a child with a disability can take a toll on couples, too. There may be conflict directly related to the parent role, as well as fallout from the stress. It is not unusual for couples to disagree about how to interpret a disorganized, impulsive child's behavior. Most of us rely on our own experiences growing up to help us determine expectations and what our children should be able to do independently. If one or both parents were strong, naturally organized students, they will likely struggle to understand a disorganized child. We often meet with parents who each have vastly different explanations for their child's underachievement and inconsistent performance. One parent may view the child as not trying hard enough while the other may see the child's difficulties as related to developmental or brain-based weaknesses. One parent may feel that the other needs to be more understanding. The other parent may feel that more strict discipline is the answer.

When parents disagree about something as basic as how to raise a child, the resulting underlying tension is sure to affect the whole family. Give these issues the attention they deserve. Each of you needs to be educated about your child's difficulties and you need to find time to discuss what your approach will be. If you cannot come to a shared agreement, seek outside input from a professional who works with parents and knows the ins and outs of daily life with a youngster who has developmental weaknesses. If your disagreements are more pervasive than just child-related concerns, seek out someone whose focus is on helping couples develop better communication and conflict resolution skills.

Even when parents are generally in agreement about expectations and their child's needs, parenting a child with special needs can be a significant source of stress in the relationship. While most of us look forward to having more time alone and as a couple as our kids get older, many children with delayed executive skills continue to require considerable parental time and supervision.

Take care of your relationship with your partner. Carve out some time for just the two of you to go out and do something you enjoy. It will make you a better and happier parent overall.

Special Situations

When the Apple Does Not Fall Far from the Tree

If you have read the first few chapters of this book, you likely understand what executive function weaknesses are and how they can make many aspects of daily life more difficult for your child. And in the preceding sections of this chapter, you have likely picked up on our emphasis on the need for adult-provided structure and support for a longer period of time than is typical. But what if you share your child's weaknesses? Perhaps organization and timeliness are not your strong suits. What if you have trouble with planning and sticking to a structure yourself? Panic may be your first response! Feelings of guilt and self-blame may follow.

Perhaps we can help you to take a different approach to your experience, because there is a silver lining to your cloud. Remember that your child has the advantage of being raised by a parent who understands the difficulties and can be a companion on the journey of learning better skills for self-management. If you have firsthand experience with executive weaknesses, you may be able to understand your child's difficulties in a way that others cannot.

However, if you have executive weaknesses yourself, you may need help to create the consistency, predictability, and order that your child needs. Enlist the aid of family members and other adults in your child's life. Although parents may be the obvious choice to provide the support that a child needs, other folks, including teachers, coaches, tutors, friends, and extended family members, can serve the same role. Seek professional resources for yourself if you need help with developing strategies for managing tasks.

Single Parents

Being a single parent presents a range of challenges. Having sole responsibility for raising a child who needs a high level of support and supervision can be tricky and exhausting. For single parents, identifying other adults who can provide daily support can offer a lifeline. Even the most patient, understanding parent needs some respite from the constant demands of caring for a child. Building a strong network of support from family, friends, and the community becomes all the more critical when you are a single parent. Seek others with whom you can share your joys and worries about your child, whether from those in your current circle or from an organization that advocates for families of children with special needs.

Divorced or Separated Parents Who Share Custody

Although it can certainly be done effectively, co-parenting a child after a divorce or separation can be challenging. Disorganized kids may have trouble transitioning between homes and may need considerable help planning which possessions they need to move between households. As much as possible, offer a common, consistent structure and daily routine at both houses, so that your child can more easily negotiate the transitions.

In addition, many students with executive weaknesses require close communication between school and home. This may mean that teachers and other school staff need to remain in contact with two sets of parents. Schools must meet stringent requirements regarding release of information, and there is likely some additional paperwork that needs to be completed to allow for parents residing in separate homes to receive all communications. We suggest that you check with your child's school to determine the best way to get this set up.

Disorganized kids and their separated parents also face the challenge of keeping track of sports schedules and social engagements. When possible, set up a shared online calendar for the child's activities. A duplicate set of cleats, textbooks, clothes, and other possessions can also help. Of course, communication and cooperation are always the goal in co-parenting arrangements.

Staying Healthy

Self-care is the cornerstone of any plan designed to help you manage the stress of parenting a youngster with executive weaknesses. Consider building into your life healthy ways to regulate your stress level. Getting outdoors in nature, regular exercise, yoga classes, and meditation are just a few of the ways to stay centered. All the things that promote your general physical health, including good nutrition and adequate sleep, also keep your mind on an even keel and improve your outlook.

To do what is best for your child, you must make it a priority to attend to your own well-being. Remember what they tell you on an airplane: If the oxygen level drops, those who are caring for others should put the oxygen mask over their own faces first.

6

Assessment

Figuring Out What's Needed

THE BASICS

- ➤ Assessment serves a variety of functions:
  - ○ Validates that the challenges are related to executive functions;
  - ○ Considers whether the executive challenges are "secondary" (related to a different underlying condition) or "primary" (occurring independently of any other challenges);
  - ○ Determines whether or not there are other, co-occurring conditions;
  - ○ Determines which executive skills are problematic;
  - ○ Defines the severity of the problem;
  - ○ Helps parents and teachers understand the whole child – strengths as well as weaknesses.
- ➤ Assessing executive functions can be challenging. To be done well, it is important for the examiner to look at multiple sources of information, including how your child performs on formal tests and functions in daily life.
- ➤ It can be very confusing to navigate the many types of testing that are completed by many different professionals.

DOI: 10.4324/9781003403517-7

One of the first steps in the process of helping a child with executive weaknesses is to figure out exactly what is going wrong and what is going well. We need to generate an individualized profile of strengths and weaknesses in order to develop a specific plan that helps the child with their challenges and builds on their areas of strength.

The Purpose of Assessment

The characteristics of executive dysfunction are generic, meaning that they are not specific to only one condition or disorder. Problems can occur for many reasons. To illustrate this, consider a child with a skin rash. A doctor needs to see what the rash looks like, learn about any other symptoms, and be familiar with the patient's health history before designing a treatment plan. A rash can signal a condition as straightforward as poison ivy exposure or as significant as scarlet fever. Just as your child's doctor first must understand the nature of a rash to treat it correctly, problems with executive skills require a thorough assessment to understand the difficulties and design a plan to help. Remember that there is no blood test or biological marker that pinpoints these conditions. Instead, we look at how the child is functioning and then use this information to make inferences about the underlying nature of the problem.

When done well, these evaluations can be quite time-consuming, and they are expensive if done by a private professional. So, why do we need them?

1. **The assessment process is important to make sure we understand the nature of the problem.**

The first task in assessment is to make sure that we understand the nature of the problem. We want to consider three possibilities when we evaluate a child or adolescent for executive functioning challenges. First, we want to determine whether or not the problems are truly consistent with a pattern of executive dysfunction. If so, then we want to consider whether the executive challenges are the primary problem, because sometimes executive weaknesses result from a different underlying issue that needs attention. Finally, if there is evidence of a primary challenge with executive functioning, we want to know if there are other problems that exist side-by-side with the executive challenges and that must be considered when we plan how to help the child.

Sometimes problems that may appear to be executive functioning challenges on the surface turn out to be something different. For example, one father sought an evaluation for his seven-year-old son, Jack. He described Jack as unable to follow through on chores and homework. He also noted that Jack was often mischievous and disobedient. To illustrate his point, he said that just the day before Jack had taken some of the tools from the shed, despite the fact that they were dangerous and strictly forbidden. Jack managed to get into the shed, even though there was a combination lock on the door! Jack admitted that he had learned the combination by standing behind his dad on several occasions when he opened the shed and watching carefully to see what numbers he used. Jack said that it took him several times over the course of three weeks to get all the numbers. The level of planning, working memory, and follow-through required to get into that shed led the evaluator to suspect that the problems were not caused by executive functioning weaknesses. Indeed, Jack's challenges turned out to be behavioral problems of a different sort.

Even when there are problems with executive functioning, these can be caused by other, more pressing concerns. In this situation, the executive challenges are called "secondary problems," and they emerge because of a different developmental issue. Problems with executive functioning can be secondary to social-emotional difficulties, weaknesses in language, or other learning disabilities. For example, a child who is anxious or depressed often has trouble with concentration, which can easily be mistaken for a primary problem with attention if the assessment doesn't look at current emotional functioning and stress levels. We also know that some kids who have trouble processing language will tune out and become inattentive to verbal instruction. Similarly, a youngster with a math learning disability may have trouble concentrating when completing math work and may rush to get the work done as quickly as possible. An evaluation will help to determine whether the individual tends to work too quickly on tasks in general, or whether rushing appears to be more related to the math disorder. When executive challenges are a secondary problem, we offer support for executive functioning while we treat the primary problem. We expect that executive functioning will improve as the child makes progress in the primary area of concern.

Sometimes, executive functioning is a primary problem that occurs alongside other independently occurring weaknesses. One problem does not cause the other; rather there is more than one developmental challenge of equal importance. These are often called "comorbid disorders." If we treat only one part of the problem, the child will not achieve the success for which we are hoping. For example, many kids with ADHD (commonly associated with executive weaknesses) also have learning disabilities and other developmental disorders. In a review of the extensive body of research on ADHD and comorbidities, Gnanavel and colleagues (2019) found that the prevalence of children with ADHD in the research studies who also met criteria for another learning, behavioral, or emotional disorder ranged from 60 to 100 percent!

By doing a thorough assessment, we can understand the various factors in play and then plan and implement effective, individualized interventions.

2. The assessment process is important to determine which executive skills are problematic and to understand their impact on daily life.

The second purpose of an assessment is to understand the child's particular profile of executive strengths and weaknesses. As outlined earlier, there are many different, but related, executive skills and it is rare for just one to be out of whack.

Understanding a child's specific profile is much more helpful than saying generally that they have trouble with executive functioning. For example, what we do to help a child with working memory weaknesses may be quite different from what we do for someone who has trouble getting started with work.

Often, for example, parents seek consultation with a treatment professional stating, "I already know that my child has ADHD, so I don't need any testing." Now, while people with ADHD make up a large percentage of those with executive dysfunction, simply knowing that someone does or does not have ADHD is not enough information for developing a treatment plan. Unless the child has recently been evaluated and the report provides the data we need, at least a partial evaluation is required for good planning. A partial evaluation might involve interviews with the parents and the child and collecting observational data from parents and teachers via structured rating scales. A more comprehensive evaluation outlines the profile of executive strengths and weaknesses both by gathering information about what others have observed regarding the child's executive functioning and by observing the child's behavior directly through testing.

For example, Eve struggles to complete writing tasks. Her teacher reported that Eve does much better when she is given a step-by-step instruction sheet to help her organize her thoughts. Similarly, her mother reported that Eve completes routines independently at home with some initial guidance to structure the task. On the other hand, Maggie most often ends up with incomplete writing assignments at school even with the same instruction sheet from the teacher. She needs reminders to read the information, and then she drifts off task quickly. Each time she returns to the task, she rereads the directions to orient herself. At home, Maggie's parents are frustrated and weary from their daily struggles with Maggie about being late for the school bus, incomplete chores, and lack of independence on homework. Maggie has difficulties with planning and organization of her thoughts, just as Eve does. However, Maggie's problems with organization are compounded by difficulty with initiating work, weak working memory, and distractibility. This important information was revealed by reviewing the history, interviews with those who know her, and structured questionnaires about executive skills.

3.   The assessment process is important to put the profile of executive skills into the context of the whole child.

Knowing about a child's executive skills does not mean that we understand the whole person. We need to place this understanding into the context of a larger profile of strengths and weaknesses. In addition to understanding the child's struggles, we want to know about areas of strength and skill. For example, a child who has challenges with executive skills in school may experience greater success in another setting, such as on a sports team, in music lessons, or in an after-school club. While these activities are often thought of as "just for fun," they also allow students to learn and apply important skills, such as taking feedback from an adult, appreciating the value of repetition and practice, or persisting through challenge.

Further, identifying preferred activities and areas of strength sets the stage for a plan that builds on areas of established success. The result is that the child is more likely to develop confidence and competence, be cooperative with the plan, and experience more significant and long-lasting improvements.

> **Tip:**
>
> ■ Although we know that kids can benefit from different types of
> services and programs, we need to balance the need for inter-
> vention with having adequate time for play, relaxation, rest, fam-
> ily, and friends.

Let's look at an example to illustrate how a properly conducted assessment can give you a comprehensive picture of your child's executive
functioning and point to effective strategies to address their difficulties.

Eleven-year-old Kent was doing poorly at school and becoming
increasingly frustrated. Kent's teacher noted that he often drifted off
task in the classroom, and he seemed unsure of how to get started on
assignments. Kent had particular difficulty getting started on writing
tasks, and he struggled to organize information into cohesive sentences
and paragraphs. Kent's parents added that they needed to provide daily
guidance and support to help him keep track of assignments and complete homework. He was cooperative at homework time, but he needed
frequent reminders to complete tasks and took an excessive amount of
time to get his work done. They also noted that Kent often had trouble
going to sleep without a parent in his room, and he had been a worrier
even as a young child. He tended to be anxious about meeting new
people or going to new places. Despite his initial hesitation with new
people, Kent was described as having several long-term friendships.
Both his parents and teachers reported that he was kind and caring to
adults and peers. Kent and the adults in his life all agreed that he was
happiest when he was drawing or when he could explore the outdoors
to discover interesting bugs, colorful leaves, and the like. An assessment
resulted in diagnoses of ADHD (predominantly inattentive presentation)
with significant executive functioning weaknesses in initiation, planning,
and organization, as well as notable anxiety. In addition to recommending that Kent's parents request a range of supports and accommodations
at school, the evaluator suggested medical consultation for ADHD and
anxiety to consider the pros and cons of medication. Further, the evaluator recommended that the family work with a mental health provider
to serve as a sort of case manager, educate the parents and Kent about
how to manage ADHD and executive functioning challenges, and also
to teach their son skills for coping with his anxious feelings. Knowing

that Kent had strong relationships, the evaluator predicted that he would connect easily with a therapist, a characteristic that would serve him well as a foundation for therapy. Further, the evaluator recommended that Kent participate in art classes and join a scouting group. These activities were included in the plan to build on his strengths and also to provide a context in which he might feel more comfortable learning to manage new people and places.

Evaluating the Role of Expectations

In some cases, we have seen children without executive weaknesses who are struggling because school demands or expectations in other settings are just too high for their typically developing executive abilities. Sometimes, the curriculum goals or the pace of instruction are advanced relative to the average child's abilities. Even when students have above average intellectual capabilities, they may struggle when the content is paired with higher-level executive demands. This can occur in any school, but we tend to see it most often in selective private schools and high-achieving public schools. For students struggling in these schools, extra educational support, accommodations to instruction, or even a change in schools might be helpful.

Sometimes, too, children with only mild executive weaknesses experience big problems because the adults in their lives are themselves so disorganized. Again, this is where a thorough evaluation that looks at all the possible contributing factors can help to pinpoint other necessary interventions. Perhaps the whole family needs help with developing organizational strategies that work. These are things that should be considered by an evaluator.

You can always do a consultation with a professional to help you figure out if a full evaluation is even needed. In some cases, you may already have a good enough understanding of the issues to move directly to intervention.

The Evaluation Process

Evaluations generally start with an initial information-gathering process. Sometimes, the problems are so clear and specific that the initial data collection process directs the interventions, and no further testing is required. In most cases, however, collecting relevant information is just the beginning of the evaluation. If this is the first evaluation of your child or if you are asking the school for help, it is particularly important that the assessment be comprehensive enough to fully delineate the strengths and weaknesses in your child's cognitive profile.

A comprehensive evaluation usually includes the following:

- Review of medical, developmental, and school history;
- Analysis of school records;
- Parent and teacher ratings of the child's behavior completed via questionnaires; older children and adolescents also complete rating scales about their own behavior;
- Interviews with the parents, teachers, child, and other professionals involved with the child (e.g., tutor, counselor, physician);
- School observation, if indicated;
- Test administration.

The total amount of time, length of each session, and specific tests vary. The evaluation is designed to find out why your child is struggling and depending on the complexity of the challenges and what the evaluator learns along the way, more testing may be needed. Additionally, children work at different rates, so it is not possible to predict exactly how long it will take for an individual child to complete the tests. The evaluator will consider your child's age, attention span, and stamina when doing the scheduling. Some evaluators conduct testing for a full day, while others break testing into smaller sessions. The evaluator can work to make sure your child is comfortable but cannot change the standardized instructions and procedures. The evaluator will be supportive of your child's needs but will also make demands of your child by asking them to perform. This is the nature of testing.

During the testing appointments themselves, the evaluator will work with your child using a variety of functional tests to learn about various skill sets. "Functional tests" are those that evaluators administer to children and adolescents during the assessment session to directly engage executive skills and the ability to manage attention. The evaluator asks questions, requires the child to complete hands-on tasks and to work independently. Some of the tests are timed, while others are untimed.

Evaluators will pay careful attention to your child's work style. How a child approaches a task is as important as how accurately they answer the questions, and important information often emerges from the observations of a skilled and experienced examiner. How does the child do on very structured tasks (such as simple questions) versus those with less of an inherent structure (such as those requiring longer responses or involving open-ended questions)? How does the child perform on tasks that require them to remember bits of information? On timed tasks, does the child get right down to work, or seem unaware of the need to perform in a timely fashion? How does the child perform once fatigue sets in? All these observations contribute to a better understanding of your child.

Evaluations are most often conducted in person. Most of the tests in use at this time were developed as in-person assessments, with a research base that relied on in-person administration to support their accuracy, consistency, and interpretation. However, testing by videoconference platform has been available to those in isolated geographic locations for many years, and the need for remote assessment increased with the COVID-19 pandemic. To answer that need, some measures have been developed with the possibility of remote administration in mind. Additionally, many in-person measures have been adapted to remote administration, and there is a growing body of research on how these fare by comparison to the original format. When remote administration is needed or recommended, it is important for parents to understand the reasons for the recommendation, the tests that will be administered in this way, the technology requirements that will support a best-practice remote administration (e.g., network demands, software, or hardware) and the evaluator's expertise and familiarity with remote administration and test interpretation.

Tests are revised and updated regularly, and new tests are published based on theoretical and research advances. Please see Appendix A for a list of some of the most commonly used measures of executive functioning.

Who Does Testing and What Do They Test?

Neuropsychological testing? Psychoeducational evaluation? Psychological assessment? Help! What do these terms all mean, how are they different, and what professionals are qualified to give me the answers I need?

Let's keep it simple. Regardless of who signs the report and what the evaluation is called, you need someone who is qualified to address the following broad areas of development:

- Cognitive ability ("I.Q.");
- Language-based skills;
- Visually based skills;
- Visual–motor integration;
- Memory;
- Attention;
- Executive functions;
- Academic achievement;
- Social-emotional factors.

A variety of professionals perform testing to determine reasons that a child is having difficulties in one or more of the above areas. In some cases, a comprehensive evaluation may be completed by one professional, such as a psychologist with specific training and experience in assessment. Often, more than one professional completes the evaluation so that the child benefits from the specialized expertise of different professionals, such as a psychologist and an educator.

When considering the often-confusing list of the various professionals who may be involved in an assessment, it is important to remember that there is wide variability within each profession. It is the combination of educational degree, experience, interests, and ongoing specialized training that lets you know whether a specific professional is likely to offer what you need. Be sure to ask if the individual has specialized training in assessment. Professional titles aside, there is overlap in what the various disciplines offer and the requirements for licensing and certification may vary from one state to another. So, the information that we provide below is necessarily general.

Professionals who might be on the assessment team include:

1. **Psychologists** (including clinical child psychologists, school psychologists, and neuropsychologists) are often a good place

to start your efforts to help your child with executive function concerns. Psychologists are professionals who specialize in understanding and treating different aspects of behavior; psychologists who conduct assessments should have specialized training and experience in child and adolescent development, in challenges that can affect development, and in treatment planning to address these challenges. Psychologists have a doctoral degree (e.g., Ph.D. or Psy.D.) or a master's degree. Psychologists are the professionals most likely to administer an I.Q. test. An experienced psychologist may also serve as a sort of case manager, coordinating the diagnostic team. Clinical child psychologists have training in a wide variety of developmental challenges affecting children and teens, particularly their impact on behavior and emotional health. They may offer both assessment and therapy for children with executive function difficulties, as well as common comorbid conditions such as ADHD, autism, and learning disabilities. School psychologists specialize in child development as it affects learning and behavior in the classroom, in treatment applications within the classroom and the broader school setting, and in understanding how schools work systemically to support a range of developmental needs. Neuropsychologists have specialized training in brain development and structures and how brain functioning affects cognition, development, and behavior. In most cases, the choice to work with a particular psychologist will depend more on the individual's particular experience and expertise rather than their title. However, at times, specific expertise may be needed. For example, if a child has a history of recent or significant concussions, a neuropsychologist may be consulted to understand more directly how this history may contribute to current difficulties.

2. **Educators** have expertise in how children typically learn and how to support children who need a little extra help. They can offer information about how your child is performing relative to peers in the classroom on everyday academic tasks and how they are progressing on curriculum goals. Special educators and private learning specialists have specific training and experience in assessing and teaching children with more significant academic problems, such as learning disabilities or other challenges that impact learning. They may have a bachelor's, master's, or

doctoral degree. Special educators have experience in adapting the general curriculum to the special needs of students with developmental challenges, as well as in teaching strategies and academic support that directly address an individual student's profile of strengths and weaknesses.

3. **Speech-language pathologists** have earned at least a master's degree. They have expertise in diagnosing and treating difficulties with verbal and non-verbal communication, including speech challenges (e.g., recognizing or producing specific sounds), language delays (understanding language and expressing oneself in words), and problems with social pragmatics (the use of language and other aspects of communication in social situations). As noted above, children who experience struggles with language can often be mistaken for children who are inattentive, and at times children with executive struggles have co-occurring language disorders. Speech-language pathologists can help tease out these concerns.

4. **Occupational therapists** have master's degrees, and they specialize in helping people with developmental difficulties to manage everyday demands. They have specialized training in the assessment of fine motor skills (movements involving the small muscles in the hands) and eye-hand coordination needed for tasks such as handwriting, dressing, and eating. Occupational therapists who work in schools assess children's abilities to participate in activities related to learning and may offer treatment or design accommodations to the physical environment to help a student to stay on task or to meet handwriting demands. They may also offer assessment and treatment for sensory sensitivity.

5. **Physical therapists** have a specialized doctoral degree (DPT) while physical therapy assistants have a two-year associates degree; they assess and treat difficulties with movement and pain. Physical therapists in the school setting concentrate on diagnosing and treating problems with independent movement that interfere with the ability to participate fully in that environment. They may offer treatment or accommodations that help with functional mobility, such as walking, climbing stairs, or benefiting from play opportunities.

6. **Psychiatrists** have a medical degree and additional training in the diagnosis and treatment of mental health issues. They

are qualified to prescribe medication, such as for ADHD, anxiety, depression, or other issues impacting emotional well-being or behavioral health. While some psychiatrists offer talk therapy and counseling, many focus mostly on treatment with medication.

7. **Pediatricians or family practitioners are doctors who specialize in the medical treatment of children and families.** They have an M.D. or D.O. degree, and they may be involved in diagnosing and prescribing medications for conditions such as ADHD, anxiety, and depression, particularly when the issues are relatively clear-cut and don't require the specialized expertise of a psychiatrist. Developmental pediatricians are specialists in understanding and treating the challenges of children and teens whose development is not unfolding according to typical expectations, including medical, behavioral, and social-emotional concerns. When children have complex developmental challenges, parents may find it helpful to consult with a developmental pediatrician for help with diagnosis and treatment planning.

Where Should You Seek an Assessment?

Public schools, as well as community-based professionals, offer diagnostic assessments to better understand your child's developmental profile and needs.

If your child is struggling to meet grade-level expectations, you have the right to request testing for your child from the public school system, even if your child attends a private school. The laws and procedures that govern assessment and specialized services for students with executive functioning challenges or other special needs are complex. We offer the briefest of synopses about these laws here.

In the United States, federal laws that cover testing, special education services, and accommodations for students include the Individuals with Disabilities Education Act (I.D.E.A., 2004) and Section 504 of the Rehabilitation Act. I.D.E.A. is designed to ensure that public schools offer educational opportunities equally to children with and without disabilities. Disabilities is a broad term here that encompasses a variety of academic, social, behavioral, or other challenges that interfere with a child's ability to benefit from instruction and to make progress in meeting educational goals. I.D.E.A. includes specific requirements for the timelines for assessment, determination of eligibility, documentation, and educational planning for students who qualify. Parent permission must be requested to conduct the evaluation, and parents must be invited to participate in the assessment process.

Section 504 is not exclusively related to education. Rather, it is a civil rights law designed to ensure that people with disabilities have equal access and opportunity to participate in areas such as education and the workplace. Equal access may include removing obstacles or requiring accommodations to allow full participation. The documentation requirements for 504 plans are slightly different than under I.D.E.A., as the focus tends to be on accommodations that promote access (e.g., extended time allowances) rather than educational interventions (e.g., specialized instruction). Parent permission is required prior to an initial evaluation; parent notification is required whenever evaluation or placement decisions occur.

Under both I.D.E.A. and Section 504, either you or the school can initiate evaluation. If your child meets the eligibility criteria, a plan will be developed to address their educational needs. The plan is known as an Individualized Education Program (I.E.P.) if developed according to I.D.E.A. requirements and a 504 plan if developed under Section 504 requirements. In either case, the plan becomes a legally binding document. So, these plans can be valuable tools that help your child to succeed. You want to be sure that whoever does the assessment for your child is familiar with the laws and knows what is needed to request consideration for services. The evaluator can also provide valuable input in the form of recommending specific, individualized suggestions to be included in the plan. Be aware that even if you do not develop a formal plan, the school may offer informal supports and accommodations.

The legislation governing these services is complex, so further resources are listed at the end of the book. In addition to educating yourself about the law, you may want to obtain information from a parent advocacy organization that focuses on your child's disabilities. Some families choose to hire a consultant who specializes in understanding individual learning profiles and collaborating with schools, such as a psychologist or private educational advocate.

We cannot tell you whether evaluation through the public school system or a private professional is best for your child; however here are some factors you should consider before making your decision:

1. **Cost:** All public education is funded by your taxes. That means that you have already paid for services through the public schools. An evaluation through the school requires no additional cost to you. On the other hand, a private professional charges you for their time and expertise. Although customary fees vary too widely for us to give specifics, it is a significant expense. Sometimes, medical insurance covers a portion of the evaluation fee, particularly for the neuropsychological and emotional (psychological) testing, if that is needed. Most insurance companies expect that testing for learning disabilities and other academic concerns will be done by schools and describe testing in those areas as "not medically necessary." If you are wondering if any of the testing may be reimbursed by your insurance company, make sure you obtain that information before any testing occurs.

2. **Scope of the Evaluation:** In accordance with federal mandates, evaluations completed by schools focus on determining whether a student meets the requirements necessary to be covered by I.D.E.A. or Section 504. Your child must officially be determined to be a student with a "disabling condition," and that condition must interfere with their ability to equally access a free and appropriate public education, sometimes referred to as "F.A.P.E." This is a somewhat different question than those posed in private evaluations which may take a broader view, including an assessment of functioning at home or in other environments outside of school. Private professionals typically pursue a complete profile, without limiting assessment to the single arena of education. The resulting profile identifies a student's strengths and weaknesses in many areas of development and makes recommendations for propelling the child toward their full potential both in school and outside of school. The school's focus on factors affecting performance in the school setting means that the evaluation will generally not include recommendations to help the child outside of school.

   At times, the evaluation can highlight the difference in perspectives of the parents and the school system. For example, in some states, special education is required to meet the needs of gifted students, but in many other states public schools are only required to help students to perform at grade level. Gifted students who perform at grade level (below their own ability) may not qualify for extra help despite significant challenges with executive functioning. (At the same time, please know that getting good grades does not preclude a student from services. Your child's disability may be evident in other ways, such as in the excessive time and effort it requires to manage school tasks.)

Parents who pursue evaluation through their public school are a part of the team that determines if testing is required, and if so, what testing will be done. However, in some instances, parents may disagree with the rest of the team's decision on what to test, or on the results of the evaluation. For this reason, some parents may seek consultation from a private professional about whether the decisions of the team are warranted or whether to appeal a decision with which they disagree.

3. **Time:** Federal guidelines define how long the school system has to complete each step of the process from your initial written request for an evaluation to completing the testing and presenting the results. These guidelines dictate the maximum amount of time that the school system may take, but the actual amount of time may be less. Be sure to ask your school team how long they anticipate it will take to get through the process and to apprise you of what the law states about timelines and your rights.

If you seek assessment from a private professional, make sure you are clear on when you will receive the results and final report.

If you are submitting a private evaluation report to your child's school team, find out how much time they need to review it before you can meet to discuss the report and the school's plan for meeting your child's needs. Be aware that public schools may decide to do some additional testing to corroborate the results of a private evaluation.

4. **Confidentiality:** When testing is done by the school system, the test results become a part of your child's permanent record and are communicated to members of the school team. The results travel with your child's file to each public school. Safeguards are built into the system regarding how the information is stored and who has access to the file, and information is not released outside the school system without the permission of the parent or guardian.

When testing is done privately, the parent or guardian owns the information. Except in unusual legal situations, the report goes only to you unless you sign a consent form authorizing release of the information to other specifically identified individuals.

5. **Weighing the Pros and Cons:** We understand that the decision to go with a public school–based evaluation or a private assessment is an important one. We have already shared our bias that obtaining more comprehensive information is often the best way to plan interventions. Additionally, parents have more direct control over the private testing process. However, some public schools do an incredibly good job and may be able to complete a range of multidisciplinary evaluations relatively quickly (e.g., psychological, educational, speech and language, and occupational therapy). Further, many families are simply unable to afford the cost of a private evaluation. Whichever route you choose, you need to be an active participant in the process. Read the section below for important information about how to be an educated consumer so that you can effectively advocate for your child.

How to Be an Educated Consumer

So, if you seek a private evaluation, how do you find a qualified professional? One of your best sources of information is other parents who have been through the testing process. You may also want to talk with professionals such as teachers, pediatricians, and others who work with children and adolescents. Local, regional, and national organizations that advocate for children with disabilities may also be able to direct you to qualified professionals. If possible, talk with a few evaluators to get a feel for their approach and an idea about the best personality "fit" with your child. Many professionals offer a brief initial phone call at no charge to help you understand what they do and their fees. In most cases, it is important to make sure that the professional understands educational law and school procedures so that any privately conducted testing covers the information that the school team needs to move forward with interventions. Ask about the person's education, training, and experience. Even if an evaluator has impressive credentials, you need to make sure that they will take the time necessary to listen to you and get to know your child.

If your child has difficulty feeling comfortable with new people or is anxious or sensitive, check to see if they can do a quick visit to the office before their first testing session. Particularly for younger children, an examiner may arrange to have snacks and prizes available to help pave the way for a positive testing experience and to reinforce on-task behavior. Parents sometimes ask how to prepare their child for assessment, whether they should practice certain skills or otherwise help their child get ready. It's important to know that the interpretation of your child's performance on tests given during a psychoeducational assessment is based on the expectation that the test questions and the format of some types of testing tasks are unfamiliar. For this reason, practice or preparation can muddy the waters and invalidate the test results. The only preparation needed for assessment is a good night's sleep, a good breakfast, and encouragement to do their best.

Once you have selected a professional to complete the assessment, make sure you clearly understand their business practices (e.g., fees, policy for missed appointments, insurance participation, type of payment accepted, etc.) and when to expect the results. It is important to agree upon the goals of testing and the scope of the evaluation. Before the first session, the evaluator should help you find a good way of explaining the testing process to your child, as it is important for them to feel comfortable and to understand how testing (and the time and effort we are asking them to invest) will be helpful. Gaining trust and buy-in is particularly important for adolescents who may be wary of any attempts to figure out what is "wrong" with them.

If you are requesting testing from your child's public school, you start by requesting a meeting, often called a "screening" or "child study meeting," to discuss possible testing with the school team. Make sure you make a formal request in writing and address it to the correct person. (Who this is varies widely among schools; you can call the school to ask who coordinates meetings to determine eligibility for evaluation.) Most schools will accept letters that are either emailed, sent by postal service, or hand delivered. Either way, you should send one copy of the request to the designated school representative and keep a copy for your personal files. Make sure you receive the school district's written guide to your rights and procedural safeguards so you will understand how to appeal the team's decision if you disagree.

We want to emphasize the importance of taking an active role in the assessment process. Ask questions at every step! If you don't understand the answer, ask again! Ask the professionals to use real-life language and to give examples if they are using jargon that is foreign to you. Be sure you understand the scope of the testing, what questions the evaluation is designed to answer, and what the test results mean.

If you are left with nagging doubts about what it all means or whether there is more that can be done, then it is time to seek a second opinion. You can check with your state's department of education to find programs that offer free or low-fee parent consultation regarding whether or not your child qualifies for services. Additionally, private professionals who specialize in this arena are frequently called upon to review evaluations completed by schools or by other professionals and to help families understand their implications.

Remember that the test scores alone are rarely sufficient to help us understand a child's strengths and needs. Scores do not always help us figure out the "whys": why a bright student keeps forgetting to turn in completed homework; why there is so much variability between math test scores; why a previously successful student has come to hate school. Many students with executive weaknesses do fine on in-office and classroom tests but have true problems with learning and performance. There is a well-known "secret" about executive function assessment: it is completed in an environment with minimal distractions, and by an evaluator who provides a high level of structure. Sometimes, this format compensates for executive skill weaknesses in such a way that the child looks more competent during the testing sessions than in real life. So, it is possible for children to have adequate scores on formal measures of executive functions and *still* have real-life performance and executive problems. This is why the clinical experience of the examiner and the input of the teacher and the family via questionnaires are essential.

Once the Assessment Is Done

Following the formal assessment process, parents are invited to discuss results of the evaluation and specific recommendations tailored to their child's unique profile. This typically happens a few weeks after testing is completed with a full written report to follow. In many instances, it is helpful for the examiner to have a brief discussion of the test results with the child, in a way the child can understand. For some kids, the parent is present; for others, it makes more sense for the examiner to talk to the child or teen alone. That review should emphasize the child's strengths as well as discuss ways of addressing challenges.

When testing has been done privately, the report is only provided to the school with written parental permission. An exception is when the school has agreed to fund an independent educational evaluation (I.E.E.) or when a special education hearing officer has ordered one; in those cases, the report will be provided to both the parents and the school.

If you obtain a private evaluation and choose not to submit the report to the school, the school may request your permission to perform their own testing so that they can determine whether or not your child needs individualized services or a change to the existing plan, if there is one already in place. In this case, you should provide a list of tests and procedures completed as part of the private evaluation, since many tests cannot be readministered within one year's time. There are generally alternate tests that the school can use to assess a particular area of development, such as I.Q. or academic levels.

Most likely, you will want to share the assessment results with your child's school. School teams are generally pleased to have more information to use to determine how to proceed. However, be advised that while the school team must *consider* the evaluation, they do not have to accept the results or follow the recommendations. If they choose to reject the outside evaluation or its recommendations, they should provide the reasons for doing so in writing.

Even if you submit the report from a private evaluation to your public school, the school team may choose to do some additional testing. Corroboration and testing from professionals in more than one discipline are generally required in schools when they are considering whether or not a child qualifies for a federally mandated, specialized educational plan.

When Testing Goes Awry

Unfortunately, even when you have done your best to obtain a good assessment, there can be problems. You may disagree with the evaluation results or may feel that the examiner really did not understand your child. Don't despair! Your child needs you to continue to advocate for them. If the evaluation was done through a public school, it may make sense to seek consultation with a state-funded educational advocacy group or to hire a private psychologist or educational advocate to review the results and, perhaps, conduct further testing.

If the testing was done privately, first discuss your concerns with the professional you worked with. If that does not result in a satisfactory outcome, seek another opinion. In some cases, you may need to consider that the assessment was accurate and that you are having difficulty accepting the information you received.

If you disagree with the evaluation conducted at your child's school, you have the right to request an independent educational evaluation (I.E.E.) or additional testing. If an I.E.E. is authorized, this will be done at the school system's expense. You may also request mediation or a due process hearing under I.D.E.A. Both options can be emotionally draining and, in the case of a hearing, expensive.

Now What?

Sometimes assessments end up in the evaluator's files or in a pile on a parent's desk with no other resulting action. We call this "So What Testing." Testing is useful only if it leads you to a clear understanding of how to help. When your child is having trouble, you want to understand what you can do. The interpretive session and the written report should directly address what needs to be done for your child.

Figuring out who should get copies of the results, how much information to share, and what kinds of follow-up services you need should all be part of the discussion after the evaluation. For example, attending school meetings is an add-on service that you may need from your evaluator. It may be especially important for the evaluator to attend a school meeting in these situations:

■ There is (or you anticipate) a disagreement with the school about whether your child qualifies for special education services and support. Under federal education law (I.D.E.A.), a child needs to be experiencing significant problems accessing and/or making progress in the general education curriculum and need special education because of the problem in order to qualify for services. Under Section 504, the child must have a disability that causes significant impairment in one or more life activities (such as learning). The evaluator can help you make that case with the school.

- There is a disagreement with the school about the overall label that should be used to qualify your child for special education services and support. Under I.D.E.A., a child needs to be found to have one or more of 13 different types of disabilities to qualify for services; these include a learning disability, an autism spectrum disorder, or "other health impairment," a category that includes ADHD. In some cases, it may be easier to get the types of supports your child needs with one label versus another.

- There is a disagreement about the types of support and strategies that would be helpful for your child. Your child's school might be used to providing only certain supports for children with certain difficulties and the evaluator may be able to persuade your child's school team that other supports are necessary.

If a school psychologist (or other school employees) evaluated your child, you should expect them to be present at any meeting discussing the evaluation results and your child's eligibility for support and accommodations.

A Note about Executive Functioning and School Plans

Just as evaluators need to be specific in assessing the profile of executive strengths and weaknesses your child is experiencing, they need to be specific in describing the types of school assignments or situations where interventions would be useful. To write a good plan, it is important to be as clear as possible and to tailor interventions to the child's profile and needs. It is not enough to say that a child has problems with working memory, for example. However, it is extremely useful to know that a child's working memory problems may mean that they will have difficulty copying from the blackboard because they forget what they need to write in the time that it takes to shift their gaze from the board to the paper. Identifying the latter difficulty leads directly to accommodations, such as providing a hard copy of the math problems to be solved rather than requiring the student to copy problems from the board. You or the evaluator may want to ask for a copy of the curriculum goals for your child's school grade, so that you can look at what your child is expected to do and use these as the basis for understanding what support or intervention will help them to develop the skills to meet expectations.

7

ADHD, Learning Disabilities, and Other Conditions Associated with Executive Functioning Challenges

THE BASICS

➤ Executive functioning can be weak in children, whether or not there is evidence of any other disorder. Executive dysfunction alone can be viewed as a performance disability that can be just as problematic as ADHD or learning disabilities.

➤ Most (but not all) children with ADHD have executive weaknesses, although the specific profiles vary.

➤ Many youth with executive dysfunction also have specific learning disabilities, meaning that they have unexpected difficulty learning in some specific content area (e.g., reading or math). However, some kids with weakness in executive functions have academic problems that are a result of their difficulties with the process of learning and performance. It can be hard to distinguish between these two causes of learning problems.

➤ Children and teens with autism spectrum disorders (A.S.D.) typically have a weakness in cognitive flexibility.

➤ Executive weaknesses are common in children and adolescents with a range of neurodevelopmental, psychiatric, and medical disorders.

DOI: 10.4324/9781003403517-8

Remember that some kids are disorganized or have other executive skill weaknesses but do not have symptoms of other underlying or co-occurring conditions. We do not mean to minimize the impact of these weaknesses by saying that these kids *only* have executive weaknesses. The "only" is used as a qualifier because for many other people, problems with executive skills are part of a larger picture of ADHD, learning disabilities, or other disorders.

As we hope we have made clear already, we have seen in our daily work that executive weaknesses alone can be quite problematic. Dr. Martha Bridge Denckla was one of the first neuroscientists to focus on executive dysfunction as a performance disability. She found that, similar to children or adolescents with a specific reading learning disability or a clear deficit in language skills, students who struggle with disorganization and other executive weaknesses have a disability that is apparent in their diminished work output and struggle to perform consistently. In her pioneering clinical work and research, Dr. Denckla showed how these weaknesses can have a profound effect on daily life and on school achievement, even for gifted children.

Diagnostics aside, the strategies for managing executive weaknesses in this book are not specific to any disorder, and we hope that you find them helpful regardless of whether your child has received any specific diagnosis.

However, as noted above, for many individuals, these challenges are compounded by other conditions. Let's take a look at some of the most common conditions.

Attention-Deficit/Hyperactivity Disorder (ADHD)

ADHD is generally associated with executive functioning challenges. While there is some disagreement in the field about whether executive function weaknesses are *always* present with ADHD, it is clear that executive weaknesses are a core challenge for the majority of those with the diagnosis. Individuals with ADHD vary in their profiles of strengths and weaknesses and the intensity of the challenges.

A very brief overview of ADHD can help you to decide if your child or teen has red flags that should be explored further. Remember that diagnostic terms and classification systems change over time as we learn more about the nature of a disorder. In the United States, the diagnostic criteria for all mental and behavioral disorders are listed in the

Diagnostic and Statistical Manual of Mental Disorders (D.S.M.) published by the American Psychiatric Association. In the most current edition of this manual (D.S.M. 5-T.R.), ADHD is conceptualized as a single disorder but with several possible different clusters of symptoms, or "presentations." In the past, these were called subtypes and were considered to be stable groups of symptoms that characterized an individual over time. However, it became clear that a child with ADHD can show different characteristics at different times. For example, a young child who seems mostly inattentive may seem more impulsive and restless at a later time. The term "presentation" was adopted to reflect that fluid development.

When people think of ADHD, they generally conjure up an image of a "hyper" kid. However, researchers and clinicians have learned over the years that this is only one of the possible presentations of ADHD.

Some children have attention problems but no hyperactivity, and they are called ADHD, Predominantly Inattentive Presentation. These individuals tend to have trouble getting started on tasks and sustaining their effort, and they may be described as "spacey." Disorganization is a common characteristic. A frequent parent and teacher complaint is that the child has completed their work but then left it in their backpack, forgetting to hand it in.

The Hyperactive-Impulsive Presentation of ADHD includes kids whose predominant problems are impulsiveness and overactivity, the "hyper kid." These are kids whose engines always seem to be racing, who act first and think later. However, individuals who fall into this group do not show symptoms of inattention. This presentation of ADHD is less common than the other presentations.

The Combined Presentation of ADHD describes kids who have elements of both of the presentations outlined above. So, they have inattention and distractibility plus problems with hyperactivity and impulse control.

Finally, when a youngster has notable difficulties with attention, impulse control, and/or hyperactivity but not to the extent or with the frequency that meets criteria for one of the three presentations, they may be diagnosed with "Other Specified ADHD and Unspecified ADHD." Specified or Unspecified refers to whether or not the clinician doing the diagnosis offers more information. So, as an example, Other Specified ADHD might be stated as "Other Specified ADHD with insufficient symptoms of inattention." Unspecified ADHD might be used when there is insufficient information for full documentation of the diagnosis.

There is an additional attention disorder that appears to be related to but distinct from ADHD. This cluster of behaviors is called Cognitive Disengagement Syndrome (C.D.S.), formerly called Sluggish Cognitive Tempo. It is characterized by drowsiness, lethargy, and excessive day-dreaming. These individuals are distracted by their own internal mind-wandering, and they may look like they're paying attention though they're actually "zoned out." The research on this disorder is sparse compared to what we know about ADHD. We do know that C.D.S. symptoms overlap with ADHD, particularly with the Predominantly Inattentive presentation. However, the low physical energy and sluggish, sleepy characteristics set it apart from ADHD. Like ADHD, individuals with C.D.S. tend to have significant problems with executive functioning, particularly with cognitive regulation.

Drs. Kathleen Nadeau and Patricia Quinn were among the first to highlight the special needs of girls and women with ADHD. Since they may be less disruptive than boys, the inattention and executive deficits of girls may not be as readily noticeable, particularly in the elementary grades. However, these girls may be quietly struggling, and their difficulties often become more noticeable when they experience the increased demands of middle and high school.

Many children with ADHD benefit from treatment with medication. While we understand that some parents have fears and misgivings about the use of medication for attention disorders, these can be a critical component of the treatment plan for many people. Stimulant medications, particularly, have been the target of much negative press over the years. People who write about medications for ADHD often have strong opinions, not always based on facts. We encourage parents to educate themselves about the pros and cons of medication and to carefully look for well-reasoned information based on scientifically sound research. Consult with your pediatrician or an experienced child and adolescent psychiatrist to determine whether or not a trial of medication makes sense for your child.

Whether or not you decide to try medication, however, knowing how to help your child with executive functioning is very important. Medication often improves attention, decreases impulsivity, and quiets hyperactivity, however its effects on other aspects of executive functioning are considerably more modest, at best, and remain equivocal. Researchers are exploring combinations of medications and use of alternatives to stimulant medications as they seek ways to improve executive functioning. However, despite these preliminary efforts, it appears that individuals medicated for ADHD continue to experience a heavy burden of challenges with executive functioning. This may contribute to frustration as a student has better focus but still cannot remember to turn in their homework. That is what the interventions in this book are about.

Learning Disabilities (L.D.)

The term learning disability (L.D.) refers to an unexpected difficulty in learning a specific academic skill or set of skills. It is unexpected because individuals with learning disabilities have all the intelligence and instruction they need to learn, yet they have chronic difficulties in mastering reading, math, writing, and/or spelling. These difficulties are believed to have a neurological origin that is subtle and not yet fully understood. Like ADHD, learning disabilities sometimes run in families.

In her work, Dr. Denckla noticed that many of the students with learning disabilities that she evaluated had some characteristics in common with kids with ADHD. What they had in common was weakness in executive functioning, and she called this shared deficit the overlap zone.

Why do folks with executive weaknesses have difficulty with academics? Sometimes, they have both executive weakness and a co-occurring learning disability. However, the very characteristics that we define as weak executive skills can lead a child to have academic difficulty – not with the content of the material to be learned, but with the process of learning or of performing in the classroom. Let's look at some real-life examples to make this distinction clearer.

Alan is a second grader who appears to his parents and teachers to be quite bright. While Alan loves math and science and does well in those subjects, he complains that he hates reading. He is reluctant to work on reading tasks and has been since he first started reading instruction. Alan has particular difficulty sounding out words and his reading is very slow and labored. He enjoys stories when others read to him, but otherwise he sticks with picture books that seem better suited to younger children.

Brianna is also struggling with reading. She tends to be inconsistent, sometimes reading the very same words differently within one sentence. She tends to look at the first letters of a word and then guess at the rest, and she reads very quickly. Sometimes, if you ask her to tell you about what she just read, she can't remember. However, when she reads with someone who encourages her to slow down and to look at the whole of each word, she does fine. With prompting to think about what she read and with encouragement to look back at the text, she demonstrates good comprehension.

In the examples above, we see profiles of two children who both have problems with reading that affect their school performance. However, Alan's difficulties are due to a specific learning disability in reading. Brianna's reading problems have all the red flags of executive dysfunction; she can actually read well but her problems with attention to detail, working memory, and pacing mirror the problems she has in many other areas.

It can be difficult to distinguish between these two different reasons for academic difficulty. However, since understanding the nature of the problem affects our understanding of how to help, it is a very important distinction to make. If your child undergoes testing, the psychologist or other evaluator will help you figure out if there is a primary problem with reading skills or if attention and executive function weaknesses are impeding their reading achievement. If testing has not been completed, you may want to talk with your child's teachers to help determine where the reading process is breaking down.

Reading Disorder

A variety of different cognitive processes are involved in the ability to read accurately, fluently, and with good comprehension. When any one of these cognitive processes breaks down, a disability may be the result. Some children have difficulty with hearing the individual sounds or units of sound in language. Some have difficulty relating the sounds to letters. Some children have difficulty recognizing letter patterns. Others have trouble with comprehension, with or without decoding problems. (Decoding refers to the ability to "sound out" words.)

As Dr. Denckla noted, research has shown that many kids with reading disabilities have characteristics that overlap with executive dysfunction. Common overlaps include: weaknesses in working memory, trouble with retrieval efficiency (meaning that it is difficult to pull information from memory when it is needed), and difficulty distinguishing between minor details and the big picture. Even when specific reading deficits are remediated, inattention and executive weaknesses can continue to compromise academic functioning.

Some kids with executive weaknesses do not have a separate reading disorder at all. As in Brianna's case, some children are so impulsive and read so quickly that they can't absorb the material. They may have trouble matching their level of effort and reading rate to the level of difficulty of the material. For example, reading a friend's social media post and reading *The Odyssey* require significantly different levels of attention and depth of processing. Although most children figure this out on their own, some need explicit instruction in how to match their effort and depth of processing to the material they are reading.

For children and adolescents who have reading disabilities, there are a range of research-supported interventions that are often effective in building improved reading skills. These can be implemented at school or by a private tutor and need to be provided by educational professionals who have specialized training and experience.

For kids with weak phonics skills, the interventions involve instruction and practice to improve the ability to sound out words. Experienced educators will often combine helpful components of a variety of specific reading interventions with a good dose of fun reading in areas of special interest to the child. The overall goal of improving reading skills is helped along by building on the fact that positive experiences enhance learning.

Other interventions target reading rate and fluency for those who have mastered most of the basics of reading but lack the rapid and automatic reading skills of their peers.

Some students with reading disorders struggle primarily with reading comprehension. For them, the goal is to teach cognitive strategies to improve how actively they are processing what they read. These interventions may include instruction and practice with summarizing, highlighting, note-taking, and other ways of helping the student understand and organize what they are reading.

The other primary means of helping kids with significant reading problems is to make the actual act of reading easier. Although most of us do best with silent reading, some people benefit from reading aloud or being read to (this means they will need to take tests at school in a separate room). When a student in mid-elementary school or above must work hard just to figure out the individual words, reading is more effortful for them than for their peers. Comprehension and learning suffer. Accommodations allow the student to get the full benefit of instruction until their reading improves such that they can manage grade-level text with the ease of peers. For example, computer programs or apps that read printed material aloud can allow the student to concentrate on understanding the material.

Many of the techniques that are helpful for kids with reading disorders can also be beneficial for students whose reading performance is compromised by executive dysfunction. For example, Matt has average reading skills but quickly loses focus when reading and has trouble determining the most important points in a textbook chapter. He has digital copies of most of his textbooks, and he reads along while using the text-to-voice program on his computer. The combination of listening and following along enhances his concentration.

If your child has difficulty reading due to executive weaknesses, you will find strategies to address these issues in the second half of the book (Chapters 14 and 15).

Mathematics Disorder

A specific learning disability in math means that the person has difficulty understanding basic math concepts or learning to solve arithmetic problems. As with reading disorders, some kids have a primary math disability and others have problems primarily with the executive skills needed for math.

Math draws heavily on attention, working memory, and cognitive flexibility. Math can be difficult for those with executive dysfunction because it often requires the ability to perform multi-step processes, remember details, and problem-solve. Weak executive functioning may show up as mistakes that are a result of inadequate attention to the operational sign on computation problems and other seemingly careless errors. Whether or not they understand the concepts, if a student makes a mistake on any part of a multi-step problem, the answer will be wrong.

Some children with ADHD perform better on more challenging problems than on easy ones because the task difficulty slows down the analysis process and makes careless errors less likely.

Math problems, particularly oral problems, often require students to hold information in mind to carry into a later step in solving the problem. Some kids with working memory inefficiencies struggle to learn basic math facts. Kids with poor task monitoring may not recognize when their answer doesn't make sense. When provided with extraneous information in a word problem, some students with organizational difficulties have a hard time focusing in on the important details.

Research on interventions, as well as training for helping students with math learning disabilities, have lagged behind reading disabilities. Nonetheless, there are many trusted interventions that are helpful in remediating weaknesses. As with reading interventions, many of the techniques that benefit kids with mathematics disorders are also appropriate for students whose executive weaknesses impair their math performance. Sometimes it is helpful to teach the child to highlight or circle math procedure signs (+, -) or to read the problem aloud before they begin working to help prevent "careless" errors. You will find more suggestions in the chapters on interventions for children who need help controlling impulsive behavior, managing weak working memory, and monitoring their own behavior.

Disorder of Written Expression (Writing L.D.)

Writing is an incredibly complex task that requires:

- Getting started;
- The physical act of writing or keyboarding;
- Using correct punctuation and capitalization;
- Spelling words correctly;
- Writing in sentences;
- Following oral or written directions;
- Staying on-track and organized;
- Working within time limits;
- Figuring out when one has done sufficient research to start writing; and
- Determining whether the final product matches the specific criteria and the overall purpose of the assignment.

Kids with problems with written expression can have difficulty because of the mechanics of writing (spelling, grammar, punctuation), the formulation of ideas, the organization of their responses, or all three. There are also plenty of students who struggle with the physical act of handwriting. (There is a separate term for people with handwriting difficulties: developmental coordination disorder or dysgraphia.)

Many kids with executive weaknesses have trouble with written expression. There is simply too much to keep track of! One teacher explained it this way:

Although many of my students may possess the ability to write well, and also have a keen and deep understanding of the topics they are asked to write about, when asked to produce any type of writing from quick paragraphs to longer analytical papers, their executive function deficits quickly cloud any talent or aptitude for the written word. Their ability to get started, to move from one step to the next, to persist through writer's block, to self-monitor progress, all essential skills in completing writing assignments, is greatly impacted by their struggles with executive functioning.

(Murphy 2020)

When faced with the executive challenges of writing assignments, these students may simplify the task by writing less complex and fewer sentences than required. These minimalists are often overwhelmed by the writing process and have increasing difficulty as they proceed through school. In our experience, it is not unusual for kids with a disorder of written expression to be brilliant poets and do well on creative writing tasks while demonstrating significant impairment when required to complete more structured writing assignments. Others do fine with factually based writing but struggle with creative writing tasks.

Children or adolescents with writing disabilities often benefit from special education services or working with a specially trained tutor. They need explicit instruction in how to do research, decide on a topic, structure sentences, organize their work, and proofread. Keyboarding instruction and the use of voice recognition software may be very useful for students with slow or poor handwriting.

The overlap between interventions for specific learning disabilities and executive weakness is nowhere more apparent than with written expression. Many kids with writing problems have trouble with initiation. It is often helpful to allow these students to dictate some or all of an assignment.

For students who have difficulty with organizing and planning their written work, there are many useful apps that allow a child to generate ideas and organize information using visual techniques, such as mind-mapping and graphic organizers.

Kids with weak task-monitoring skills need to learn to review their work by reading it aloud or using supportive software, as it is very hard to "catch" errors when reading silently. If you are the parent of a child or adolescent with a disorder of written expression or executive weaknesses, you or a tutor may need to continue to serve a quality control function with regard to editing written work.

For students whose writing problems are secondary to executive weaknesses, review some of the many suggestions in the second half of this book. You may be particularly interested in the chapters that focus on how to help children with problems with working memory and with planning/organizational skills.

Case Study: Putting It All Together

Simone is a fifth grader who has been diagnosed with ADHD (predominantly inattentive type) and a reading disorder (problems with decoding). Although she has benefited greatly from intervention to improve her decoding skills, she remains a slow reader and struggles with spelling. Simone also struggles with concentration. She is not impulsive; in fact, she tends to work deliberately and process information slowly. Simone's strengths include her strong intelligence and exceptional persistence – she will keep working until the job is done! However, with each new grade, her reading and attention weaknesses make it harder and harder for her to keep up with her peers. Although she doesn't complain, she spends an average of three hours each day on homework while most of her friends are done in an hour or less. Simone often has to re-read information due to weak working memory and inattention. Given her fatigue at the end of the day and the energy and time needed to complete homework, she has stopped participating in extracurricular activities, like gymnastics and choir.

Simone's mother is understandably concerned about how her daughter will manage the increased demands of middle school. She requested an evaluation by a psychologist in order to help her daughter plan for this important transition. Simone's many strengths (including her pleasant disposition and admirable work ethic) were identified along with her weaknesses in reading rate, phonological processing, spelling, working memory, planning, and organization. Recommendations included specific remediation in reading, experimenting with assistive technology (e.g., text-to-speech programs), modifications and accommodations in the classroom, and a medical consultation to consider the pros and cons of a trial of medication to address inattention. Her mother was advised to share the evaluation results with the school and to request appropriate accommodations and modifications.

Students with learning disabilities and/or executive dysfunction are at notable risk for academic underachievement and developing secondary emotional, behavioral, and self-esteem problems when they do not receive appropriate support. There are many local and national advocacy organizations that provide information and fellowship to parents of children and adolescents with learning disabilities and ADHD. Further, we provide specific suggestions in later chapters to address weaknesses in initiation, working memory, planning, organization, and self-monitoring that may be apparent in students with learning disabilities.

In addition to providing specialized interventions to build academic skills, an important way of helping kids with specific learning disabilities is through reasonable accommodations and modifications. These are designed to "even the playing field" and include adjustments to instruction, testing, and expectations. For example, a student with a reading disorder whose testing shows that they benefit from extra time may be allowed extended time on tests. They may have accommodations for homework, such as completing as much reading as possible within one hour rather than being expected to complete a set number of pages. Remember that expectations need to be revisited regularly so that we are promoting growth and independence while still providing the support and accommodations that are needed.

Autism Spectrum Disorders (A.S.D.)

Autism is increasingly in the spotlight in educational forums and in the arts. This has helped to bring greater awareness and, hopefully, understanding. It's important to know that there is a broad range, or spectrum, of this disorder. Children with autism spectrum disorders (A.S.D.) have delays in the development of reciprocal social interactions and language skills, and present with ritualistic, repetitive activities or interests. Many people with A.S.D. have a preoccupation with very specific things, such as the Civil War, emergency vehicles, or train schedules, and many demonstrate idiosyncratic behaviors including repetitive speech or habits. In milder expressions of A.S.D., these characteristics may be much more subtle.

Social characteristics of people with A.S.D. include difficulty interpreting the unspoken rules of social interaction. The routine give-and-take of peer interactions requires nuanced understanding of what drives human behavior and the ability to put oneself in the other's place.

Particularly in adolescence, it becomes critical to attend to verbal and nonverbal cues to figure out how other people are feeling. Problems in this arena may be compounded by executive weaknesses in self-monitoring and impulse control.

Most children and teens with A.S.D. also have trouble with flexible thinking and problem-solving. They tend to be somewhat rigid and have trouble with transitions and adjusting to change. Furthermore, they may have trouble generalizing, or transferring previous knowledge and skills to new situations. Since people with A.S.D. tend to become anxious and overwhelmed when faced with unfamiliar demands, they may need extra support in new situations. Even small environmental changes can result in emotional and cognitive overload.

The later chapters on impulse control, cognitive flexibility, and self-monitoring will be of particular help to those parents with children on the autism spectrum. Additionally, there are many books available devoted to intervention strategies geared specifically to this audience. Some are included in the reference section at the back of this book.

One important issue in advocating for and supporting your child with A.S.D. is helping teachers, coaches, and therapists understand the role of executive function and other cognitive differences in behavior and response to stress. For example, Cheryl, a ten-year-old with mild A.S.D., becomes extremely upset whenever there is a substitute teacher or other unexpected change in her school routine. When managing her anxiety with an unfamiliar teacher, she may be less available for learning, unable to complete classwork or participate in class discussion. These must be interpreted within the context of her A.S.D. and related cognitive rigidity. For a typically developing peer, a lack of work completion may warrant a behavioral consequence that would not be appropriate for Cheryl.

Other Conditions Often Associated with Executive Function Weaknesses

Although outside the scope of this book, we want you to know that executive function delays and deficits are commonly experienced by children and adolescents with a range of other neurodevelopmental, psychiatric, and medical conditions. These include nonverbal learning disability (N.L.D.), Tourette syndrome (T.S.), seizure disorders, traumatic brain injury (T.B.I.), and sleep disorders and deprivation. A number of genetic syndromes also involve executive weaknesses as part of the profile, including Fragile X, Velocardiofacial syndrome (V.C.F.S.), and Turner syndrome.

Some degree of executive dysfunction is typically found in children and adolescents with psychiatric disorders, including but not limited to anxiety disorders (including obsessive-compulsive disorder, or O.C.D.), depression, bipolar disorder, and psychotic disorders, as well as kids experiencing notable emotional distress due to situational stressors. Finally, children and adolescents who experienced early abuse, neglect, and/or institutional care are at significant risk for difficulties with self-regulation and other executive skills.

Wrap-Up

People often ask us how many children and adolescents have delays or weaknesses in executive functioning. That question is essentially impossible to answer because there are many developmental and acquired conditions that include executive function weaknesses. This is further complicated by the comorbidity among these conditions (that is the clinical term for the overlap between different types of neurodevelopmental disabilities).

We want to emphasize the need to analyze and understand each student's profile in order to determine how to help them rather than relying on diagnoses and labels. Telling us that a 14-year-old has autism spectrum disorder or ADHD (or both!) does not tell us about their personality, information-processing skills, academic functioning, interests, family and school environments, or specific executive skills. While such terms are often needed to obtain appropriate supports and services at school, they are not sufficient to help us plan effective interventions and supports. As many parents have helped us appreciate, their child's diagnosis often tells us little about their strengths and needs.

II

What You Can Do about It

How to Help

An Overview

> ➤ Our approach to building executive competence involves balancing two goals: helping the child manage demands in the short run; and building independent skills for long-term self-management.
>
> ➤ All short-term strategies are designed to lighten the load on the executive system.
>
> ➤ Long-term strategies focus on strengthening the executive system by building a repertoire of effective self-management skills to compensate for executive weaknesses.
>
> ➤ Figuring out how to help begins with clearly and specifically defining the problems and deciding where to start.
>
> ➤ Interventions do not come in a one-size-fits-all package. They must be tailored to the child and the setting.

There are many steps we can take to improve the chances that children and adolescents with executive weaknesses meet with success in life. In this chapter, we lay out a general approach to helping your child. In the next chapter, we provide some basic principles of

DOI: 10.4324/9781003403517-10

behavior change to guide your treatment planning. The chapters that follow provide specific strategies or interventions that we have pulled together from our own experience, and learned from other clinicians and researchers to target various areas of weakness within the executive system.

The Two-Pronged Approach

Parents and teachers have two primary roles in helping kids with executive weaknesses. The first is to help children to be successful in their daily lives. The second is to teach the skills and approaches that allow the children to be independent in the long run. If we only provide temporary support, we may be reinforcing overdependence and learned helplessness. However, if we don't offer adequate short-term support while our kids build better executive skills, they may experience a range of negative academic and emotional consequences with long-term effects.

Short-Term Goals: Building a Prosthetic Environment

Just as we provide prostheses for someone who cannot walk otherwise, children with executive weakness need adults to adapt their environment and tasks when they do not yet have the executive function abilities to succeed on their own. For this reason, Dr. Russell Barkley refers to the process of accommodating kids as building a "prosthetic environment."

External support, limits, and supervision can all be types of prostheses. The supports that are needed change over time and, hopefully, eventually are not needed at all.

All these short-term strategies are designed to lighten the load on the executive system, allowing the child to be more successful in daily life. We do this by modifying the nature of the task, providing support, or supplementing the child's executive system. Although we call these strategies short-term, it is important to understand that many kids may need support for years, with the goal of eventually learning to independently manage tasks and demands.

One important outcome of good accommodations is that we generate a model for the child of how to manage the task. When we walk a youngster through a process, we help them in the moment, but we also help them to create an internal template that they can call on in the future.

Jim has trouble organizing and planning written reports. It takes him a long time to get started, and then he often neglects to check his work for correct spelling, punctuation, and capitalization. In the past, Jim's father worked with him on every long writing assignment. Together, they worked their way through each step of the writing process, including helping Jim to develop an outline and use a proofreading checklist. In this way, Jim was introduced to an approach to completing writing tasks and he was able to be successful, though not independently. Now Jim is working with a writing tutor who is helping him to develop strategies that build on his growing independence. He uses writing software to produce a graphic organizer (a visual display of what he will write about) and then uses another program that reads his work aloud so that he can catch mistakes. Jim still needs his tutor or father to proofread lengthier or more important papers so that he receives support as he continues to build independent writing and executive skills.

A prosthetic environment provides opportunities for children to continue to take part in experiences that further development. For example, a child with executive dysfunction might benefit from the sense of belonging and the outdoor group activities associated with participation in Boy Scouts or Girl Scouts. Even children who have difficulties initiating and independently organizing the projects required to earn badges can get a lot out of the group. Accommodations in the form of extra support from a parent and from the troop leader can allow children to be a part of the many developmental experiences that scouting can provide.

Finally, and perhaps most importantly, helping a child to be more successful on a daily basis reduces the risk of serious secondary problems, such as depression, anxiety, and low self-esteem. These secondary problems can arise from the constant demoralization caused by failure to meet expectations day after day.

For adolescents with weaknesses in impulse control, extra parental support and supervision may be needed to help them stay on a stable and positive path. These teens tend to be more vulnerable to the temptations of substance abuse and other risky behavior. Offering support that allows teens to participate in healthy activities, build on their strengths, and feel hopeful about their future provides a foundation that may help to counter the risk factors.

Sometimes parents who provide appropriate support for their children with executive weaknesses are accused of trying to protect them from the realities of life. We think it makes sense to provide a level of protection and a buffer from demands when a child does not yet have the skills to independently manage them. If we do not provide this, even very bright, talented kids may come to view themselves as incompetent and ineffective. Depending upon temperament, they may become overly self-critical or give up due to their inconsistent performance. Without appropriate expectations and support to even the playing field, these youngsters may experience academic underachievement, underemployment, and interpersonal problems.

By experiencing success when the support is in place, children learn that it is possible to succeed. With adult guidance, these children can begin to understand the kinds of support they need and where to find them and then, over time, learn to choose and use support for themselves when needed. By combining short-term support with interventions that focus on skills needed for independence in the long run, we can help children and teens to build competence and confidence.

For most of the people we have worked with, the self-awareness and maturity to recognize the need for help and to seek appropriate support comes late in the game. Often, parental guidance continues to be needed into high school and, for some, into the college and young adult years. This guidance must be balanced with the need to allow the emotional and practical independence that our adolescents and young adults are seeking. That is no easy balance! It is important that adults evaluate on an ongoing basis whether they can scale back their direct involvement. In Chapter 10 we discuss ways to accomplish this balance.

Going the Distance: Building Executive Skills

If we only focus on short-term goals with our kids, then we are only doing half of our job. It is also important to provide the explicit teaching and the practice vital to increasing their executive competence. Building skills can be done with help from parents, teachers, tutors, therapists, and other important adults.

Long-term interventions focus on strengthening the executive system by building a repertoire of effective self-management skills to compensate for executive weaknesses. These interventions allow our children to be competent as they move out into the world on their own.

One of the most effective ways of building executive skills is by developing habits and routines that eventually become automatic. Building habits requires repetition, repetition, and more repetition.

Here's the good news: Once you no longer have to think about doing something, you largely bypass the executive system. Here's the bad news: It really does require repetition, *ad nauseum*, for kids with executive weaknesses to internalize these behaviors. Remember, this is not a knowledge problem. As with adults who are trying to change their behavior (have you ever tried to lose weight?), kids often know what they should do, but tend to revert to their old ways. Once behaviors become automatic, they no longer require conscious effort. Until that point, independent performance of the desired behavior is likely to be inconsistent. This is why it is so important to provide a prosthetic environment while the skills are still developing.

Using Habits and Routines to Manage Your Life

Let's move away from talking about kids for just a minute and look at the role of habits and routines in our adult lives. When you walk in the door to your house, where do you put your keys? When you are ready to leave the house again, do you have to look for them? Most adults have a designated place for their keys, having learned by experience the importance of putting them in the same place every time. Do you have a hook by the door? Or a basket or table where you drop them? Whatever your special place, it is probably so automatic at this point that there is no effort involved in this small detail of your day.

Now, if you move to a new house, you will likely be disoriented until you build new habits. You will once again have to think about your keys. As simple as it sounds, building habits and routines is one of the most powerful ways to manage repetitive tasks efficiently. Routines can also be applied to much more complex tasks such as schoolwork and study habits. The more you can help your child to develop habits and routines that meet their own individual preferences, the more likely they are to be able to manage demands independently.

As children get older, it is increasingly important that they learn how to manage daily life's demands and know what to do to compensate for their executive weaknesses. We must actively engage them in experimenting with various strategies to see what works and suits their particular style. Still, helping children develop better executive functioning is not just about teaching strategies. Rather, we must highlight the importance of starting tasks by thinking about a plan. When we focus on helping children and teens plan *how* they will complete a task, we help them with the sort of executive thinking that will allow them to be independent.

Designing Interventions

The Detective Phase

Designing interventions begins with a detective process. Success at any given task generally involves a whole chain of behaviors. If a child is not succeeding, we must figure out exactly what link in the chain is broken.

Kevin often gets low grades in school because he does not turn in homework. In an interview with Kevin and his parents, it was determined that he does not write down homework assignments consistently. He also forgets to bring home the materials needed to complete assignments.

Debbie also gets low grades due to failure to turn in homework. She writes down all of her assignments and generally finishes some of her work each night. However, she tends to underestimate how long assignments will take, so she starts too late to complete the work.

Understanding where in the cycle the process breaks down is an important first step. We use this knowledge to target the problem. We can then address the problem using specific strategies. For example, teachers may comment that a student needs to hand in assignments on time. Sound simple? Not so much. Turning in homework is a process that requires accurately recording the assignment, bringing the necessary materials home, completing the work, and submitting it online or putting the assignment in a backpack and bringing it to school and to class. Once the student, teacher, and/or parent identifies the step(s) in the process at which the child falters, specific interim steps and strategies to achieve the goal can be developed to help the child mend the missing link in the chain of behaviors. So, the overarching goal of turning in assignments would be the same for both Kevin and Debbie. However, the steps to achieve these goals (sometimes referred to as interim objectives or short-term goals on school plans) would be different. For example, short-term goals for Kevin might look like this: "Kevin will record daily and long-term assignments in his agenda book. In the margin next to each assignment, he will list all materials needed to complete the work. Kevin will present his agenda book to each teacher at the end of class to be initialed for completeness." For Debbie, support and strategies are quite different: "Debbie will meet with her advisor each Monday and will develop and record a plan for completing all assignments and studying for tests. The written plan will include an estimate of the time needed for the work and when the work will be done." These goals and objectives may be part of an informal plan developed with the teacher and family, or if Debbie and Kevin are eligible for a more formal plan (see Chapter 6), these goals and strategies can be written into their 504 plan or I.E.P.

Creativity at Work

The first step in helping kids is to define the problem or the behavior to be changed. (See Chapter 6, Assessment: Figuring Out What's Needed). We can be most helpful when we specifically identify behaviors (e.g., "they lose their assignment book") rather than focusing on broad characteristics (e.g., "they are forgetful"). Once we have a target behavior defined, there are many different ways to intervene. There is no one set of interventions that suits all children or all settings.

An important part of helping disorganized kids is deciding what is most getting in the way of academic or social adjustment and giving priority to these. For example, although it may drive you crazy as a parent, your child's messy room may be less of a priority than their disorganized backpack. To be effective and supportive, we need to work on only one or two goals at a time. Otherwise, we and our children are at risk of becoming overwhelmed or sidetracked. Tackling just one or two skills or issues at a time is not only practical, but it also helps adults and kids to remain focused and hopeful.

Interventions are most likely to be effective when the child or adolescent plays an active role in brainstorming solutions. Inviting collaboration can be challenging, particularly when adolescents are doing their best to separate from their parents. Sometimes the most unconventional approaches are the most effective. If a disorganized student remembers their binder because they put it next to their lunch in the refrigerator, that is fine as long as it works for them!

Helping kids with executive challenges can surely be frustrating, but it's also an interesting and creative effort. The number of possible interventions is limited only by our ability to think outside the box.

In the next chapters, we present some of the interventions that we have found helpful for children with whom we have worked. Our goal, though, is for you to understand the principles well enough that you can design interventions that work for the specific challenges you and your child face. So, at the beginning of each intervention chapter, we list the general principles we apply to build better functioning in that particular area of executive weakness.

A Few More Things about Interventions

Interventions are not:

- Doing everything for the child;
- Excuses for inadequate effort or bad behavior;
- Praising or rewarding all behavior.

Interventions often:

- Involve setting different expectations for a given child;
- Change as a child encounters new tasks and demands;
- Evolve as a child becomes more competent;
- Require ongoing monitoring of effectiveness and adjustments as needed.

Behavior Change in a Nutshell

THE BASICS

> Kids are most likely to be successful when we teach using real-life tasks rather than trying to teach skills in the abstract.

> Guided practice will allow your child or teen to learn the skills needed to perform a task and then to practice them until the steps become a habit.

> Teaching new skills to children and adolescents with executive skill weaknesses may require a different approach than teaching skills to other children. Natural consequences and typical behavioral interventions may not be as effective.

> Change happens in small steps, not in giant leaps. It is important to recognize the effort and accomplishment involved in even small steps if a child is moving in the right direction.

If you are going to be the architect of your child's intervention plan, or even just an informed reviewer of the plan, then you need to know some basic principles of behavior change. Here are some essential principles to guide you.

DOI: 10.4324/9781003403517-11

Use Real Life to Teach

Skills learned in the context of real-life activities generally have better sticking power than skills taught in the abstract. For example, helping a child with the planning and organizing for a school or home project is more effective than a study skills class in the summer that teaches basic principles of how to organize things. Kids may learn something from those classes, but there are some definite pitfalls to the classroom approach.

The most important thing to know is that children do not necessarily apply skills that they learn in an isolated environment. It is the daily application of skills and tools that forges good habits over time, and that is where real life offers the best opportunities.

Rather than talking about the importance of keeping their room clean, for example, clean the room with your child. You can help by breaking the task down into individual steps necessary to complete the job well. "How should we do this? First, let's sort the papers. Then, we can throw away the trash and put papers that you need to save in this box for now. Next, let's deal with your clothes. Dirty clothes go in the hamper, and clean clothes go in the closet or folded and placed into the proper drawers." Create a plan that defines each step and create a written template. Now your child has a checklist that they can use until the steps become routine. You have also emphasized the executive thinking process, thinking about how to accomplish the task before jumping in. Once your child or teen gets better at this approach, they will participate more in creating the plan. Of course, the long-term goal is for them to take over and do it all themselves, in time.

Take a Teaching versus a Punishing Approach

Remember that the origin of the word *discipline* comes from the Latin word that means "to teach." While thoughtful punishments certainly have a role in raising children, they are useless if the child's delayed development means that they cannot perform the desired behavior independently and consistently. You would be up in arms if the first-grade teacher yelled at your child for not knowing how to read. Instead, you expect your child to be offered instruction that teaches the foundation skills and then moves to more advanced lessons as their abilities progress. Do the same with executive skills.

As parents, we are at risk of getting weary and falling back on verbalizing our unfiltered first thoughts. "How many times do we have to go through this? Why do we always have to remind you to pick up after yourself?" It will help you and your child if you focus instead on what you want to teach. In very specific behavioral terms, tell them what is expected. "You need to go back and pick up your coat and hang it on the hook," is specific and effective for children who need daily instruction. This repetition should change over time to prompting the behavior, rather than directing it. "Jack, what are you supposed to do when you come in the door?"

It is frustrating to see your child make the same mistakes over and over again, but lectures, threats, and harsh comments are ineffective at building skills.

Collaborate with Your Child

Your child is most likely to be successful in making changes when encouraged to be an active participant in developing goals and deciding how to reach them, as we noted in the previous chapter. Consider your child's ideas and input and reinforce them for being willing to experiment with a range of approaches. As children get older, they are better able to generate new ideas for building habits and changing behavior. However, even younger children often respond positively to being asked to help with problem-solving and monitoring how things are going. Kids can also help us understand what is getting in their way.

Focus on the Desired Outcome

Focus on helping your child to achieve a relevant, meaningful behavior rather than focusing on what is getting in the way. For example, squirmy and distractible kids often have trouble completing their schoolwork. Adults may assume that the problem with work completion is that the child needs to sit still and keep their attention on the worksheet. So, the child might be rewarded for sitting quietly in their seat and keeping their eyes on the paper. Unfortunately, that does not mean that the child is getting more work done!

If you want your child to complete more work, then focus on the goal of getting more work done! Now, there may need to be some other changes to allow that to happen. Ben may need to be moved away from the kid who encourages misbehavior. Ana may need to get up and walk around for a few minutes; she may be asked to hand out papers, run an errand, or be allowed to get a drink of water. Peter's concentration and work completion may be enhanced by letting him suck on a hard candy, chew gum, or use a fidget toy such as a squishy ball or piece of clay. However, after trying these approaches, the child should be evaluated to determine whether they are getting more work done. After clarifying the goal, think creatively to generate possible ways to achieve it.

Raise the Stakes

Concrete rewards, point systems, and the like are all aimed at increasing the importance of a behavior from the child's perspective. Positive reinforcement for new and difficult behaviors helps the child to maintain interest and sustain effort. Kids don't necessarily see the value of what we are trying to teach them; if they don't see the value, they aren't likely to put much effort toward the goal. So, sometimes we need to make the behavioral goal more important to the child by pairing it with a preferred reward, or tethering failure to perform the desired behavior to a loss of desired privileges. Further, particularly when children and teens are working on behaviors that are hard for them or building complex, multi-step chains of behavior, such as a long-term project, rewards for interim steps help to sustain motivation for what may seem like a distant long-term goal.

We understand that many parents have concerns about rewarding or "bribing" kids for what they theoretically *should* be doing. However, if a child does not yet have sufficient skills to complete the task consistently and independently, using rewards can be very effective and appropriate in helping to build skills, routines, and habits. After all, most adults are motivated by earning a paycheck, even when they enjoy and value their work. At the same time, adults are motivated to work when they feel appreciated and valued for what they do. Likewise, when incorporated into daily life with a spirit of compassion and respect, home rewards are more than just transactional. An individualized reward system can be a useful tool that is validating to the child.

Of course, our long-term goal is to increase independent performance as children mature through adolescence and into young adulthood. Over time, practice and repetition of executive skills and compensatory strategies, combined with maturation, bring our children to a phase where they are primarily motivated by their own goals and have most of the skills necessary to reach them. However, this development may be delayed in individuals with executive functioning weaknesses.

Reward Even Small Steps in the Right Direction

Change happens in small steps, not in one giant leap. It is important to recognize the effort and accomplishment involved in even small steps toward a goal. For example, Matt often ended up at soccer practice without his soccer bag. His mom worked on helping him develop a checklist of things that he needed to pack into the soccer bag and planned with him to put the bag into the car the night before practice. At first, Matt tended to rush the process by packing from memory and then tossing the bag into the car without double-checking that he had all that he needed. His mother praised him for getting the bag to soccer practice, and then encouraged him to use his checklist, too, so that he would have all the things on his list when he got to practice.

It is a basic principle of behavior change that any behavior followed by a positive result is more likely to recur, and any behavior followed by a negative result is less likely to recur. So, if Matt completed one step of the process, and his mom yelled at him for not doing the other steps, can you see how that would discourage the small, but positive, change Matt had made?

Use "Tried and True" Behavior Modification Techniques

Behavior modification is the process of applying the basic principles of behavior change in a systematic and planned manner. When informal behavior modification techniques are insufficient to bring about desired behavior change, then more formal systems may need to be used. These systems are built on the same basic principles outlined above: any behavior followed by a positive event is more likely to recur, and any behavior followed by a negative event is less likely to recur.

For many kids and teens, behavioral plans help to build confidence, because they provide concrete evidence of their own accomplishments. When their small successes are praised and rewarded, the approval from others highlights what they are doing right. Even though they might not meet all the goals, they may feel more hopeful that they're making progress toward the standards. In this way, systematic recording of achievements helps guard against sweeping criticisms and self-rebuke.

Further, parents are less likely to make global, negative attributions about behavior when they see success in some areas. The specific definition of goals on a behavioral plan can help parents to see evidence of improvement.

Tomas' mother said that he was "never" on time in the mornings, despite his behavior plan. Most days, he raced out of the house in the mornings without making his bed or eating breakfast. Tomas countered, "But I haven't missed the bus at all in over two weeks!" This was a significant improvement for Tomas, and the daily recording of his behaviors helped him to claim it!

Behavioral plans range from simple agreements, targeting just a few behaviors, to comprehensive plans that lay out expectations for the entire day at school and home. The more comprehensive plans are helpful for children who are unable to regulate their behavior without step-by-step guidance. Some kids also need the concrete and immediate feedback that a detailed behavioral plan offers. The key here is matching a plan to your child.

Matching a plan to the individual also includes choosing age-appropriate rewards for older children and teens. Reward systems work best, in general, when the child or teen contributes to the design of the plan: they should be involved in the consideration of behavioral expectations, identifying personal goals, and determining meaningful rewards for improved performance. Particularly with teens, getting buy-in is critical. Perhaps a teen wants to work toward more driving practice time with a parent or credit for in-app purchases on a favorite video game. Perhaps they could save up points for an outing, like lunch at a favorite restaurant. Likewise, they should be invited to identify their own goals. Research on helping teens with executive weaknesses confirms that interventions are most effective when parents listen to what is motivating to their child (Sibley 2017).

Most plans incorporate a menu of rewards, since working toward the same reward repeatedly becomes less appealing once the novelty wears off. Reward menus for more comprehensive plans generally include some choices that require fewer points, such as what might be earned in a single day, as well as choices that would require points to be saved over a longer period of time. (For a clear explanation and step-by-step guide to creating a behavioral plan, see Barkley 2020.)

For children and teens who are having behavioral issues at school, it is important that parents and teachers collaborate so that there is consistency and communication from one setting to the other.

The overarching goal of any formal behavioral plan is for the person to perform the desired behaviors so reliably and consistently that the plan is no longer needed. For many older children and teens, earning their way off the system is the biggest reward of all!

You will notice that the use of basic principles of behavior change, in general, and explicit behavioral plans, specifically, are incorporated into the suggestions provided in Chapters 11 through 16.

Trust Your Child's Own Developmental Urges

Developmental unfolding is a powerful phenomenon, and most children have a strong need to be competent. When you move out of a punitive perspective and align yourself with the part of your child that wants to grow up and be successful, you have fewer power struggles. How do you do this? Here are some words to practice that will help you to avoid power struggles and help your child to "own" their behavior.

"Wow, you do have a problem. Now you are missing two assignments. What do you think you can do about it?" Apply as needed when your child forgets to bring their book home from school, arrives at the beach in the summer with no bathing suit, etc. Help with problem solving, as needed, rather than taking over the problem or getting stuck in chastising, lecturing, or punishing.

When Should You Allow Your Child to Experience Natural Consequences for Behavior?

Allowing your child to experience natural consequences *can* be a very effective way to motivate behavior change. For example, when a teen calls ahead of time to invite a friend over, their planning and initiation may be reinforced by the desired natural consequence because the friend was free to come over. Likewise, sometimes negative natural consequences can motivate a child to seek new skills or try strategies they have resisted in the past. For example, Matt might start using his checklist to pack up his soccer bag if he has to sit out a game or two because he did not bring his shin guards. However, deciding whether to allow negative consequences to occur can be tricky.

When we consider whether to let a child suffer negative natural consequences, we must be attuned to two factors: whether success is within reach; and what the cost of experiencing the negative consequences would be.

Since many children and adolescents with executive function weaknesses do not yet have the foundation skills they need to independently perform the desired behaviors, "learning from experience" may not happen by withholding support. In such situations, negative natural consequences may be at best discouraging, and at worst devastating to continued development and success. At times, we advise parents to intervene so that their kids do *not* experience the natural consequences of their behavior. Instead, we focus on defining the requisite skills and building competence one step at a time.

As an example, let's consider the developmental task of learning to cross the street independently. We assume that almost all kids eventually will be able to cross the street without a parent present. This requires considerable executive skill as not all drivers are predictable and the child needs to be able to judge the situation in real time. All kids quickly learn the rule for street crossing: stop, look both ways, cross if it is clear. However, being able to recite the rule does not mean that a child is ready to perform this behavior. Is there a universal age at which all kids can cross the street? Of course not! Some kids master this skill at seven, while others do not do so until age ten. (There are even some teenagers we worry about!) Now, the natural consequence of failure to cross the street according to the rules is simply too steep a price to let a child go if they are not ready, so we take an active role to make sure the child is safe.

Just as we would not allow a child to cross the street without guidance before they are ready, we should not expect a child to independently complete a project, get ready for the day, or plan for the coming week before these skills and habits are developed to an adequate level of mastery.

Change Does Not Occur in a Smooth or Steady Uphill Manner

Expect slow progress with ups and downs along the way. If you have ever tried to lose weight, then you know how slow behavior change can be. If you have been successful at losing weight, you have learned to set realistic goals, to celebrate small victories, and to recover when you have a setback. These are principles that guide all behavior change. (And is it ever helpful to have someone chide or make fun of you when you had that piece of chocolate cake or skipped your scheduled exercise walk?)

While frustration and exhaustion are normal parts of the parenting experience (and the child's experience), these are even more pronounced when your child has executive skills challenges or other developmental delays. Similarly, children and teens with challenges can become weary of the extra effort required to manage daily demands. Your child needs your empathy, understanding, encouragement, and support to recover from missteps and move forward. In this way, you set the foundation for healthy adjustment despite the challenges.

If at First You Don't Succeed, Try a Few More Times Then ... Change Your Expectations!

THE BASICs

> Knowing where to set the bar for a child or adolescent who is out of sync with peers is a challenging job.

> Setting realistic expectations requires careful observation of your child's performance and a willingness to frequently reevaluate based on how things go.

> Setting the bar too high can be as detrimental as setting it too low.

> Expectations must be based upon the child's unique profile rather than age or grade.

> You may need to adjust the height of the bar.

For children and teens with weaknesses in executive functioning, the journey to adulthood can be rocky. As their peers are handling increasingly complex tasks with greater independence, children with executive weaknesses may continue to rely heavily on adult-provided structure and guidance.

When you know that your child is out of sync with the standard expectations for their age, what guidelines do you use to set expectations? How do you know if the expectations you set are realistic for your child or teen's unique profile of strengths and weaknesses?

DOI: 10.4324/9781003403517-12

Don't Try to Keep Up with the Joneses

The good news is that you are *the* expert on your child. You have watched your child grow over the years and understand what they need to thrive. Don't listen to your coworker or sister who says that your child will never develop responsibility unless you demand more of them. For kids with executive weaknesses it is often the case that the intent and desire are there to meet age-appropriate goals, but the means for achieving those goals is not. Remember, executive dysfunction is a performance disability: there is a gap between knowledge and the ability to apply that knowledge independently and consistently.

The Limbo Game of Setting Expectations

How do you know where to set the bar for your child? Here are some clues to help you figure out if your expectations are where they should be:

Clue #1

If your child continually underperforms or does not meet expectations, it is likely that the bar is set too high. Perhaps your child "should" be able to accomplish the task according to developmental timetables for typical kids. However, the fact that your friend's child did something when they were your child's age, or that your child's older brother did not need extra help with the same task, are not the criteria to use to set the bar.

Clue #2

If the bar is set at the right height, your child should hit the goal more times than not. Don't expect your child to be 100 percent consistent; inconsistent behavior is the hallmark of executive dysfunction. This poses real challenges for setting fair expectations. It is like a trick; for example, your child might amaze you by remembering to take out the garbage two out of seven times. If your child can do it sometimes, why can't you expect them to manage the task successfully every time? Similarly, perhaps sometimes your child's essays are brilliant, while at other times it is hard to believe that the essay was written by the same child. Maybe you've noticed that your child sometimes spells a word three different ways within the same paper.

Though it may be tempting to assume your kid is just trying to get away with something, try to shift your perspective. To paraphrase Dr. Russell Barkley, sometimes our kids do something well, and we hold it against them for a lifetime. Of course, we're not looking for perfection, but you will know that you've set the target correctly if the "hit" rate improves with practice and repetition.

Clue #3

If everyone in your child's life seems to disagree about how your child or teen is doing, you may need to confer with a third party. Teachers, coaches, and other adults that you trust and who work with your child can offer observations of your child or teen from a different frame of reference. These observations can provide a much-needed perspective on how your child is performing in an everyday context.

It is also instructive, though potentially misleading, to ask students how they think they did on a paper or test. Many kids with weaknesses in their executive system are very poor judges of their own performance because they think they put forth adequate effort and did what was asked of them. Imagine how discouraging it is to believe that you studied hard but then to receive a D because you inadvertently overlooked a whole section of an assignment or made careless errors on a test. Don't assume that your child is avoiding telling you the truth on purpose. They may be clueless! (That is not to say that kids with executive dysfunction do not sometimes try to cover their tracks, just as their peers do.)

Clue #4

If you feel like you are on the brink of losing touch with your child, consider that they may be having difficulty living up to expectations. Often kids with executive weaknesses cope with embarrassment and shame by pretending that they just don't care about school or whatever standards you have set. This is a self-protective maneuver. It often feels more comfortable to say "I just didn't try" than to admit you tried and didn't succeed. This is particularly true for people with weak impulse control, who sometimes behave in ways they didn't intend and then must deal with the consequences. Be cautious about assuming that your child really doesn't care about being successful. This may be the mask that your child wears to save face. Consider ways to bolster your child's success rate to see if that affects their behavior and attitude.

You may need to lower the bar just a bit to allow for more success. Sometimes simplifying your child's life by eliminating an activity or demand helps to relieve some of the pressure.

Sometimes your child needs more help in one particular area. At other times, they may be overwhelmed trying to manage many demands. To improve their success rate, you can consider reducing the challenge level or adding more support. Here are two brief examples:

Tina, a third grader, was brought in for consultation due to increased stress that showed up as tearfulness, difficulty sleeping, and complaints about going to school that she had never expressed before. With some exploration, it was determined that these difficulties had started following a change in Tina's placement in language arts and math class. After monitoring her performance, the classroom teacher had moved Tina from the standard groups to the accelerated groups in these areas. Even with some time to adjust, Tina continued to be overwhelmed by the increased pace of instruction. Her symptoms subsided once her parents requested that she be moved back to the standard group for language arts. She remained in the advanced group for math, a subject she particularly enjoyed, and she became an enthusiastic student again.

A different plan was developed for Andre, a high school junior who also began to show signs of stress. Andre's stress emerged as a change in attitude toward studying and planning for college. His interest in researching his college options diminished, and he began to shrug off increasingly poor performance at school. Since these changes were uncharacteristic for their son, Andre's parents shared their concerns with him and asked what was going on and what they could do to help. They learned that juggling the demands of school, along with the added pressure of managing the college application process, was overwhelming Andre. They decided together to enlist the school guidance counselor to help him lay out the process and timeline for steps in the college application process. They also obtained a tutor to help him keep up with his classes and to learn the organizational skills he needed to track all of his demands. With these supports in place, Andre began to feel more in control, and his attitude changed.

If You Need to Change Expectations

If you feel that demands so exceed your child's abilities that they cannot succeed, then you may find yourself going against the current in realigning expectations. Today's culture, at least here in the

United States, seems to be characterized by a more-is-better approach. If reading at age six is good, then reading at age four must be better! If being good at school or athletics or music is an advantage, then doing all three must be even better! There are many factors at work that lead to this general competitive climate for kids (and adults!), and it is far outside the scope of this book to explore these. However, as you consider scaling back your expectations, be forewarned that you may meet with resistance from others in your child's world.

Indeed, we hope it is clear that we are not arguing for coddling kids, setting low expectations, or any of the other ways to describe undervaluing our kids' abilities to rise to a challenge. However, if you have carefully looked for the clues outlined above, including by obtaining the opinion of a third party if you are unsure about expectations, and you feel that the bar is set too high, then go ahead and swim against the current!

Your Child's Expectations

Another tricky aspect of setting realistic expectations for kids with executive weaknesses is that they may resist accepting the support they need. Especially for adolescents and young adults, the societal pressure and internal drive to succeed independently are very strong. But the reality is that you can only do as well as you can do. Children with delayed development of executive skills need and deserve external supports and accommodations so they can fairly demonstrate their competencies. Just as we wouldn't expect a child with a physical disability requiring a wheelchair to compete in a footrace with typically developing peers, we shouldn't ask a child with executive dysfunction to independently manage certain tasks and situations before their own abilities unfold.

You can best support your child by helping them understand that the executive functions are brain-based skills and that difficulties with them are *not* moral or personal weaknesses. As a parent, you likely have great ability to understand your child and their needs. When you are unsure, consultation with a psychologist or other mental health professional may be useful.

Your Partner's Expectations

Don't be surprised if you and your significant other have divergent views on your child and where to set the bar. One of you may want to back down on expectations, while the other one may think that providing stronger consequences is in order. This sort of disagreement is quite common and may lead to a situation in which it makes sense to consult with an objective third party. Last, but certainly not least, blaming yourself or your partner as the biological source of your child's executive weaknesses is never productive. Feel free to take credit for your child's strong intelligence and artistic talent and acknowledge your shared executive weaknesses, if that is the case, but don't spend too much time there. More important is how you all move forward together.

Fading Support

Once your child is performing the desired behavior consistently with external supports in place, the next step is to "fade" out supports. Fading supports means that you gradually and systematically reduce the amount of external support to the point where you are no longer involved at all.

For example, perhaps you are working with your child on a daily basis to empty their backpack, sort the papers, and then organize them. To fade support, you might move first from doing the job with your child to observing and cuing as your child does it. If that goes well, then you can back off from cuing, but ask to see the backpack and notebook after they are organized. Then you might move to reviewing this every other day, then to random checks. If your child continues to complete the task consistently and does the job relatively well, then you know that they are independent on this task. However, if they falter at any step of the fading process, be prepared to back up to the last level of support at which your child was successful.

It is very important to view this as an experiment rather than a "pass-fail" experience. If your child has developed sufficient independent skills, you will not need to keep providing support. However, if they cannot yet manage independently, reinstate the structure and guidance until the pattern of consistent performance is re-established. After a time, you can "test the waters" again.

11

Helping Children Control Impulses

Impulse control = *The ability to stop and think before acting. Impulse control is also called inhibition. Disinhibited kids are those who lack age-appropriate impulse control.*

O ften when people talk about a person who is inhibited, they are referring to someone who is constricted or uptight. While this extreme of too much inhibition is generally agreed to be a negative characteristic, a good amount of inhibition *is* essential for behavioral control. The ability to stop and think provides a cushion of time between impulses or feelings and a behavioral response. Thus, impulse control is critical to self-regulation.

Young children are not expected to consistently control their impulses or their thoughts and actions; they rely heavily on adults to help them control their behavior. They require immediate and concrete guidance. As kids mature, we expect them to internalize rules and to develop better and better self-control so that they are not at the mercy of their impulses. However, those who are disinhibited are slower to develop these controls. Their neurological systems seem to be hard-wired to prefer immediate reward over long-term goals. Despite their knowledge of rules and expectations, they are often unable to control their behavior in the moment. These children and teens need extra support and teaching over a longer period of time in this critical arena of executive functioning.

DOI: 10.4324/9781003403517-13

Strategies reviewed in this chapter help children who:

■ Have trouble controlling verbal impulsiveness (e.g., talking excessively, interrupting others, blurting out);

■ Have trouble controlling physical impulsiveness (e.g., grabbing things, pushing and shoving others, hitting);

■ Have trouble controlling irritating behavior;

■ Run off in stores or other settings; and

■ Have problems doing homework.

Below are some general intervention strategies that you'll want to employ with your child or student with impulse control issues. Further down, we've provided advice for dealing with more specific scenarios that you're likely to experience with your child or teen. Note that depending on the issue you are addressing with your child, you will typically use only a subset of the strategies discussed in this chapter.

Summary: General Strategies to Help Your Child Control Impulses

■ **Provide external structure** in the form of general guidelines, specific rules, and clear labels in plain language to convey expectations and teach acceptable behavior.

■ **Offer support** (e.g., visual cues, verbal prompts) to bolster the "stop" function. Use brief phrases to cue the desired behavior in the moment.

■ **Plan in advance** for potentially problematic times by identifying what leads to loss of control and providing extra support in those situations.

■ **Teach alternatives** to negative behaviors. For younger children, practice behaviors that interfere with impulsive physical responses. For older children, work together to brainstorm more positive responses to the situations.

■ **Build on the older child's desire for more freedom** by directly connecting this desire to the behaviors needed to maturely handle the desired privileges. Align yourself with your child's strong developmental urges and take a teaching rather than a punishing role. Trade on good control to enhance motivation.

■ **Use rewards (tangible, verbal, or otherwise) to motivate desired behavior.** If rewards alone do not work, you may also need to take away privileges or allow the natural consequence to occur. Be sure to let your child know in advance that they may lose privileges.

■ **Ensure your child's safety.** If your child's impulsive behavior puts them at risk of physical harm, drop all other priorities, forget teaching anything, and grab that kid!

Strategies to Help a Child Manage Verbal Impulsiveness (Talking Excessively, Interrupting Others, etc.)

1. Provide external structure by teaching rules that can be applied to a variety of situations. For example, you might tell your child:

   • "When you walk into a room, stop and listen to see if the grown-ups are talking. If they are, say, 'Excuse me,' then wait for the go-ahead before you jump in."

   • "If you want to join a group of kids who are talking, listen first to what they are talking about, and then you can add a brief comment on that same topic."

   • Or, for older kids: "Don't jump right into the conversation. Just say hello and stay nearby. See how they respond. What would you notice in their words or body language if they're receptive to you?"

   • "Do not talk when the teacher is talking. Raise your hand and wait for the teacher to call on you."

   • "When you're with your friends, listen as much as you talk. Give your friends as much airtime as you take."

2. Provide specific rules and clear labels in plain language to convey expectations. For example:

   • "I need some quiet time now. Please find something quiet that you can do on your own for 15 minutes." For young children, you may need to be more creative with your language: "My listener is full right now. I need some quiet time to rest my listening."

- "This is adult talk time. You may stay in the room if you can play quietly without interrupting."

- "Dad and I have a few things we need to discuss alone. Please find something to do in another room until we have finished."

- "Maria, I need to participate in an important video conference in a few minutes. This is work time for me and free time for you. I'll be tied up for 30 minutes. I'll open my door when I'm through."

3. Offer support to bolster the "stop" function. Work out some private cues with your child, so that you can help them know when to stop. For example:

   - Put a finger to your lips or hold up a hand, traffic-cop style, to indicate "No talking."

   - Use a visual image to indicate "No interruption" time in the classroom, such as a laminated picture of a big ear to show this is listening time or a mouth with a line through it to indicate "No talking."

   - When a student interrupts while the teacher is talking, the teacher can raise their hand as a simple and gentle reminder for the student to do the same.

   - In classrooms, the teacher may turn the lights on and off when too many students are talking at the same time. This can also work at home when kids tune out verbal reminders to sit quietly.

   - Adults can also use physical proximity to cue the child or teen that it is not an appropriate time to talk. Many teachers find that it helps to stand near a student's desk, perhaps putting a hand on the student's shoulder. The goal is to be subtle enough to avoid embarrassing the student.

   - A parent or a teacher can provide an agreed-upon nonverbal cue to halt talking out of turn.

   - Use verbal prompts to help children think about the rules:
     - "What is the rule for entering a room when people may already be talking?"

- o "I need to make some work phone calls now. What's the rule about interrupting when I'm working?"
- o "Remember, quiet activities only if you are going to stay in the room. Are you ready with some things to do?"
- o Create some brief phrases to cue the desired behavior: "Work time, now, Jake. Talk time is in 15 minutes." "Hold that thought or write it down for now."

When you see that your child is already about to boil over, provide support by briefly validating their feelings and then reminding them of the rules and possible consequences. "I can see that you have a lot to say. I wish I could listen now, but I have to get to my meeting online. Please keep it quiet out here for 30 minutes. Otherwise, I'll need to start scheduling a sitter again."

J.P. is a 16-year-old who lives and breathes soccer. He gets very upset when a teammate's pass is off target, or a peer misses a goal. He routinely responds with loud disapproval and strong language. Although he is a valued player, J.P.'s behavior has gotten the coach upset enough to suspend him from games. Even his close friends on the team are starting to resent his negative comments. J.P. understands that his behavior is inappropriate, but he has trouble containing his strong reactions in the moment. In private talks, J.P., his parents, and his coach have come up with a variety of strategies that are helpful. The coach prompts J.P. and the rest of the team before games: "Have fun out there and support your teammates!" In practice, the coach teaches the team appropriate things to say when they get upset at themselves or a teammate who plays poorly. "I did my best." "Good effort." "Get back out there and try again." Knowing how hard it is for J.P. to stay in control, the coach is careful to praise him and the other players when they support each other. Additionally, the coach seeks out visual contact with J.P. when he is upset and offers a quick thumbs-up to help the teen stay on track with his efforts to manage his strong feelings.

4. Plan in advance. When possible, head off problems by setting the scene ahead of time and laying out the guidelines. For example:
   - "After dinner we would like some adult talk time with Grandma and Grandpa. Please think about what you would like to do. You may stay in the room if you can play quietly without interrupting.

Or you could work on the puzzle in the family room. However, it will be grown-ups only for half an hour after dinner."

- In classrooms, hand out note cards to students and instruct them to write down questions or thoughts during uninterrupted lecture times.

- Ask talkative kids to think ahead of time of something to do during long drives, waiting during an adult appointment, or other times that are ripe for excessive chatter. Bringing a book or loading a tablet or smartphone with music or movies can make for a more successful outing. (Remind them to pack headphones, too!)

- Encourage kids who come on too strong in social situations to practice laying low. "Laurie, remember that when you go into Jan's house she may have other girls over, too. I know that sometimes you feel left out if others are not including you in their conversation. That's when you might jump in too quickly. I want you to think about laying low. Listen first, and then slowly offer some comments on their topic."

- Warn your child in advance when you are going to impose a limit that is likely to spark a verbal outburst. "Okay, guys: brace yourselves. I'm going to tell you something you're not going to like, but you need to remember that whining, fussing, or screaming is only going to make matters worse for you. Take a deep breath. Here comes the news: we need to leave the park in five minutes."

Try This!

Sometimes we prescribe a short, prearranged period of whining or complaining for kids. Sound strange? Here's how it works. If you have a child who tends to respond to some commonly occurring event with a verbal outburst, you can set up an opportunity for them to complain in advance. "Sam, I know that you really don't like it when I tell you that it's time to put your toys away and start on your homework. So, from now on, I'm going to let you know ahead of

time, and you will have five minutes to complain. You must use that
time to complain, and I encourage you to use the full five minutes so
that you really get your feelings out. I will let you know when complaining time is over."

It is important that this be done without condescending to or
demeaning the child in any way. It is a real, if humorous, task that
teaches children that they do have control over their complaining.
After all, if they can turn it on and off for a prearranged time, then
they can control it at other times, too! Don't lecture the child about
the purpose of the task. The learning will occur from the experience itself. Generally, over time the child will become less and less
interested in complaining about whatever it is that used to get them
started!

5. Use rewards to reinforce successful behavior. For example:

- When your child responds to the guidelines and
  plays quietly during adult conversation time,
  respond immediately by offering to play a game
  or do something of their choosing as soon as the
  adults are finished talking. If this is a new behavior
  that you are just starting to work on, do not wait
  until the end of the adult time. Go over after just a
  few minutes and whisper to your child that you are
  very proud of how well they are doing and encourage them to keep up the good work.

- For students with a history of calling out in class,
  reinforce them for raising their hands with a smile
  and by calling on them.

- Sometimes, a wink or a thumbs-up is just the right
  subtle way to reinforce a behavior.

- For kids who have a really hard time inhibiting
  the urge to talk, a formal behavioral plan may be
  necessary. There are many versions of these, but
  all involve using age-appropriate rewards for the
  desired behavior (e.g., a sticker for each half-hour
  period in the classroom without interruptions, or
  perhaps coupons toward pizza with the teacher for
  an older child). We provide more information about
  behavior modification techniques in Chapter 9.

Tips:

- Remember that spontaneous sharing is one of the joys of human interaction. Differentiate between excessive talking in the form of routine chatter and occasions when something exciting or upsetting has happened.

- If a child interrupts and you say you will be with them in "just a minute," then you need to do just that! Otherwise, you will have no credibility the next time, and the phrase "wait a minute" will rightfully be understood as just a way to put the child off. If it will really be five minutes, then say that. You may need to use a clock or timer to keep yourself honest!

Strategies to Help a Child Manage Physical Impulsiveness (Grabbing Things, Pushing and Shoving Others, Hitting, etc.)

1. Provide external structure in the form of general guidelines and specific rules. Teach rules that can be applied in a variety of situations. For example:
   - "David, it is not okay to hurt people. No hitting. Not ever. Unless your life depends on it. If you are angry, there are other ways to handle angry feelings. Let's discuss some options."
   - "Sarah, if someone grabs something from you, you can look them in the eye and say, 'That's mine. Give that back.' But we do not hit other people in this classroom."

2. Provide specific rules, and clear labels in plain language to convey expectations and teach acceptable behavior. For example:
   - "Jack and Susan, you will each have a turn with the new pool toy. I am going to use my watch to keep track of the time. Ten-minute turns each then switch time. If you grab the toy before switch time, then you will lose your next ten-minute turn."

3. Teach alternatives to negative behaviors. That is, replace a negative behavior with a different, possibly unexpected, behavior. For example:

    - A creative teacher of a small class of young children instructed all her young students to hold onto their pants legs when they lined up to leave the classroom. This positive directive ("Hold onto your pockets!") engaged the children in a behavior that counteracted the pushing and shoving that so often occurred when the children moved to a different location.

    - A speech-language pathologist found it difficult to set up her materials at the beginning of group intervention sessions. Seated across from her at the table, the students' little hands darted out to reach for the novel, interesting materials as she took them out of her bag. She devised a simple, very effective approach to helping the children manage their impulsiveness. Before taking out her materials, she directed the children to hold on to the edge of the table, rewarding them with a sticker on every hand that was holding on.

    - After a few missteps when her daughter texted a friend during dinner at her grandparents' house, Ann's mom implemented a new strategy. Before getting out of the car, everyone in the family turned off all notifications on their smartphones and placed the phone into a designated place (purse, pocket). If Ann removed the phone during dinner, then it was placed in Mom's purse until they get back to the car.

Try This!

One way to teach alternatives to impulsive physical behaviors is by stopping the action and doing a retake. "Whoa, what's going on here, David? I can see that you are angry, but it is not okay to hit when you are angry. You can say, 'I'm mad,' and stomp your foot, but you cannot hit. Let me hear it. Say, 'I'm mad!' Good, now tell me what you are so mad about." Thus, the adults go through a pre-set problem-solving conversation: they identify the feeling triggering David's unacceptable behavior, restate the rule, provide an alternative, and then require immediate practice. As David starts to use the new behaviors spontaneously, they will encourage him to build a broader repertoire of skills by brainstorming different ways to handle strong feelings.

4. Build on an older child's desire for more freedom by tying the use of proper behavior to an independent activity. For example:

    - "Tonya, I know that you want to stream that new karate video. My concern is that you are already having trouble controlling yourself when your brother irritates you. Show me that you can control your temper with your brother and find other ways to solve your conflicts with him besides physical fighting, and I will reconsider whether you can watch the video. We will talk about this again at the end of the week."

    - Teach children and teens that driving is a privilege, not an automatic right based on chronological age. To earn that privilege, teens must demonstrate that their behavior is under their control and that they can manage their impulses in the service of safety. "I'm concerned about the way that you react when you disagree with our rules. You have to show us that you can tolerate rules without making a fuss before we can trust you to drive and follow the rules of the road." (For specific information regarding teens, driving, and self-regulation, see Snyder 2001.)

Tip:

■ Impulsive physical responses to frustration must be differentiated from dangerous physical aggression. The latter is quite problematic – whether at home or in a classroom – and will require targeted intervention beyond the scope of this book.

Strategies to Help a Child Stop Irritating Behavior

1. Provide external structure by teaching rules that can be applied to a variety of situations. For example:
   - "It is hard for others to listen to the teacher or get their work done when there are distracting noises. No mouth sounds except for talking at the agreed-upon times when you are in the classroom."
   - "It is rude to grab things off a serving plate. If you would like a cookie, you need to ask for someone to pass the plate. Then you may gently take one."
   - "Pushing in line is not polite. You must wait your turn. When you stand in line, you need to stay in your own space. Do not push against the people ahead of you."

2. Provide external structure in the form of specific rules and clear labels in plain language to convey expectations and teach acceptable behavior. For example:
   - "Rachel, it looks like we will have to wait in line for a little while. I expect you to stand here next to me until it is our turn to order food. No pushing and no running off."
   - "Jack, your brother needs to get his homework done now. No talking to him or crawling around under the table. He needs quiet time and a calm space until he is done."

3. Offer support to bolster the stop function. For example:
   - Use simple, nonjudgmental language to cue the child to stop:
     o "Arthur, tapping your pencil bothers the other kids. You need to stop."
   - Work directly with the child to create an unobtrusive nonverbal signal to cue the need to stop the behavior of concern. For a pencil tapper, perhaps holding up a pencil would do the trick. Or tapping once or twice on the student's desk. Consider this a collaborative, trial-and-error effort between you and the child to figure out what works.

- Use a verbal prompt to help the child think about the rules, for example:
  - ○ "Matthew, that's too loud for the music teacher's house. What are the rules while we wait for your brother to be done?"

4. Plan in advance. When possible, head off problems by setting the scene ahead of time and laying out the guidelines. For example:
   - "Sarah, before we leave the car we need to talk about guidelines for when we are in the doctor's office. I know that it is tempting to sing along to the music you're listening to on your phone, but please keep the music in your head. No singing out loud in the waiting room."
   - "Emma, we are going into the restaurant in just a minute. Remember, when you swing your feet under the table, you end up kicking other people. We will try to give you some extra space by putting you at the end of the table. Please try to keep your feet under your own chair."

5. Teach alternatives to negative behaviors. That is, replace a negative behavior with a different, possibly unexpected, behavior. For example:
   - "Jared, here is a pipe cleaner for you to hold in your hands while we wait for the show to start. You may not poke your brother or pull on my sweater. Keep your hands busy with the pipe cleaner instead." (Many different quiet, soft toys work well in this regard. Look for "fidget" toys that have some texture or other kinesthetic property of interest. Kids who like to draw or color can learn to keep a small notepad or coloring book with them so they have something to do during downtime.)

6. Use rewards to reinforce successful behavior. For example:
   - When working with a child to build better control of a specific behavior, it is important to reinforce periods of good control. The more difficult the situation or entrenched the behavior, the more important it is to offer praise or provide concrete rewards.

● For specific behaviors that recur, a behavioral plan can help the child by reinforcing good control. As noted above, there are many versions of behavioral plans, but all involve using age-appropriate rewards for the desired behavior (e.g., five minutes of free time for each half hour of quiet work). Build in success by using frequent rewards and adjusting the goal to start the child at a level that allows them to meet expectations a large percentage of the time. You should continue to adjust expectations upward as the child's abilities increase.

Try This!

When we work with families with impulsive children, we often introduce them to the metaphor used by authors Patricia Quinn, M.D., and Judith M. Stern, M.A., in their book, Putting on the Brakes. Even young children can understand that some kids, like cars, have weak brakes. We explain to the child that they must exercise their brakes to make them stronger and that their parents will help them to do so. It is a metaphor that translates into immediate understanding and lends itself to brief, direct verbal prompts. "Denise, you are moving so fast that you are bumping into people. You need to put on your brakes."

Strategies to Help a Child Control Running Off in Stores or Other Settings

1. Provide external structure by teaching rules that can be applied to a variety of situations. For example:
   ● "Jake, when we go for a walk, you must always be within my sight. We need to be able to see each other's eyes. It is dangerous for you to run off where I cannot see you."
   ● "Sally, in a crowded place, it is easy for me to lose track of you or for you to lose track of me. So, in crowded places, you must stay right with me.

'Right with me' means that you are within one arm's length. Let's practice that so that I am sure you understand what it means."

- "Ted, you must always ask for permission before you leave the classroom to get a drink from the water fountain or for any other reason. I must know where you are at all times."

Try This!

Set up scenarios with your child to role-play desired behaviors. For example, children who are impulsive may not think of their own behavior in a store as "running off," but rather as "just looking at something." So, set up the scene at home where one of you is picking out groceries and the other goes to look at something down at the end of the aisle. Can you both still see each other? What about if one of you goes around the corner? What if a couple of people come into that aisle and block your view? What should you do then? Work out what is acceptable and what is not. Giving your child the opportunity to play the role of the adult sometimes may enhance learning (and fun!). Then, the next time you are in the real-life situation, offer praise when your child shows you that they have learned from your role-playing.

2. Provide specific rules and clear labels in plain language to convey expectations and teach acceptable behavior. For example:
   - "Jake, this is just a quick trip into the grocery store. We need just three things, and we need to get done as quickly as possible so we can make it to the post office before they close. You must stick right with me. In and out in ten minutes. Stay right next to me; we're moving fast. Do you think we can do it?"
   - "Andrew, I know you like to ride ahead a bit when we go bike riding. But we have to cross a busy street here to get to the bike trail. We will walk our bikes over to the trail together. Stay right with me until I say that it is safe to get back on your bike and ride ahead. Okay, now right next to me for this part."

- "Brianna, it looks like the kids are all playing outside. The Smiths have a big backyard, and you kids can have fun playing there. But you may not leave the backyard, even if some of the bigger kids go down to the creek. You must stay in the back-yard and come talk to me first if you want to go anywhere else. I will be right here on the patio or inside in the kitchen."

- "Jack, the restrictions on your provisional license will be lifted soon. When you are out in the car, we will need to know where you're going at all times. So, if you drive over to a friend's house, that's where we expect you to be unless you call or text us. If you want to go anywhere else – like to a different friend's or to get something to eat – you need to let us know. No cruising around in the car without letting us know."

3. Offer support to bolster the stop function. That is, work out some private cues with the child so that you can help them know when to stop. For example:

    - Ted's teacher has taped a large red stop sign to the inside of the door to remind him of the rule to ask permission before leaving the classroom. He prompts Ted verbally, if needed. ("Stop at the stop sign, Ted.")

    - If Sally starts to drift too far away at the mall, her mother gives her a simple reminder. ("Sally, arm's length please.")

    - Sarah's field trip group leader prompts her verbally before they get off the bus. "Sarah, we are getting off the bus soon to enter the museum. Do you remember the important field trip rule we talked about earlier? What was that rule?"

4. Plan in advance. When possible, head off problems by setting the scene ahead of time and laying out the guidelines. For example:

    - "William, we are going into the grocery store in just a minute. Remember the grocery store rules: You stay right with the cart and me, and only the things I say go into the cart. If you do not stay near me, then you will need to sit in the cart while we shop. Now, you tell me the store rules before we go inside."

- "I know that you and your friends prefer to sit together without a grown-up in the movie theater. I will let you girls sit alone, and I will sit in the back of the theater. If you go to the bathroom or to buy snacks, you must go with at least one other person. I will lay low until the movie is over unless I see you getting too wild or not following the rules."

- "Sarah, I know how excited you get when the class goes on a field trip, and that you get so interested in things that you just can't wait to see them all. But this is very important: you must stay with your group leader at all times. No exceptions. If you want to look at something in the museum, you must wait until the group moves on together. If you or one of the other girls needs to use the bathroom, you must tell your group leader and you will all go together. Okay? I want to make sure that you understand the rules of the day. You stay with the group leader. No exceptions."

5. Teach alternatives to negative behaviors. That is, replace a negative behavior with a different, possibly unexpected, behavior. For example:

- A creative preschool teacher was faced with the task of keeping a small group of impulsive children together. She fashioned a long rope with four loops on it. Whenever they went anywhere as a group (e.g., down the hall or out to the van), each child was instructed to hold onto a loop.

- In the grocery store, parents often find that keeping kids involved prevents boredom and the accompanying tendency to wander off. "Jake, I need your help to get everything on my list. Right now, I need carrots. Can you go get one bag of carrots, please? Put them in the basket and then I will tell you what to get next."

- "Alex, the class is going to the bus now. I need a helper to count off as each person heads out the door. Would you please stand next to me at the door and be my head counter? Then you can be my partner as we go to the bus."

6. Use rewards to reinforce successful behavior. For example:

- Try verbal praise. "Jake, you are doing a great job following the grocery store rules. Keep up the good work."

- Use tangible rewards. "Ashley, there is a sticker waiting for you when we get on the bus if you follow all the rules for lining up and leaving the building. Remember those rules? Stay with your partner and stay behind the buddies in front of you in line."

7. Ensure your child's safety by using hands-on tactics. Running off is simply too risky a behavior in some situations. If the situation is dangerous, then you just need to ensure that the behavior will not happen. That is why we hold small children by the hand in a parking lot. However, with impulsive children, the hands-on approach is often necessary in other situations as well. For example:

- Sammy's mom often endured the disapproving looks of other shoppers when she took her young son to the mall. Knowing that he would run off to explore things he found interesting, she used a children's safety harness and tether that she attached to the back of his overalls. In fact, she was always careful to dress Sammy in overalls for risky outings so that she would have a way to attach what she called her umbilical line. Ensuring her son's safety and her own peace of mind always outweighs her desire to blend in with the other parents at the mall.

- Amanda had no fear of the water, even though she could not swim! Whether or not she had her "floaties" on, Amanda would run off and jump in the water. Amanda's parents developed a no-exceptions policy when near the pool. They put her floaties on her before she left the car. If Amanda took them off at any time they were at the pool, they immediately packed up their things and took her home for the rest of the day.

Tip:

■ When you impose a consequence in response to your child's behavior, let the consequence do most of the teaching rather than over-talking the issues or getting into an argument. A simple restatement of the rule and the consequences, followed by action, is what is needed. "Amanda, you are not allowed to take off your floaties when we are at the pool because it is too dangerous. We will need to go home now." Your child may get upset and argue about the consequences or promise to do better the rest of the day. ("I won't do it again! I promise! I'll be really, really good!") As difficult as it can be (particularly if it is a nice day and you want to stay too), your child will learn best if you follow through with a minimum of words and emotion. "Sorry, Amanda. You didn't follow the rule. You will have another chance tomorrow." Experiencing the consequences for the problematic behavior is the source of the learning.

Strategies to Help a Child Manage Homework Problems

1. Provide external structure by teaching rules that can be applied to a variety of situations. For example:

   • "Drew, during homework time your computer is only to be used for schoolwork. I know how tempting it is to message your friends. But you lose a lot of time when you jump into chats online. So, before starting your homework, you must close down the class chat."

   • "Sarah, homework comes before electronics and telephone time. You can take some time to unwind a bit when you get home. Have a snack and hang out for a while. However, you must finish your homework before you get digital privileges."

   • "Alex, after band practice you need to come home so you can get your homework done. No last-minute decisions to go somewhere with your friends. You must come right home after practice."

- "Jen, getting enough sleep to be well-rested is important for all of us. All of your homework needs to be done early enough that you have time to settle down for bed. So, homework must be done either in the afternoon or right after dinner. We'll see which one works best. What would you like to try first?"

- Or, for a teen: "Allie, I am happy to help you with your homework when you need it, but I really need my sleep to be able to function well the next day. So, any input you want from me has to happen before nine o'clock. You do your best work before then, anyway, and you really need to wind down before bed. But if you choose to do your homework later, then you're on your own."

- "Ed, I know how frustrated you get with homework. But it is not okay to treat others badly because of your frustration. When you get upset, you need to take a short break to get yourself under control."

2. Offer support to bolster the "stop" (or in this case, the "review") function by working out some private cues with the child so that you can help them review work. For example:

- When Jim finishes work quickly and turns it in ahead of most of the others in his class, his teacher prompts him to review the directions and make sure all questions have been answered. His teacher also reminds him to proofread his answers and lets him step into the hall so he can read his work aloud.

- Ed's mother often previews his homework with him and encourages him to monitor his frustration level as he works. "That looks like some tough work because I know that writing can be hard for you. Remember, take a break if you feel yourself getting all worked up inside."

3. Plan in advance. When possible, head off problems by setting the scene ahead of time and laying out the guidelines. For example:

   - "Saundra, today you have a dentist's appointment after school. That means that you must come straight home after school. No stopping at Sheila's house on the way home and no hanging out at the bus stop talking to friends. I expect you to be home by 2:35."

4. Teach alternatives to negative behaviors. That is, replace a negative behavior with a different, possibly unexpected, behavior. For example:

   - Melanie often rushes through her work and does not read the directions thoroughly. So, Melanie's dad took her to the store and allowed her to choose her own brightly colored highlighting marker. Now when she sits down to do an assignment, she is required to first highlight the most important words in the directions. Before she starts the actual assignment, her parents review the highlighting to be certain she has done that task thoughtfully and has chosen the key words or phrases.

   - Melanie was also taught to circle or highlight the operational sign before starting a math calculation problem.

   - Jonas makes many careless errors on tests because he jumps in and starts writing before reading the whole test question. Jonas's teacher now begins each test by asking students to read each question and underline key words (e.g., not, all, except).

   - Cassie often asks her mother for help with homework, but then gets irritable and rejects her mother's input. Cassie's mom has introduced the concept of "frustration breaks," brief times to step away from the homework and cool down. "Cassie, you're getting really frustrated. Take a few minutes and I'll wait for you here."

5. Use rewards to reinforce successful behaviors. For example:

   - Melanie's new behaviors (slowing down and reading directions all the way through) are rewarded. If she completes the items on a page according to the directions, then she is allowed to skip the last one or two problems, depending on the length of the assignment. (Of course, this plan had to be preapproved by the teacher.)

● When Jim independently and accurately underlines key words on his homework assignments, he earns points toward rewards. He can trade in his points for weekend privileges (e.g., a trip to the mall) or save them for longer-term rewards (e.g., a day at the water park).

Tips:

■ Reward systems should be created with your child or teen's input. If they have selected the possible rewards (with your approval, of course), then they will be a lot more motivated to work toward those goals. In fact, if they also participate in creating the target behaviors that will be rewarded, there is an even greater likelihood of success!

■ If the reward system that you create is not working well, you might benefit from a more systematic approach to your plan. Seek guidance from a psychologist or behavior specialist. You can do this indirectly through reading up on reward systems (see *Your Defiant Child: Eight Steps to Better Behavior* by Barkley and Benton, 2013). Or, if you need more direct help, seek a professional consultation.

Case Study: Putting It All Together

Trevor is a young boy who often interrupts his parents' conversations. A bright, verbal, and exuberant child, he both charms and irritates people with his constant stream of chatter.

Now, when Trevor comes bursting into a room, talking as he enters, his parents remind him to stop and listen to see if others are talking. They have taught him these rules: listen first, say "Excuse me" if others are talking and he wants to say something, then wait for the go-ahead. They still need to provide reminders, sometimes several times a day. ("Trevor, did you listen as you came into the kitchen?") Sometimes, they just put a finger to their lips to quiet him. When Trevor's excessive talking gets to be too much, they request quiet time. ("Trevor, my listener is feeling full right now. I need some quiet time for a few minutes. Please find something quiet to do on your own.")

When possible, Trevor's parents warn him ahead of time if they know they will need some adults-only conversation time. They help him to think ahead and to plan some things to do while the adults are talking.

Trevor's parents are very conscious of providing frequent feedback, praising him for controlling his talking. Trevor has been begging to have a sleepover with a friend in a tent in the backyard. He and his parents have worked out a system in which Trevor's self-control earns him points toward this goal.

Transitioning from Short-Term to Long-Term Goals

For children who struggle with impulse control, the goal is for them to learn ways to interject a brief moment of thought before acting. This time helps them more accurately interpret events. ("Maybe he didn't mean to push me. Maybe he just got jostled by all these kids in the hallway.") It also allows for consideration of consequences. ("Jack is a nice guy. I could really mess things up if we get into a shoving match when he really didn't mean to do it.")

Remember that better behavioral control comes about as the result of both learning and brain development. This means that the younger and more impulsive your child is, the longer the trajectory will likely be for developing control. There is no quick fix here.

We start teaching better impulse control by providing clear guidelines for behavior. This external structure provides the model for the internal structure we want the child to eventually develop. Short-term goals include ensuring the child's safety, preventing a loss of behavioral control (and negative social-emotional consequences), and allowing the child to engage in experiences necessary for healthy development. Following the general principles for behavior modification, we use concrete reinforcers and frequent verbal praise for following the rules and putting on the brakes. We use reasonable consequences for serious lapses in behavior. Ultimately, we are trying to move our children toward internalized controls, but this is done step by step.

When your child responds impulsively, use the incident to reinforce expectations and to suggest better ways to handle the situation.

This helps your child begin to build a repertoire of behaviors that will serve them in the long run. Once your child begins to show evidence of even rudimentary self-control, then you can best support this growth by verbal or concrete reinforcement. The amount of self-control is not fixed; children's behavior will vary from one setting to another. Prompt your child with verbal or physical cues.

You are working toward fading out the prompting, and this should happen in tandem with your observations of your child's development. What eventually replaces your prompting? It is a sort of internal dialogue that you may be aware of, at times, even as an adult. The voice that we (hopefully) hear in our heads as we are on the edge of yelling at our spouse or the person with a cartload of groceries in the express checkout lane tells us that behaving badly will not help the situation. Sometimes, we may even hear the voice of a parent or other teacher. So, consider this your reminder to choose your words carefully when you teach your children. What words and what tone of voice do you want them to hear in their heads when they think of you?

Educate Others and Advocate for Your Child

As you educate yourself about your child's behavior and the role of the executive functions, you will surely notice that you understand and handle your child's impulsive behavior differently than you did before. If you provide information to other adults in your child's life, it will promote sensitive handling of their executive weaknesses in the various settings in which they operate.

You can educate other adults informally, such as in conversation with the babysitter when they complain that they had to tell your daughter three times in one day to use words rather than her hands when she was upset. Or, it can be done in a more systematic manner, such as by giving them articles to read (or lending them this book).

Working with impulsive children can be very frustrating, as they tend to repeat the same behaviors over and over in spite of knowing what they "should" do. They may also show great variability (inconsistency) in their behavior, depending on the day and situation. The inconsistency in the behavior can lead others to mistakenly assume that it is a lack of motivation that causes the problem. ("He did well yesterday, but today he chose to ignore the rules.") It is important for adults to remember that the behavior of impulsive children occurs in the moment. By definition, they do not think before they act.

Talk to your child's teacher about their issues and get a feel for how the behavior is being handled at school. Just as important as how the teacher handles lapses in control is what is being done to support and teach better self-control. In many cases, you will want to ask for a meeting with all the school staff dealing with your child. If your child has an I.E.P. or 504 plan (see Chapter 6: Assessment for more information about school plans), you will be meeting with the team at least once a year to plan goals, supports, and accommodations, but you can also request a meeting anytime when you have significant concerns about your child's ability to benefit from their educational program.

Conveying your understanding of impulsiveness and what to do about it can be the lead-in to a cooperative relationship based upon the shared concern of all involved with your child's well-being. As we have hopefully made clear, we do not mean to suggest that understanding your child means giving them a free pass on meeting behavioral expectations. It is sensitive and informed handling that you are working toward.

Final Thoughts

Although parents often resort to lecturing to kids, this is not effective if a child's primary weakness is impulse control. Instead, stay focused on the specific behavior, apply the principles of intervention, and try to stick to a straightforward, nonjudgmental, problem-solving approach. And know that you will repeat yourself often, because developing self-control requires practice and maturation over time.

It is important to remember that much of your child's irritating or impulsive behavior is not intentional. Prepare yourself in advance of difficult situations by setting your own intentions. Think of a few key words to keep yourself calm and plan your own internal response for impulsive behavior. ("Keep your cool." "Terry is impulsive because it is his nature, not because he intends to do it." "Don't lecture him; just tell him what he needs to do." "Stop and take a calming break for both of us if we need it.") Perhaps your child is not the only one working to develop self-control. Do you find yourself yelling whenever your child has lapses in control? Do you physically grab your child when they do something impulsive? Do you respond with unsafe driving behavior when someone pulls out in front of you? Then you, too, must learn better control. (If control of emotions and behavior is an ongoing problem in your family, then you may benefit from reading Chapter 17: Emotional Regulation.) Don't neglect your own needs. As the parent of a child with executive dysfunction who may perhaps be struggling with it yourself, you need to seek out support, even if all you can manage is a cup of coffee or a phone call with a sympathetic friend. If you continue to have difficulty controlling your own responses to your child, and practice does not help you to build a more thoughtful, systematic approach, then you may need the help of a mental health professional to learn these parenting skills.

12

Helping Children Shift Gears

Cognitive flexibility = *The ability to adapt to new or unexpected situations. This includes the ability to generate a variety of ways to view a situation or solve a problem.*

Even when children have a well-established routine, life at home, at school, and with peers is filled with changes and unexpected events. Children who are inflexible have great difficulty adapting to change and generating new ways to solve problems. They cling to familiar approaches and routines, so they may become unsettled when faced with unexpected changes.

Cognitively rigid children may be critical of others, as these children expect absolute adherence to the rules. As with other areas of executive functioning, a child may be very intelligent and still lack cognitive flexibility.

Strategies in this chapter help children who:

- Have difficulty with transitions;
- Have difficulty adapting to new situations or environments;
- Become upset when their peers "break the rules" or behave in unexpected ways; and
- Are frustrated when their first attempt to solve a problem isn't successful.

DOI: 10.4324/9781003403517-14

Below, we've listed general intervention strategies that you'll want to employ with your child or student who has trouble being flexible. Further down, we've provided advice for dealing with more specific scenarios that you're likely to experience with your child or teen. Note that depending on the issue you are addressing with your child, you will typically use only a subset of the strategies discussed in this chapter.

Summary: General Strategies to Help Your Child Shift Gears

- **Create a consistent, predictable environment** as much as possible.
- **Create visual cues** for routines and schedules.
- **Highlight changes to the routine** and help your child build a bridge from the familiar to the unfamiliar.
- **Provide additional support** during transitions and when new concepts, tasks, or environments are introduced.
- **Allow additional time** to adjust to changes in routine.
- **Teach the child to walk through new situations and changes.** This includes teaching self-talk (e.g., "This is different but that doesn't mean it is bad" or "I need to figure out the best thing to do even though this is new") as well as determining when to seek external assistance.
- **Model multiple ways of approaching a task or situation.** When you are faced with one of the many changes in routine (both expected and unexpected) that occur in your life, model a flexible approach for your child. Talk it through aloud, narrating your thinking.
- **Provide a place for self-calming** during stressful times and teach self-soothing techniques.

Strategies to Help Children Manage Transitions

1. Create a consistent, predictable environment to the extent possible. Try to build in continuity from one day to the next, even in the midst of change, and minimize the number of exceptions to the general schedule. For example:

- David's mom started his school year with a daycare arrangement that she thought would work well. The daycare was run out of a private home and was able to accommodate her unpredictable shift changes at work, allowing her to send David or not each day just by placing a call to the daycare mom. After a difficult few weeks that clearly challenged her son's flexibility beyond his ability to adapt, she set up a new plan that involved providing after-school care for him and two other neighborhood children in her own home. By sharing the expense, she could afford to have David in a situation that allowed him to come home to his own house every day.

- Rachel's divorced parents have an amicable relationship, and they are able to accommodate one another's schedule preferences from week to week. However, their daughter has demonstrated that she is not able to handle these changes well. They now keep a very systematic, predictable schedule so that she knows exactly what days and times she will be with each parent. While there are changes for various unavoidable events or for vacations, they are generally able to keep to a consistent schedule.

- Sam receives speech therapy and occupational therapy at school. Due to his difficulty with transition, the school team found that it works best to pull him from his regular classroom at natural transitions in the school day rather than once an activity has started or in the middle of instruction.

- Whenever possible, Matthew's mother schedules doctor's appointments for the beginning or end of the school day so that he does not need to deal with both leaving and returning to school mid-activity.

2. Create visual cues such as schedules and calendars for routines. For example:

   - Post a daily schedule. This is generally done in classrooms, particularly in the early grades. A daily schedule, perhaps less detailed, can be helpful at home, as well. Use drawings or cut out pictures to create a schedule for nonreaders. For example, draw a picture of a clock showing the times that events will occur. Pair it with a picture representing the event (e.g., pictures of clothing to symbolize getting dressed and a picture of a school bus to symbolize time to be at the bus stop).

- Provide your child with a calendar to keep track of the larger picture.
  - o Let your child select a calendar in a favorite theme as a holiday present at the end of the year. For younger children, the adults can set it up by filling in important events. Older children and adolescents can use a paper calendar or a calendar app to track events. If your child routinely uses an app to track school assignments, it works best to use a single platform for personal and school schedules.
  - o Include vacations and extracurricular events such as band concerts or sports practices and add doctor's appointments and birthday parties as they arise. If your child spends a significant amount of time at another parent or a grandparent's home, include words or pictures to indicate whose house they will be in on each day.
  - o Teach your child to use the calendar. When they ask about upcoming events, refer to the calendar or encourage them to check their app. If your child is too young to use the calendar without help, build in an evening ritual that consists of crossing off each day and then looking ahead to the next day or the weekend.
- For younger children especially, who have difficulty making transitions throughout their day and in the classroom, commercially available devices like the Time Timer or apps like the Children's Countdown Timer can help by creating a visual image of time passing. Making the passage of time concrete, these tools can help students *see* how much time they have before free play time is over and silent reading begins.

Tip:

■ When you set up calendars or schedules for your child or teen, involve them as much as possible in the process. A younger child may enjoy decorating a calendar that you create, either on the computer or by hand. If you have an older child or teen who uses a calendar app, create a time to sit down together to ensure that they enter important dates. Involving your child in the process promotes a sense of control and prepares them to independently manage their time.

3. Highlight changes to the routine. That is, let children know about changes to expected routines in advance. For example:

    ● Trial and error helps children or teens learn how much time is needed to prepare for changes. The general guideline of "not too far in advance but not at the last minute" has to be customized for the age and temperament of each child.

    ● Be very explicit about highlighting what will be the same and what will be different. "Look at the calendar with me, Katrina. You see you will still visit Daddy on these three Tuesdays, but on *this* Tuesday, Daddy will be out of town for work. Let's cross off the word *Daddy* from that day and add it here to Friday. Daddy will be home then, and you will visit him that week on Friday."

4. Provide additional support during transitions. For example:

    ● At school, assign a peer buddy for transition times. The buddy can serve as a model for what to do next and becomes a calm companion as the child moves through the transition.

    ● Assign the child a job to help them focus during transitions (e.g., carrying the volleyballs outside or turning off lights and closing the door to the classroom).

    ● Stay near the child during transition times.

    ● Preview the transition and then provide verbal support through the process. ("Sarah, we are going

to be leaving soon to head home. When it is time
to go, you will need to clean up the toys, get your
coat on, and say goodbye to your cousins. Got that?
Okay, time to start cleaning up.")

- Provide advance warning to allow the child to
  prepare for upcoming transitions. ("Alice, you will
  need to clean up in ten minutes.") Let your child
  know when they are at the five-minute and then
  the one-minute mark.)

- Focus on what is starting, rather than what is end-
  ing. (Rather than, "Put the game away so we can go
  to dinner," try "We're going to go get your favorite
  pizza now. Do you think you want mushrooms
  on your pizza again? Great! Once the game is put
  away, we're off!")

Strategies to Help a Child Adapt to New Situations or Environments

1. Highlight changes and help your child bridge from the familiar
   to the unfamiliar. For example:

   - "You have a different teacher and a new classroom
     this year. But your new classroom is in the same
     wing of the school as your classroom last year, and
     you will use the same entrance. Would you like me
     to see if we can visit the school and see your new
     room?"

   - "Abby, this is a new doctor, but her job is to help
     us just like Dr. Smith did. She will talk to us about
     how things are going at home and at school, and
     she will help us if we are having any problems."

   - "Matt, my work schedule is changing, and I will
     need to stay late on Thursdays. That means that
     I won't be home for dinner. Sarah will be home
     before your bus gets here, so she'll come down to
     the bus stop to meet you. This is just a Thursday
     change, and no other days will change. On

Thursdays, you and Sarah will eat dinner, do the dishes, and start on your homework, and then I'll be home."

2. Provide additional support. That is, provide something or someone who is familiar when your child is faced with an unfamiliar situation. For example:

- Have a parent or other trusted adult accompany your child and walk through the new environment.

- At school, assign a familiar peer buddy.

- Young children often carry a favorite "snuggly" or familiar toy. These are sometimes referred to as *transitional objects*, and they help children master the transition from the familiar to the unfamiliar. Sometimes older children benefit from a transitional object, although the object needs to be something that does not set them up for ridicule by peers. One girl kept a photo of her mother in her pocket to provide the extra measure of security that she needed. Another pre-teen carried a small piece of material cut from her childhood blanket in her pocket. It was the textural feel of the material that soothed her.

3. Preview the situation and be very explicit about what will happen whenever possible. For example:

- "Jack, your new teacher may ask you to do things differently than Mrs. Miller did. Your job is to follow your new teacher's directions and to ask her if you are unsure or confused about what she wants you to do."

- "Annisha, when we get to the party, there will be a lot of people. We will know some of them, and we won't know a lot of them. The first thing we are going to do is find the table with the cards that tell us where we will be sitting. I know that we will be sitting with Aunt Liz and your cousins, but we will need to find out the table number when we get there."

- Using puppets, superheroes, stuffed animals, or other toys, set up the scene and act out what will happen. (In fact, if you observe your child's imaginary play, you may notice how often your child already rehearses life situations through the use of play. Sometimes play is the child's work!)

- Many children, and certainly most teens, are uncomfortable with imaginary play with toys. Try role-playing instead. You can also use your smartphone to make a video together of the scenario; role play how you expect things to go and what each person will likely be doing. When teaching new behaviors, it works well to reverse roles so the child takes the adult role and you play the child dealing with the new situation or change.

- Expect and accept that your child will likely feel stressed by changes. Don't try to talk them out of their feelings or treat worries as forces that need to be cast out. It's important that children learn that feelings, including uncomfortable emotions, are part of life. Acknowledge the feelings, provide verbal support and encouragement, and soldier on.

4. Allow additional time to adjust to new situations. Set up a "dry run" in advance to familiarize the child with the situation, if possible. For example:

- Ask the school to schedule a visit with the new teacher a few days before the start of the school year if this is not already done routinely. For some children, this is included as an accommodation on the child's education plan or in the formal school meeting notes.

- Take your child to play on the playground of a new school ahead of time, just to build some comfort and familiarity.

- Visit with a new tutor or daycare provider for a short time a day or two in advance of when the services start.

- Take your child to observe a karate class or other activity before they start lessons.

- As much as possible, try to keep the routine stable when your child is in the midst of major changes, like getting braces or transitioning to a new school.

5. Teach your child to walk through new situations and changes. This includes teaching self-talk (e.g., "This is different, but that doesn't mean it is bad" or "I need to figure out the best thing to do, even though this is new"). Also help them learn when to seek assistance. Teach your child to identify their own characteristics in a straightforward, nonjudgmental manner. For example:

  - "Denise, this is one of those times where your distaste for change might get in the way. These changes just take a long time for you to get used to, don't they?"

  - "Anthony, it looks to me like you have your 'new situation jitters.'"

  - "Sally, you have never been to a sleep-away camp before. Of course, it will take a little while for you to feel comfortable there. But those are your 'new place blues' kicking in. I think you will have a great time once you settle in. Your counselor is aware that you might have some discomfort, and you know you can always call me if you need to talk."

6. Model multiple ways of approaching a task or situation. When you are faced with one of the many changes in routine (both expected and unexpected) that occur in your life, model a flexible approach for your child. Talk it through aloud, narrating your thinking.

  - "I'm a little nervous about starting my new job. I think I'll see if I can go in sometime this week at lunch to meet my coworkers and find out more about what to expect. It would be helpful to know where my desk will be and where the bathroom is in advance!"

  - "Dad and I are going to a party at the new neighbor's house this evening. I'm not a big fan of large, loud parties, so I hope they don't have the whole neighborhood over! I guess if it's a large group I could just find one person I know and talk to that person. It's supposed to be really nice weather, so I could also just sit outside on the deck and enjoy the warm night air while I check out what's happening."

7. Help your child learn strategies to manage various situations and initiate their own coping skills. For example:

    - "Ella, I know that vacations start off being hard for you because of all the new things. But after a day or two, you usually feel better. Let's brainstorm about things you can do to help those first few days go more smoothly."

    - "Chris, I know that you are used to my being at home when you come home after school on Tuesdays. Now, it will be Dad who is here on Tuesdays instead of me. Is there something we can do to help you feel more comfortable with the change?"

    - "Ashley, you have an overnight band trip coming up. Do you think this is one of those times when you would like me to go along as a chaperone? Or is there someone else that will be going that you could count on for help if you need it?"

    - "Jack, birthday parties are exciting, but they also mean that you will be going to a house that you have not been to before. Sometimes it helps to have a friend when you go to a new place. I spoke to Mike's mom, and he will be going to the party too. How about if I offer to drive Mike so you have a friend with you when you walk in? I can stay at the party and talk to the grown-ups, too, for a little while, if you'd like."

8. Help your child understand how discomfort can affect overall behavior and mood. For example:

    - "Jackie, you are really grumpy today. Sometimes that happens when people are worried about something. I know how hard changes are for you.

Do you think that you are worried about going on vacation?"

- "I know that you have had trouble falling asleep the past few days. I think you might be a little worried about the start of the school year. What do you think?"

- "Monique, I don't think it's me that you're angry at, but you do seem troubled. Is there something happening that's making you feel unsettled? Maybe hearing that you're going to have a new swimming coach this season?"

Tip:

■ Whether or not your child acknowledges that they're feeling uncomfortable with change, your words still provide a perspective that can help build self-awareness and provide a model going forward. Don't belabor the point with your child. They don't need to acknowledge the feelings in words to benefit from what you are saying.

Strategies to Help a Child Who Becomes Upset When Peers Break the Rules or Behave in Unexpected Ways

1. Provide additional support, verbally. For example:
   - "Chris, Kate is drawing her picture the way that she wants to. And you can draw yours the way that you want to. Both pictures show what spring is like, but you seem to be thinking about different aspects of spring. They are both just fine."
   - "Do you remember that I said that kids can sit wherever they like? So, Jack decided that he wanted to sit in a different seat today, and he chose the one that you usually choose. Now it is your turn to pick a different seat. Perhaps this one, right at the same table?"
2. Teach the child to walk through new situations and changes. This includes teaching self-talk (e.g., "This is different, but that

doesn't mean it is bad," or "I need to figure out the best thing to do even though this is new") as well as determining when to seek assistance. Teach the child to identify their own characteristics in a straightforward, nonjudgmental manner. For example:

- Teach specific guidelines and practice the words. Examples of helpful self-talk include "I'm only in charge of me," or "It's not my job to tell the other kids how to behave. That's a teacher's job."

- For younger children, ask them to draw a picture of what the new situation may look like. Remind them that the drawing can be changed after they see what actually happens.

- "Ada, when you get to camp, there will be all kinds of kids there. Some of them will do things differently than you are used to. That's probably going to make you uncomfortable, because it is hard for you when people do things that you are not used to. As long as they are not hurting you or anyone else, you can just let it be. But if you are unsure of what to do at any time while you're at camp, what do you think you could do? Is there someone you could ask to help you? I'm thinking that your counselor would be a good 'go-to person.'"

3. Provide a place for self-calming during stressful times and teach self-soothing techniques. Once your child has a meltdown, as so often happens with these issues, it is important to help them return to a calmer state before even talking about the issues. For example:

    - Teach self-soothing techniques, such as counting to ten or deep breathing. Self-soothing refers to the ability to calm yourself down when you start to get anxious or upset. The teaching part generally starts with either modeling a technique when your child is not upset or by doing it with them when they need calming. ("Let's breathe together. Big, deep breaths now. In through your nose and out through your mouth.")

    - Many children need to get physical distance from a stressful situation, and they respond best when you've agreed in advance on a special place where they can take a break when they feel out of control. (This is *not* a time-out or a punishment, and adults must be cautious to guard against lapsing into a punishment framework.) For young children, the special place is often a small, contained space such as one of the child-sized fabric tunnels available as playthings or a beanbag chair. One teacher provided a small tent in the classroom, and the child added a few favorite books. Sometimes, children spontaneously seek such a place when upset, such as under a blanket or under their bed. Give them some time and praise their efforts to calm themselves when you do approach them.

- Be clear and direct, but gentle, when your child is overwrought. "Your feeling brain has taken over, and you need to quiet your body so you can hear your thinking brain again." Your calm, authoritative tone sets the stage for calming, whereas a stressed-out and overly emotional response will escalate the situation.

- Trial-and-error will teach you whether or not your child needs more personal space once they're upset. Many children having a meltdown respond like a cornered animal when someone gets too close to them. This is when they often strike out at a parent or teacher. Unless the child or those around them is in physical danger from their actions, give the child space and allow them to take the lead in rejoining you once they feel calm.

Strategies to Help Reduce a Child's Frustration When Their First Attempt to Solve a Problem Isn't Successful

1. Provide additional support verbally. For example:
   - "These problems are really frustrating, aren't they? Try to slow down and let's see where you got off track."

- "If you already knew how to do everything, then you wouldn't need to be in school. This one is a hard one. It may take a few tries to figure it out."

- "Jamie, it looks like the part of you that wants things to be easy is fighting with the part of you that knows what it takes to learn new things. Try to hold on to that new learning mindset here."

2. Teach the child to walk through new situations and changes. This includes teaching self-talk (e.g., "This is different but that doesn't mean it is bad," or "I need to figure out the best thing to do even though this is new") as well as determining when to seek assistance. Teach the child to identify their own characteristics in a straightforward, nonjudgmental manner.

    - "Emily, you are having trouble with the homework. Remember, when you are feeling frustrated with a task, you need to remind yourself that this is all about learning. It is hard, but it is not impossible."

    - Teach your child to modify their thinking by changing their words. "Remember to add 'yet' at the end of that sentence, Lily. I can't do this … yet."

    - "Justin, you are getting a bit irritable with me over this homework. What do you need to do to get back into the right frame of mind? Do you think you need help with the work now or time to calm down?"

3. Provide a place for self-calming during stressful times and teach self-soothing techniques. As noted above, be clear and direct, but gentle, with your child when they are overwrought.

    - "It looks like you are getting really frustrated with this writing prompt. Maybe you need a brief break to get your thoughts together. Would you rather hang out in your room or play with the dog?"

    - "Alan, you are losing it. Time to calm yourself down. How about taking 15 minutes, maybe listen to music or go sit on the deck."

    - "Lana, remember how you learned to pull inside your shell like a turtle to give yourself a mental break? I think it's turtle time."

- "Jack, maybe this is the time to use what you learned from the school psychologist. Use your imagination to take yourself to your favorite place. I'll be in the kitchen. Let me know when you feel calmer and ready to tackle this again."

Try This!

We have found it very helpful to teach kids that strong emotion can interfere with thinking. Let your child know that different parts of the brain are responsible for feelings and problem solving. Teach them that strong feelings lead to temporary changes in a person's brain and throughout their body. When that occurs, the person may not be able to think as clearly as they need to in order to solve problems. To get back to our "thinking brains," we first need to calm ourselves. A framework for understating their emotions may help to provide the perspective they need to be successful.

Case Study: Putting It All Together

*J*oanne is a seven-year-old who tends to lose control when her normal routines are interrupted. When plans change, she becomes agitated and often defiant, unable to relinquish her expectations. Both at home and at school, Joanne is thrown by any change in routine. For example, if the cafeteria runs out of the pizza that she eagerly anticipates on Fridays, she may cry and refuse to eat anything else. She is likely to be irritable for the rest of the day. Having a substitute teacher is very hard for her, even one she has met before, because the substitute does not do things exactly the same way as the regular teacher. Although Joanne enjoys playing with other kids, her cognitive inflexibility makes it hard for her and for them. For example, she has trouble switching gears if a friend suggests playing outside instead of completing their board game. Vacations are hard on the family because Joanne really prefers to stay within her familiar surroundings. The rest of her family enjoys going to new places and trying new activities and restaurants, but Joanne balks at the changes in routine.

Like many children with cognitive rigidity, Joanne is thrown by changes and unexpected events. When feasible, her parents review the daily schedule and point out possible changes or other times when she may be at-risk for becoming overwhelmed. They also plan ahead to help her manage changes that have proved problematic in the past. Her parents and teacher have discussed with Joanne the possibility (yes, it might happen again!) that there will be no pizza on Pizza Friday or that the cafeteria may run out of other menu items on other days. Joanne's parents have brainstormed with her to create a list of options that are available in the cafeteria that serve as backups. Using dolls to act out the scenario, Joanne and her mother have practiced ways to handle the initial upset feelings that occur when she finds out that there is no more pizza.

During play dates at her house, her parents remind her that her guest gets to decide what they play. If she follows that rule, once Joanne's friend leaves, she is rewarded with an extra hour of playtime during which she can decide what she and her mother do. When Joanne is at another kid's house (particularly one she doesn't know very well), her parents may first talk to the other parent(s) to share that she needs some extra time to move from one activity to another and to request that the parent stay somewhat close by in case she needs a bit of support.

Joanne's parents use their own disappointments to model cognitive flexibility. Recently, the family had to forego a planned visit to a friend's beach house, because their friend got a nasty case of the flu. They were all disappointed, and they talked together about their feelings, when they could reschedule the visit, and what they could do to make the weekend fun in other ways.

Joanne has benefited from instruction that teaches her that there are rules and exceptions. Rules apply most of the time, while exceptions apply some of the time. She does best when a trusted adult or peer helps her manage the exceptions to the rules. Joanne needs these guidelines to be explained very clearly and at times when she is feeling calm and in control. For example, the general rule is that we don't scream. However, it is fine to scream at a baseball game or when someone needs help. Since Joanne still needs a trusted adult to help her when she is unsure of how to behave, there is a designated "go-to person" in each setting, such as the guidance counselor at school, her soccer coach, her religious school teacher, and her parents.

With the help of these accommodations, Joanne is learning to manage her initial tendency to react strongly when something unexpected happens. She is learning to calm herself, and then to generate acceptable ways to handle the situation. She is getting better at problem solving, and the adults reinforce this by praising her when she is able to move on without incident.

Transitioning from Short-Term to Long-Term Goals

Our ultimate goal is to increase children's flexibility in thinking and problem-solving. Younger children need considerable warning and preparation for changes. As kids get older, they may be able to respond to changes in a more controlled manner.

The shift from short-term to long-term strategies happens by gradually moving responsibility for problem solving from the adult to the child. This gradual shift occurs in stages based upon the child's abilities and developmental status.

First, the adult generates the intervention. ("It's raining, so we won't be able to go the playground today. Why don't we play a game together instead?")

At the next stage, the adult generates the intervention, but narrates the process of problem solving to model the behavior for the child. ("It's raining, and that means a change in plans since it's not a very good playground day. I'm really disappointed, and I guess you are, too. Let's think about some other special, fun things we could do together instead. I'm thinking that we could play a game together, or bake some cookies, or go visit Grandma. Do you have any other ideas for how to handle our change in plans?")

Next, the adult might shift to just prompting the child by initiating the process. ("Look at the weather out there. What do you think that means for our plans?")

Eventually, most children internalize the process and need less and less adult input. Our ultimate goal is to increase children's flexibility in thinking and problem-solving. When this is not possible, we aim to have them adapt more quickly to changes and more readily accept different points of view.

Educate Others and Advocate for Your Child

Kids who are less cognitively flexible than their peers may encounter notable difficulties at school, with other children, in the community, and at home. When inflexible children or teens face transitions or unexpected events in settings away from home, their strong reactions may be hard for others to understand. While most kids we work with learn to handle these changes adequately by the time they are in middle school, some continue to need support into their middle school years and beyond. Helping others to understand the nature of your child's difficulty will pave the way for the types of accommodations that allow them to effectively deal with change. Even relatively simple accommodations, such as advance warning of what will happen, can make a big difference in the daily life of a child who struggles to be flexible.

To advocate for your child, you will need to offer your perspective on their behavior. ("Actually, it's not just changing classes that is likely to be difficult. Elise sometimes gets upset with smaller changes too. Can I suggest a few techniques that seem to help?" Or, "Sometimes it may seem that she is being rude. Usually, that happens because she walks away to get some space and calm herself down.") At school, accommodations for an inflexible student can be initiated informally or may be part of a formal I.E.P. or 504 plan. Grandparents, babysitters, sports coaches, and others who spend time with your child will benefit from your perspective as well.

Final Thoughts

It is impossible to prepare your child for all the situations requiring exceptions to rules or to ready them for all unpredictable events. Of course, your goal is to help your child learn to manage these situations on their own, and this happens for most kids over time. However, some kids with cognitive rigidity have so much difficulty that they need a higher level of support even into high school. If your child falls into this category, you will need to offer what they need to be able to manage the settings in which they must operate. Some of the interventions and supports described in this chapter to help kids who tend to be inflexible would be accurately viewed as "coddling" or "enabling" for other kids. However, while most kids can adapt to a change in the school menu, others, like Joanne, need a different approach that allows them to build their competence at their own developmental pace.

Although all of the executive functions may be viewed as helping people effectively adapt to changing environmental demands and conditions, cognitive flexibility plays a key role in figuring out how to manage our ever-changing world. As such, it is an important focus of intervention.

13

Helping Children Get Started on Homework and Other Tasks

Initiation $=$ *The ability to begin a task independently and in a timely manner.*

Think of initiation as you do the ignition in your car; it is the mechanism that activates our system so that we get moving toward our goals.

The ability to get started on a task is important for functioning well in school and for successfully managing daily routines. Of course, all children begin life heavily dependent on adults to let them know when it is time to begin (and end) certain activities. We don't know any two-year-olds who hop up from their play to independently brush their teeth! However, as kids get older, we expect to see a gradual transition from relying on external cues to trigger the "start" function to managing this essential executive skill internally. When children and adolescents lag behind their peers in their initiation skills, they are very likely to be viewed as lazy or unmotivated, when, in fact, they may have specific delays that lead to procrastination.

In addition to difficulties with initiation, other executive challenges may contribute to procrastination. For example, if a child has problems with planning and organizing, they may not be able to envision the steps that they need to take to get started. (We incorporate ways to help with this in the current chapter. See Chapter 15 for more ideas on how to help kids with planning and organizing challenges.)

DOI: 10.4324/9781003403517-15

Children and teens who have trouble getting started on tasks often feel that they've disappointed others and themselves in the past. So, their difficulties can be compounded by hopelessness about their ability to get the job done in a timely manner. When faced with a new task, they may struggle against an emotional barrier that keeps them stuck. ADHD and Executive Functioning Coach Brendan Mahan labeled this barrier "The Wall of Awful" (Mahan 2016). When kids have difficulty getting started on tasks, it's important that we help them with both executive functioning and emotional barriers to initiation.

Strategies reviewed in this chapter help children who:

- Have difficulty starting homework;
- Have problems completing chores and routine activities without prompting; and
- Put off major projects, even if important to them.

Below, we've listed general intervention strategies that you'll want to employ with your child who has trouble initiating tasks. Further down, we've provided advice for dealing with more specific scenarios that you're likely to experience with your child or teen. Note that depending on the issue you are addressing with your child, you will typically use only a subset of the strategies discussed in this chapter.

Summary: General Strategies to Help Your Child Get Started

- **Develop a designated work time and place** to avoid mood-based decisions and to build habits and routines. (Once an activity becomes automatic, the need for the initiation function is significantly reduced.)
- **Use technology.** Alarms, timers, smart speakers, and other external aids can help cue the "start" function.
- **Incorporate supervision and remain in close proximity** to help children and teens get started on tasks.
- **Start the task with your child** (e.g., topic sentence, chores).
- **Help procrastinators develop a step-by-step plan for each task.** (Do you know what you need to do? How will you do that?)
- **Use rewards (verbal and/or tangible) to motivate desired behavior.** If rewards alone do not work, you may also need to

> take away privileges or, when appropriate, allow the natural
> consequence to occur. Be sure to let your child know in advance
> that they may lose privileges.
> - **Help your child learn ways to get activated for difficult tasks.**
> - **Teach the student to start small – a small step or a small
>   amount of time** (Dolan 2014).

Strategies to Help Your Child Get Started with Homework

1. Develop a designated work time and place to avoid mood-based decisions and to build habits and routines. (Once an activity becomes automatic, the need for the initiation function is significantly reduced.) For example:

   - Set up a daily homework time that is consistent from one day to the next (at least as much as other activities and demands allow). You may need to experiment a bit to determine what time works best for your child (e.g., after they've eaten a snack or had a chance to decompress after the school day).

   - Provide verbal reminders to help your child monitor the time until the behavior becomes a routine. ("Jessie, it's 3:30 now. If you want a snack, now is the time. You have 15 minutes before homework time.")

   - Create a homework station. Going to the designated workplace helps to cue the start function. For many children and teens, it works best to be in a central area, such as the kitchen or dining room. Others may need a quieter location, away from siblings or dinner preparation and other distractions. The right place to work is wherever the child is most productive, and it may take some trial and error to determine the best spot.

   - Plan ahead to ensure that the designated location has what's needed for homework. Does it provide access to an electrical outlet for a tablet or computer, if necessary? Also consider other routine supplies that will be needed. Stock the station with a basket of pens, pencils, and other supplies.

- Situational cues can also set the stage for work time. Be intentional about helping the child develop routines. Just as an adult might have a routine of making a cup of tea or coffee before they sit down to work, children may benefit from grabbing a water bottle or setting up their computer as they prepare to do homework.

- Managing social media, texts, and chats can also be an important step that becomes part of the routine for initiating homework. For students who are often on their phones interacting with their peers, we sometimes get pushback on this one (particularly from teens). "My friends will think I'm being rude!" "What if my friends are planning something and I don't answer? They'll think I'm not interested!" We have had success with many of these teens by teaching them to send a text to their friends before starting homework. "I'm starting homework isolation time. I'll be back online at 7:30."

- For many children and teens, unpacking their backpack and previewing the homework for the day with an adult is an important step in the homework routine. This first step transitions naturally into work time, and it also teaches kids how to manage homework demands.

Try This!

Some children tend to rush through their homework in order to get to free time. For these children, we recommend that you designate not just a start time for homework, but schedule a homework hour (or more, if this is an older child who often has more than an hour's worth of daily homework). So, homework time might be from five to six o'clock. If your child finishes their homework with time to spare, they can read a book. Only homework and reading are allowed during the designated hour. That way, your child is less likely to rush through their work to get to video games or other favorite activities.

2. Use technology. Alarms, timers, smart speakers, and other external aids can help cue the "start function." For example:

- A timer or watch with an alarm can be set to cue your child to begin the designated task. Watches with countdown timers can be set so that an alarm goes off after a specific time interval, so that your child knows when playtime is over and work time starts. There are also a variety of digital watches that can be set with multiple alarms and text messages that serve as prompts. Some vibrate rather than using an auditory alarm. Some individuals also benefit from a visual time tracker that communicates the concept of elapsed time with an easy-to-understand graphic depiction of time remaining. By making the passage of time concrete, a tool like this can help your child visualize how much free time is left before homework hour begins.

- Older children who carry cell phones can use the alarm function that is already built in, or they can use a specific timer app on their phone or tablet. There are a variety of apps available for different ages and preferences.

- To encourage independence, move from being the timekeeper to having the child set a timer, or watch. Consider teaching your child to use a smart speaker if you have one. "Remind me to start my homework at 4:00 today." Or they can use the smart speaker to let them know when the designated work time is over "Set a timer for one hour." Be sure to offer lavish praise when your child starts homework without being cued!

3. Incorporate supervision and remain in close proximity to help children and teens get started on tasks.

- Just having someone nearby who is aware of what the child is doing often helps them to get started at the agreed-upon time. These observers are sometimes referred to as "accountability partners," since they help children and teens to be accountable for their behavior and their time.

- Adults who work from home or who have other paperwork or emails to answer may find that having a shared work time is the best way to create accountability. For younger children, create a routine for "going to work" that involves children and adults getting settled at their workstations.

- Teens sometimes work best in a study group, since the group offers the built-in accountability of meeting at a specified time and for a specific purpose.

4. Start the task with the child.

- Some students spend an inordinate amount of time staring at their papers or computer screen, particularly when faced with a writing assignment. For such students, try talking through the assignment with them. Talk about what they will write, possible opening sentences, and then sit with them until they have started writing. For some kids, this becomes a transitional approach that morphs into using the dictation function on their digital device to help them get rolling.

5. Help procrastinators develop a step-by-step plan for each task. (Do you know what you need to do? How will you do that?)

- Sometimes tasks seem overwhelming for those who have executive challenges, particularly multi-step tasks and projects. Creating a plan can help the child or teen to break the work down into steps so that they see a path to completion. Once they have a plan, the first step may seem more obvious and doable.

- Laying out the plan together is also a way that you and your child can find out if there are gaps in their understanding of the assignment or the content, and you can help develop a plan to get the information, if necessary.

6. Use rewards (verbal and/or tangible) to motivate desired behavior. If rewards alone do not work, you may also need to take away privileges or, when appropriate, allow the natural

consequences to occur. Be sure to let your child know in advance if they are at risk of losing privileges. For example:

- Play "Beat the Clock." Measure how long it takes for your child to start a task once they have been given a directive. Reward them for improving on their best time. For example, if your child tends to sit at their desk for a long time before starting homework, chart how long it takes to get started and reward them for reducing that time. (This would probably not be a good strategy to use with a child or adolescent who is overly anxious.)

- Reward completion of homework with the opportunity to spend time doing a favorite activity. "Once you finish your homework hour, you can go back outside to play."

- Use natural consequences to motivate behavior when those consequences are reasonable and appropriate. "Homework has to be done before TV time. I know you want to watch the basketball playoffs. The game starts at eight o'clock, so get moving or you'll miss the start of the game."

7. Help your child learn ways to get activated for difficult tasks.

- Brief interludes of activities that are known to be activating can jumpstart people into work mode. These include aerobic activity, time in nature, and listening to upbeat music. Laughter is also a great way to shift into a cheerier frame of mind and helps some to get started on work. Brainstorm with your child to come up with some ideas to include as part of their preparation routine or to try when they're stuck.

- Some kids respond best to novelty when they are having difficulty getting started on a task. One teenager we know came up with an idea that combined novelty and an accountability partner with a reward. He and his father went to a local frozen yogurt shop and sat in a booth there while he got started on a long-term project. He went to the eatery for the sole purpose of working on his plan, and he earned a yogurt sundae for completing the task!

8. Teach the student to start small – a small step or a small amount of time (Dolan, 2014).

- Help your child learn ways to make tasks less overwhelming by starting small. They might start by targeting a single, manageable task. For example, a small step might be to complete just the topic sentence on the first day of a writing task. Or perhaps the goal would be to write a single paragraph or do a single page of problems in a math packet.

- Another way to start small is to plan to work for a small amount of time on a project, perhaps just ten minutes. It's not unusual for kids to choose to continue working once they've gotten going.

Strategies to Help Your Child Complete Chores and Other Routine Activities

1. Develop a designated work time and place to avoid mood-based decisions and to build habits and routines. (Once an activity becomes automatic, the need for the initiation function is significantly reduced.)

- Provide specific work times and deadlines. "You need to clear the table right after dinner" or "All your chores need to be completed by seven o'clock."

- Designate a chore time and give it a clear label to lock in the ritual. "Kitchen clean-up duty happens right after eating." "Saturday afternoon is room cleaning time. First is lunch, then room cleaning time, then free time."

2. Use technology. Alarms, timers, smart speakers, and other external aids can help cue the "start" function.

- Set up alarms for the start of chore time. For example, "Okay, Google. Remind us that it's time to start our chores at ten."

3. Incorporate supervision and remain in close proximity to help children and teens get started on tasks.

- Stay nearby at chore time to encourage children and teens to start chores or routine tasks. "It's time to brush your teeth. I'll wait here for you."

- Often older children and teens have time on their own after school until an adult gets home. This seems like a good time for them to complete homework and chores. Unless it isn't! If you find yourself repeatedly arguing about the fact that your child did not get their work done while you were gone, then you may need to accept that they are not yet able to initiate non-preferred tasks on their own. If that's the case, then perhaps you can flip the schedule so that the unsupervised time after school is free time, and work time starts when you get home. As they demonstrate better ability to get started without supervision, you can do a trial period of changing up the schedule again.

4. Start the task with your child (e.g., topic sentence, chores).

- Help your child or teen to jump into the task by starting with them. "Would you like to start with the dirty clothes? If you toss those into the hamper, I'll put away the clean clothes from the pile on your dresser." "I'll clear the dishes from the table and put them on the counter. If you load them into the dishwasher, we'll be done in no time."

- Provide the needed materials and let the child get started from there. "Okay, here is your bread, peanut butter, and jelly. Once you make your sandwich, we'll add a piece of fruit and put everything in your lunch bag."

- If kids tend to stop the job while you continue, remind them of the "partners rule." "I'm happy to work *with* you, but I don't work *for* you. Get back to the job, Amelia."

5. Help procrastinators develop a step-by-step plan for each task. (Do you know what you need to do? How will you do that?)

- The broad directive to "do your chores" can seem overwhelming to kids who have trouble getting started, even when the chores are familiar to them. Sit down with your child and create a checklist of all the jobs to be completed.

- Create reusable templates for repetitive chores. These make it easier to get started. ("Pick up trash. Put dirty clothes in the hamper. Put away clean clothes from laundry basket. Put drawing things in art box...")

6. Use rewards (verbal and/or tangible) to motivate desired behavior. If rewards alone do not work, you may also need to take away privileges or, when appropriate, allow the natural consequence to occur. Be sure to let your child know in advance that they may lose privileges. For example:

- Tie completion of chores to meaningful reinforcers. "You need to clear the table and load the dishwasher before electronics time. Bath time is eight o'clock, but if you get your kitchen chore done in time that leaves a little free time. You need to get a move on if you want to have some electronics time tonight."

- Provide an additional reward for completing chores without being reminded. (If you have established a point chart or other behavior management system with concrete reinforcers, build in bonus points for self-initiation.)

- Use natural consequences if they are reasonable and appropriate. "We need a few hours if we are going to go to the mall, and we need to be home by dinnertime. So, if you want to go shopping today, you need to be finished with your chores by 3:30. Otherwise, we just won't have time."

Tip:

■ Sometimes, the obvious natural consequences for a behavior are simply too undesirable. For example, if your child misses the bus repeatedly because they hit the snooze button on their alarm and oversleep, you may end up driving them to school regularly. (We are assuming that you have already tried such interventions as placing a second alarm farther away from their bed as a backup.) The natural consequence for missing the bus might be having them walk to school on their own, but then they would be late. Naturally, you end up driving them.

So, what would be a reasonable consequence? Think about a consequence that accounts for the extra time you devote to driving them to school. Here's how you might present this: "John, when I drive you to school, it takes me 20 minutes round trip, and that is 20 minutes that I would have used to get my own work done. So, each time I drive you to school, you owe me 20 minutes when you get home from school. You will spend those 20 minutes helping me with the housework that I usually do, like laundry or cleaning." After following through with those natural consequences once or twice, your son might want some help thinking through ways to get an earlier start in the morning.

7. Teach the student to start small – a small step or a small amount of time (Dolan 2014).

- Checklists and templates lend themselves to "starting small." For example: "Jack, there are six steps on the laundry checklist. I want you to do the first two today. Gather your dirty clothes and bring them down to the laundry room."

- Choose a reasonable amount of time and help your child get started on the task by focusing on that. "I suggest you start with ten minutes of clean-up time today. You can do more tomorrow."

Strategies to Help a Child Who Puts Off Major Projects

1. Start the task with your child.

- Working with your child on the first step of a major project may help them get into gear. Creating a plan is an important starting point; offering input at this stage can serve as a way to help your child get started while also teaching the importance of starting a project by making a plan.

- For many children who have problems with initiation, choosing a topic from among a large range of options can be quite difficult. Help your child to narrow the field of choices. "It looks like you need to choose two novels from the list of books you've read this semester and then write a comparison paper. Have you decided which books? Were there any that you particularly liked?"

- For many people, the structure inherent in a group effort (e.g., breaking down the work into subtasks and assigning them to team members, developing a team timeline, the accountability of meeting at a specified time to review progress) compensates for executive skill weaknesses. Also, working in a small group allows the person to gain momentum from the energy and focus of other team members. Working together with another child to earn a scouting badge, for example, can be easier than working alone.

2. Help procrastinators develop a step-by-step plan for each task. (Do you know what you need to do? How will you do that?)

- Large projects can be intimidating, even to those without executive challenges. As children move through middle and high school, large projects and long-term assignments are a more common demand. Older children and teens may need help with breaking down their projects into manageable chunks and developing a timeline for completion of the steps.

- Deciding what the first step will be and when it will be done can help kids who have trouble getting started. When you review daily homework with your child, be sure that due dates for tests and long-term assignments are entered in the agenda book. You can further help by prompting your child to enter each step of the project in the agenda book on the day they plan to get that task done.

- Encourage your child to use a single organizing system for tracking all projects, including non-school demands. The information might be recorded and tracked in an agenda book, on a calendar or whiteboard, or in a homework app. The important thing is that for some people with initiation difficulties, the "out of sight, out of mind" principle operates a bit too well. These folks need constant, concrete reminders of things that are due.

- Trouble with initiation can have consequences in activities outside of school and home, as well. Jim is a Boy Scout who has earned only a few badges because of his tendency to procrastinate. Jim's parents have talked with his troop leader and together they've developed a plan that includes working with an adult to plan the work and brief private check-ins on his progress before each troop meeting.

Tip:

- If discussions about starting homework and projects have become a battleground, try a different approach. Children and teens are often defensive about their tendency to procrastinate, and busy adults may become impatient with what seems like willful avoidance. Interactions about project due dates and missing assignments can become confrontational. If this is the case for your family, try taking a step back. Reach out to your child with curiosity and a collaborative spirit. Focus on understanding. "Wow. You seem to be having a lot of trouble getting your paper done. Where are you getting stuck?" "Wasn't that project due last week? What's up?" "I got an email from your teacher. She said that you have several missing assignments. Sounds like maybe you've dug yourself into a hole. Want some help figuring out how to climb out?" "How can I help?"

3. Use rewards (verbal and/or tangible) to motivate desired behavior. If rewards alone do not work, you may also need to take away privileges or, when appropriate, allow the natural consequence

to occur. Be sure to let your child know in advance that they may lose privileges. For example:

- If your child or teen has a history of missing due dates, then brief verbal praise or a fist bump for getting started and/or sticking to a plan is surely in order. Sometimes parents are reluctant to offer praise for something that they feel the child should be doing without it being a big deal. It's important to remember that the more difficult something is, the more we all desire validation for getting it done.

- Older students benefit from setting up their own rewards for completing work. One college student we know used a concert ticket as the incentive for completing a major project on time. Here's how that worked: Jack and his friends bought tickets to see a favorite band in concert. However, the concert was the weekend before a major school project was due, and Jack knew that he often needed those last few days to finish (or even start) his work. So, Jack gave his concert ticket to a trusted friend with the instructions that the friend was only allowed to give it back if he had emailed the project to the professor before the concert. He also had to send the project to his friend for verification. If Jack didn't deliver, the friend was to invite someone else and use Jack's ticket. (Jack did complete the project!)

4. Teach the student to start small – a small step or a small amount of time (Dolan 2014).

  - It can be tempting to push your child to do more than a small step when you see the complexity of the task ahead. However, the goal here is to just help them to get started. If your child gets started, that constitutes success at this stage!

  - Small steps with big rewards might include reading the assignment packet and underlining the important tasks and due date, making a timeline or writing a topic sentence.

  - Small amounts of time might include 15 minutes of work on a math packet or 20 minutes of review time before a big test.

Try This!

Sometimes, despite their best efforts, parents find themselves stuck in a pattern of power struggles about homework and projects, particularly with older children and adolescents. If that's the case, it can help to remove this work from the context of the parent-child relationship. If you find yourself engaged in constant struggles over managing project demands, consider engaging the help of a tutor or ADHD coach. Outside help can also be a good step if you are concerned about your child's progress toward independence.

Just like a coach can help improve your child's basketball or chess skills, there are a growing number of professionals who work with children and adolescents to help build executive skills. By definition, the coaching relationship is collaborative and is most successful for children and adolescents who can identify their areas of weakness and are open to experimenting with strategies to build their skills. Coaches may offer services via online platforms or in person.

Coaches come from a range of backgrounds and professions, including teaching, counseling, speech-language therapy, and occupational therapy. Some coaches were licensed in a mental health profession before seeking the training as a coach. Although there is no licensing process for ADHD or executive coaches at this time, several organizations including the International Coaching Federation (www.coachfederation.org) and the ADHD Coaches Federation, or the A.C.O., (www.adhdcoaches.org) provide credentialing and practice guidelines. Unlike tutoring, coaching does not focus on academic content (e.g. math or other specific academic areas). Instead, coaches build specific skills but can be very helpful in addressing problems with school performance, including initiation difficulties. If your child needs both tutoring and coaching, then an academic tutor with specific expertise in executive functioning will be the best fit. Sometimes, therapists or counselors who specialize in working with people with ADHD incorporate coaching techniques into their work.

Case Study: Putting It All Together

*M*ark is a 13-year-old boy who has many friends, but he often found he had no one to play with. He repeatedly complained to his mom that whenever he called a friend to come over, that person already had plans.

Mark's parents told him repeatedly that he might get better results if he called in advance rather than on the day he wanted to get together, and Mark said he would do that. However, he didn't follow through.

Mark's parents could see that he really wanted more time to hang out with friends. Still, it was frustrating for them because Mark seemed to know exactly what he needed to do, but he just didn't seem to get around to initiating social activities until the last minute.

So, Mark's parents started taking a more active role in helping him arrange to get together with his friends. Whenever he complained to his mom that he was bored and wanted someone to do things with, she helped him to identify who he wanted to invite over and then she reminded him of the right-now approach. "Do it right now, so that it gets done." She sat down with him while he texted his friend. She encouraged him to offer a number of different options, so that they could make alternate plans if the initial proposal did not work.

Mark's parents also reviewed the calendar with him every Monday afternoon. They found that using the calendar app on his smartphone worked best. With his parents' oversight, Mark entered the phone numbers for his friends into the contacts list on his phone so the contact information was easily accessible. Looking ahead for the week, they identified the afternoon and weekend times that Mark would have free time. Their Monday routine included contacting friends to arrange for at least one weekday and one weekend time to get together. Planning in advance meant that his friends were more often available, and so the natural rewards reinforced the behavior of initiating the calls. After a while, the Monday routine became part of the weekly ritual, and Mark initiated it on his own with only occasional reminders.

Still, on a variety of other tasks at home and at school, Mark's parents and teachers continue to provide a relatively high level of external prompting and support. They recognize that his internal "start" switch is hard to trigger and that his lack of initiation and resulting procrastination are due to executive weaknesses rather than insufficient motivation.

Transitioning from Short-Term to Long-Term Goals

When children or teens have difficulty with initiation, we first build routines and reinforce the children for sticking with them. We create a structure for important activities, such as when homework needs to be done, and we actively ensure that the child follows the routine. Often, as routines kick in, the struggle over initiating a particular task diminishes. Over time, you should do less direct prompting ("Time to start your homework") and instead prompt your child to think about the rule ("It's four o'clock. What's the rule about homework time?"). The next step is to prompt your child to use more independent strategies. ("How about if you set your alarm for 3:55 p.m.? That will be your cue to come inside and start doing your homework at four o'clock.")

To move toward the long-term goal of building independence, children who struggle with initiation need to learn to regularly use tools such as watches, schedules, and calendars. For these to become habits, we need to encourage their regular and consistent use, so we reinforce the child for using them.

It is also important for your child to gradually move from thinking about a particular task (e.g., doing today's homework) to developing effective ways of independently managing demands in a timely manner (e.g., daily review of their schedule and what needs to get done). You can help by first suggesting a strategy ("Jack, did you make a list on your whiteboard of the things that need to get done today?") Then, move from suggesting a strategy, to encouraging your child to come up with one on their own. ("Jack, do you have a plan for getting started on your science project?")

We need to continue to heighten the child or teen's awareness of how long things take and the importance of thinking in terms of time limits. ("We are leaving on Saturday for vacation. What is your schedule like this week? When do you plan to start your packing?") Even when your child has developed pretty good routines that help them get started, be prepared to provide help from time to time, particularly during times of increased stress. ("I know that moving to a new house so close to final exams isn't going to be easy. Let's figure out how I can help without nagging.")

Perhaps most importantly, we encourage people with initiation difficulties to shift from vague plans ("Oh, I don't know, I guess I'll do it sometime Thursday or maybe Friday afternoon") to specific deadlines ("I'll be home from football practice at two o'clock, so I'll shower and start my packing by three o'clock on Thursday"). As one professional project planner recently stated so succinctly, "Nothing ever gets done without a deadline."

Observation of a youngster's hits and misses helps us to know more about their status as far as progress on initiating tasks independently. For example, one teenaged client looked forward excitedly to his first band trip with the middle school. He talked about what he needed to take and eagerly showed his mom the packing list that had been given to all the kids, but he seemed to get nothing accomplished toward getting ready to leave. So, it seems unlikely that this boy was being "lazy" or "unmotivated." The obvious and most effective solution was for his parents to step in to help him get started. (For the next band trip, however, it would be more helpful to develop a "packing plan" in advance, with target dates for specific tasks that needed to get done by specific dates.)

As your child matures, they will learn from experience about their tendency to wait too long, to start too late, and to come up short. You can then gently call upon their experience to inspire new approaches. ("Jack, my last-minute son, I just don't see how you will be done packing on time if you don't get started really soon. Remember the last time we went on a trip? You were so surprised by how long it took to get ready and you were racing around at the last minute. You got really frustrated because you forgot your bathing suit and your cell phone charger. What do you think would be a better way to handle this?")

Overall, what you are doing is a form of scaffolding – teaching skills that build on each other and that work together to allow your child to reach a higher level of performance. Your child may start to balk at your involvement, and that is an opportunity for you to consider whether you are doing too much. Give them some room to show you what they can do on their own. If you need reminders of the guidelines for how to adjust expectations, take a look at Chapter 10 again.

With maturation, experience, and teaching, most children and teens we have known have risen to the challenge of starting tasks in a timelier manner. However, difficulty with initiation can be a stubborn problem. Some people with significant executive function weakness continue to need a high level of support to help them start important tasks through high school and even beyond. Achieving independence may sometimes require finding someone other than yourself, the parent, to be an accountability partner and to help your child set and stick to their own deadlines. Procrastination is often the issue that leads adults with ADHD to seek counseling or coaching!

Educate Others and Advocate for Your Child

Kids with initiation or activation weaknesses may be viewed as "passive," "lazy," "unmotivated," or "dependent." If you've heard these words used to describe your child, you may need to share what you have learned with the school staff or other adults involved with your family.

Be cautious about the use of natural consequences. Sometimes, natural consequences serve as powerful motivation, leading to the development of important new learning. However, when children or teens do not have the skills to perform the desired behavior, then natural consequences (such as failing a class) are simply unreasonable.

When you can collaborate with other adults in your child's life (your spouse, life partner, school staff, etc.), you will have the best chance of effectively thinking through what will help your child move forward and become more independent. If your child's difficulties with initiation are interfering significantly with learning or performance in the school setting, they may need school-based instruction and/or accommodations through an informal plan or more formally through an I.E.P. or a 504 plan.

It's important to be aware that sometimes initiation difficulties are more apparent at home than at school since the classroom setting is more structured with fewer opportunities for children to choose when things get done. Share your observations of your child's behavior at home with your child's teacher and discuss possible interventions that will help with homework, such as breaking large tasks into smaller chunks and having interim deadlines for portions of larger projects. This may include first turning in an outline, then making a timeline for each part of a paper or project.

While we do not want children to suffer unreasonably harsh consequences for behavior that they do not yet have the ability to change, parents must be mindful of the tendency to work too hard to protect their children from the world. Parents must be open to examining their own actions to make sure they are doing the best job they can to promote independence.

Final Thoughts

We can all think of times when we just couldn't start on something that needed to be done. Often it is the looming deadline that finally launches us into action. This is also true for kids with executive weaknesses, but the frequency and intensity of the problem is on a different scale. Since people with executive weaknesses have difficulty keeping the long-term picture in mind, more immediate rewards can often help them get started.

Parents often have questions about whether their child is choosing to avoid a task or is having real difficulty getting started. Wouldn't anybody rather watch a video than take out the trash? Fortunately, many of the ways to help kids get started work equally well whether it is executive weakness or behavioral factors that are leading to work avoidance. Try the types of interventions offered here without judgment or blame. Hopefully, you'll see progress, whatever the source of the problem!

14

Helping Children with Working Memory Challenges

> ***Working memory*** *= The complex cognitive process that allows us to hold information in mind as we work towards a goal. It is a dynamic process that involves capturing new information and retrieving previously stored information, all while we manipulate and update the data on our mental scratch pads.*

Working memory is a complex system that allows us to hold on to information and to work with it while we move toward a goal. Think of working memory as an internal scratch pad that provides us with a place to store information we will need to use for the next step of a task, but that we do not need to store beyond that time. The scratch pad is a dynamic one, because we continuously update and work with the information stored there.

Like other executive skills, working memory does not operate solo. Working memory acts in concert with other executive processes involved in allocating attention and selecting relevant versus irrelevant information.

Working memory tasks can be as straightforward as remembering small bits of information, such as simple directions. ("Go get your coat and hat.") However, working memory is also involved in much more complex tasks. For example, consider the deceptively simple classroom task of learning from a classroom lecture. Students must take in the information, prioritize relevant over irrelevant information, hold that

DOI: 10.4324/9781003403517-16

information in mind long enough to take notes, all while connecting the new information to what they already know, using the new information to revise their current understanding, and while the teacher continues to present information!

For those with weak working memories, it is as if their scratch pads are much smaller than expected, so that they cannot hold as much information in mind as others do. Further, the lettering on the scratch pad seems to be written in disappearing ink, so the words or images fade more quickly than for others.

A common problem for those with weak working memories is that it is hard to think creatively while they are trying to remember directions for a task. The child may falter on some tasks because of the complexity involved in holding on to the information from the directions, generating creative ideas in response and then capturing those ideas in order to complete the task. The scratch pad is simply overloaded!

Working memory challenges are particularly problematic because so much everyday information is communicated orally. We give directions or other information aloud, and we expect that the listener will hold on to what we say. However, words are a fading stimulus that may leave the listener's awareness as soon as the sound waves dissipate. Information presented orally leaves no trail; that is, there is nothing concrete to reinspect if the listener needs to review the information. It's easy to see how an inadequate internal scratch pad can make managing many of life's tasks difficult!

We'd like to offer just a brief note here about working memory training. Various programs and tools have emerged over the years with the promise of improving working memory, however research suggests that they do not live up to the promise. At this time, it appears that working memory training in isolation from real life is not likely to be useful. So, in this chapter, we focus on ways to help children by accommodating the individual's needs and by teaching workarounds that will improve independent functioning over time.

Strategies reviewed in this chapter help children who:

- Have trouble following directions;
- Have trouble with written expression and other complex, multistep tasks;
- Interrupt others so they won't forget what they want to say;

- Need to reread or relearn information – it just doesn't stick; and
- Have trouble taking notes in class.

Below, we've listed general intervention strategies that you'll want to employ with your child or student who has trouble remembering things. Further down, we've provided advice for dealing with more specific scenarios that you're likely to experience with your child or teen. Note that depending on the issue you are addressing with your child, you will typically use only a subset of the strategies discussed in this chapter.

Summary: General Strategies to Help Your Child with Working Memory Challenges

- **Modify the presentation of auditory information** so that it is easier to remember.
- **Use multisensory strategies** such as pairing verbal instructions with visual cues. Multisensory teaching is the process of connecting multiple sensory inputs to the new material. This involves the use of strategies that connect new learning with input from the eyes, ears, voice, and/or hands.
- **Focus on the use of external scratch pads** to create a way to store information that takes the burden off the weak internal storage system.
- **Teach strategies and techniques to aid recall.**
- **Provide templates for repetitive procedures or routines.**
- **Accommodate working memory challenges** by providing reasonable support.

Strategies to Help a Child Who Has Trouble Following Directions

1. Modify the presentation of auditory information so that it is easier to remember. For example:
   - Simplify the directions so that the most essential information stands out. "Jackie, I want you to get

your coat, get your library books from the dining room table, and come back here to the kitchen. Got that? Coat. Library books. Kitchen. Go."

- Slow the pace of your language, so that your child has time to process the information. Rapid-fire information can get lost as your child works to hold onto and make sense of what you've already said.

- Organize the information in a manner that creates bullet points to aid in recall. "Remember, you have *three* important points to write about: what was the problem, how did the people solve it, and what was the outcome. Remember, I want to see three points." Or "Johnny, this morning we have some clean-up to do around the house before we can go swimming. You have *three* things you need to get done. Here they are: First, put all the dirty clothes into your hamper. Second, bring the hamper down to the laundry room. Third, put your superhero figures away. Got it? There are three things on your list. Do you remember what they are? You tell me so I am sure you've got them all."

- Give directions for a single goal at a time, and offer information related to that goal only. For example, if the goal is to leave the house to do errands, then focus on the action steps for that goal. To illustrate, here are two ways to present the information. Which one do you think will be most helpful? (1) "Sam, we need to be ready to go in 15 minutes. Put your shoes on, if you can even find them in all that mess on your floor. And where do you think you'll find your school supplies list? Did you even save that? Because I don't want to end up at the store and not know what we're supposed to buy like last year. What a pain that was! I'm not sure what we're going to do if you can't find it. Have you talked to any of your friends to see if any of them are in your class so we can ask for a copy of the list? Oh, look at the time! Get going! We need to get out of here, so we have time to get done at the store and still pick up your sister." Or (2) "Sam, we need to be ready to go in 15 minutes. Please find a pair of shoes and your school supplies list. Let me know if you need my help with finding your shoes or the list."

Tip:

- To organize and simplify directions, you need to take a moment to focus in on the goal yourself, so that you can distill the information down to the most important points. Eliminate extraneous information by stating only what you expect the child to do. Simplifying the message makes it less likely that your child will get lost in the words and in the complex emotions and worries that you convey. Focus on the action steps and you will automatically narrow in on the essential information.

2. Use multisensory strategies such as pairing verbal instructions with visual cues. Multisensory teaching is the process of connecting multiple sensory inputs to the new material. This involves the use of strategies that connect new learning with input from the eyes, ears, voice, and/or hands.

For example:

- "Let's sing the directions."
- "Tap the table for each step you need to do."
- "Let's make a picture list of all the things we need to get done before Grandma and Grandpa get here."

Try This!

Set your simplified directions to song, rhythm, or dance steps. If you have a playful style to begin with, capture that occasional, spontaneous silliness to punctuate your serious parental efforts. A few verses of "Shoes, coat, cha-cha-cha" with the accompanying dance steps may help you all get out the door with smiles on your faces!

3. Focus on the use of external scratch pads to create a way to store information that takes the burden off the weak internal storage system. For example:

- For young children, make a to-do list or schedule using pictures. This can also help kids who have trouble keeping track of steps in their morning and evening routines. Print the steps in checklist form or write them on a whiteboard so your child can check off each step as it is completed. Older children and teens benefit from to-do lists and visual schedules, as well, and they can help to create the list. Whatever their age, most people find that checking things off of a list is satisfying and highlights their successes.

- Teach your child to write down oral information. The written information becomes a concrete cue that can be reinspected whenever necessary, long after auditory recall fades. For example:

  o "Marina, I need you to run into the grocery store and buy a few things while I pick up the dry-cleaning next door. Do you have paper? Great! Here are the four things we need. Write them down."

  o "Richard, I agree that you need a new notebook. You also mentioned yesterday that you need new socks. Write the things you need on the whiteboard in your room to remind us of the errands we need to get done this weekend."

- Teach your child or teen to jot down a few notes as the teacher gives directions aloud. Writing down a few key words can ensure that they are doing the requested problems and not wasting time on the wrong page.

- Use technology to compensate for weak working memory. For example, "When you think of something you need to do, record a message on your cell phone, send yourself a reminder text, or call your voice mail and leave a message."

- Ask your child's teachers if they are okay with having their lectures recorded. For a child who has difficulty focusing on what is being said while writing notes, having a recording that can be stopped and started later can be a big help.

4. Teach strategies and techniques to aid recall. For example:

- Teach the child to visualize. ("You need to pack for your ski trip. Imagine yourself walking through a whole day of vacation and think about what you will need from the time you wake up until you go to bed and then get each item as you think about it.") You might even suggest that the child make a list while they're visualizing, and *then* have them collect each item and check it off the list. If your child is younger or needs more support, offer to be the list-maker while they dictate the list. Then, you can check off each item as they pack it.

- Teach your child to repeat directions several times in their head in order to lock in the information. "Turn to page 15 and take out my notebook and pencil. Page 15, notebook, pencil. Page 15, notebook, pencil."

- Teach your child to use mnemonic devices in the form of short rhymes or special words to recall lists if this strategy does not appear to tax their working memory, too. "You can remember the line notes in the treble clef by repeating 'Every **g**ood **b**oy **d**eserves **f**udge.'" Or "Remember the list of stuff I'd like you to pick up at the store by thinking of the word "beam": **b**read, **e**ggs, **a**pples, **m**ilk."

5. Provide templates for repetitive procedures or routines. A template details all the steps required to complete a repetitive task and can be useful for a variety of home and school demands. Templates are particularly helpful for those who have trouble with planning/organizing in addition to working memory weakness. The templates can be faded out when the procedure becomes automatic. However, this should be monitored carefully so that the template can be brought back if it appears that it was discontinued too soon. For example:

- Use chore cards to keep your child on task, as suggested by Dr. Russell Barkley. These index cards list the steps to complete a particular job. You and your child can create a chore card together when you first introduce a new job. A simple numbered list of all the parts of a task works well. For example, cleaning up the bedroom might include these steps:

1. Throw away trash.

2. Put dirty clothes in hamper.

3. Put clean clothes away.

4. Books on bookshelf.

5. Toys in correct put-away place.

6. Make bed.

- Then, at chore time, you hand the child the card or pull up the template on their digital device. "Byron, here is your chore card for this morning. Just follow the steps on the card. Bring the card back to me when you finish everything on the list."

- Create a visual template by taking a photo after the chore is successfully completed. For example, once your child has cleaned their room, take a photo. The next time they need to do this chore, hand them the picture with a reminder that shows what the room should look like once it's clean. (See Ward and Jacobsen, 2014, for more on this approach.)

- Provide a template for specific academic skills. For example, create a template that delineates the steps for long division. This relieves the student of needing to remember the steps while they are trying to understand the process of division.

- You can create a template for any daily routine. This can be helpful for kids who tend to leave out steps when packing their backpacks, doing their basic morning hygiene routines, settling into the classroom, or packing up materials that will be needed at home.

6. Accommodate working memory challenges by providing reasonable support. For example:

- Expect to repeat the directions, as necessary, and do so in a patient, sensitive manner.

- For adolescents, ask how you can provide reminders or cues without bugging them. Be flexible and willing to try any reasonable way of helping.
- Prompt for good listening skills. ("I am going to give you the directions. Please look at me so I know that you are focusing.")
- Request accommodations in the classroom that focus on creating backup for your child's weak memory. These could include such interventions as having the teacher provide a written copy of directions and assignments, and having the teacher review and initial the student's agenda book to indicate that the assignment has been written down fully and correctly with no omissions.
- Teach your child the importance of having the phone numbers of at least two students in the class so they have someone to call or text if they need to check on an assignment. Teach your child to select kids who are good students, not necessarily a best buddy if the buddy also has trouble keeping track of assignments!
- Offer understanding and support when the child experiences frustration or failure:
  - "It can be hard to keep track of so many tasks at once. Would it help if we make a list together so you can check off each one as you complete it?"
  - "Sometimes it's hard to manage complicated directions. Let's read these aloud and then take it one step at a time."
  - "It sounds like you were so focused on remembering the directions for your essay that you missed what the teacher said about when it's due. Maybe Max got that information."

Tip:

■ Parents sometimes avoid talking with their children about the difficult feelings and frustrations of life with weak executive skills. However, by avoiding discussion of these emotions, you may indirectly send your child a message that their feelings are too scary for you to acknowledge. Model for your child that even difficult feelings can be looked at and discussed openly. Validate your child's feelings with a simple observation. "You look really sad when we talk about all the information that you need to remember." Or "I'm guessing that you are really frustrated by that grade." This gives them an opportunity to say more, if they choose, and helps them feel less alone with their feelings. It is not your job, nor is it possible for you to take away their feelings. Your job is to listen, to try to understand, and to ask if they would like help with thinking through how to handle the situation.

Strategies to Help a Child with Written Expression and Other Complex, Multistep Tasks

1. Focus on the use of external scratch pads to create a way to take the burden off the internal storage system. For example:

   ● Separate the process of brainstorming ideas and remembering them from the mechanics of completing the project. Teach your child to take notes, either manually or using brainstorming software, while formulating ideas. For younger children, you may want to take notes while you talk together about their ideas. Some students benefit from voice-to-text software on their tablets, computers, or phones.

   ● Those with working memory difficulties often find it helpful to use the same mind mapping apps and software that help with planning and organization difficulties. Designed for brainstorming and organizing ideas into a visual schema, they can be a helpful tool for capturing thoughts that evaporate too quickly from the minds of those with weak working memories. Popular programs such as Kidspiration (for early elementary school ages), Inspiration, Coggle, and MindManager are great tools for laying out written assignments (see Figure 14.1). See Chapter 15 for more examples of how this software can be helpful.

- Many schools now teach students to create visual organizers as the first step of the writing process. This is a way of formulating ideas and then working with those ideas to create a written response. The concrete visual format helps to reduce the amount of information that must be held in mind while creating the response. Learn what types of visual organizers are used in your child's classroom so that you can support this learning and use the same techniques at home (see Figure 14.1 for an example).

2. Provide templates for repetitive procedures or routines. For example:

- Templates for writing tasks can be a valuable tool for some students. They free the student from needing to think about the steps in the writing process while working on the content of the written assignment. For example, teach students to recognize what type of writing is being called for and to choose the template that fits (e.g., compare-and-contrast paper, persuasive essay, etc.). An experienced educational professional that we know teaches middle and high school students to use PowerPoint, Inspiration, or other software for writing because these have features that cue the user to choose the purpose of the writing and then provide a template that walks through the steps to achieve the desired product.

3. Accommodate working memory weaknesses by providing reasonable support. For example:

- Thinking and writing at the same time can tax working memory. If your child's oral responses are consistently more elaborate and complete than their written work, consider requesting accommodations that help get those thoughts onto paper.

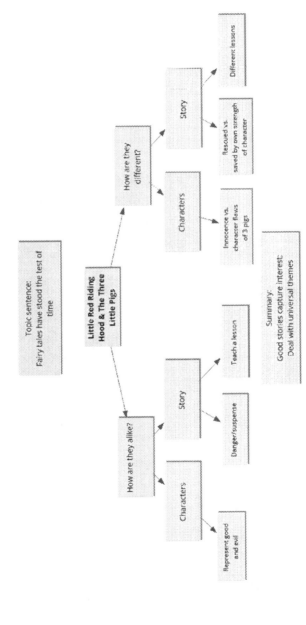

Figure 14.1 Mind map for compare and contrast paper. Created with Inspiration®

Request that the school allow your child to dictate responses to you for homework assignments. You can take notes or type the information into the computer, and then your child can work from those notes. This does not mean that you write the paper for your child – your job is simply to serve as a scribe or note-taker. Alternatively, teach your child to use voice-to-text software.

Tip:

- It makes good sense to teach computer keyboarding skills to children in the elementary school years. Using a computer for writing saves children from having to recopy work when they add to it or correct it. However, working memory challenges, motor skill delays, or problems with visual-spatial processing can make it harder for some children to become proficient at typing. These kids will require more time and practice to become proficient, and some will need to use dictation (voice-to-text) to work efficiently. For the large majority of those who are able to become proficient at typing, the computer provides opportunities that make written work less burdensome. Since learning to type is tedious and taxes working memory in the early stages (until the typing process is embedded in muscle memory), you may need to build in some meaningful reinforcers for practicing this skill. There are many resources online for learning to type, including engaging games that teach skills and monitor progress. Many schools teach keyboarding, although you might want to accelerate the pace of learning by building in practice at home or making it a summer project.

Strategies to Help a Child Who Interrupts Others So They Won't Forget What They Want to Say

1. Focus on the use of external scratch pads to create a way to take the burden off the internal storage system. For example:
   - "Here's a notepad. Jot down a few words to remind you of what you want to say, and it will be your turn to talk once I am done."

2. Accommodate working memory challenges by providing reasonable support. For example:

- "Tell me your question now, and when I am done talking, I will answer it."

Strategies to Help a Child Who Needs to Reread or Relearn Information

1. Modify the presentation of information so that it is easier to remember. For example:

- Introduce new material by previewing the lesson. This creates a structure that will help the student to organize and retain new information. ("We are going to be talking about three important events in the Civil War.") Use the structure to keep the student oriented as you continue. ("So, that was the first of three important events that we are talking about today. Now, let's talk about the second one.")

- The same approach helps for nonacademic material. ("Listen up, Sally. I need to tell you about the choices for what we can do tomorrow when your cousins are here. I thought of three things you all might enjoy. Here's what I came up with… So that was my second idea. Here is the third.") You can anchor the structure by holding up one, then two, then three fingers as you count out each of the three ideas.

2. Teach strategies and techniques to aid recall. For example:

- Teach the use of simple mnemonics, specific aids for memory. A common type of mnemonic for remembering lists is to use the first letter of each item to create a word. For example, one mnemonic that is often used for remembering all of the Great Lakes is HOMES: **H**uron, **O**ntario, **M**ichigan, **E**rie, and **S**uperior. Encourage students to develop their own shortcuts to memorize facts, lists, and other rote information. For example, "The plan for understanding what you read is SQRRR: **S**urvey,

Question, Read, Recite, Review." Monitor the effectiveness of mnemonics to ensure that they don't add to the burden on working memory.

- Encourage the child to be an active learner by teaching ways to work with the material as they read it. ("When you read, write a brief sentence or two to summarize each section of the chapter.")

- Teach the child to use a highlighter to underline key words and points. (The student may need instruction and practice to determine what to highlight.)

- Teach the student to preview the material before jumping in to reading. The goal is to create a general framework upon which they can hang the specifics of what they read. ("Let's go through first and read all the subheadings, look at any pictures, and read text boxes.")

- Teach the student to orient themself before reading a chapter by first reading the questions at the end of the chapter.

3. Use multisensory strategies. Multisensory teaching is the process of having students use more than one of their senses (not just hearing or sight) to understand new material. This is done using strategies that connect new learning with input from the eyes, ears, voice, and/or hands. For example:

- Some kids who have trouble remembering what they read benefit from hearing the material. For these students, using text-to-voice software, being read to, or even just reading the material aloud, can improve learning.

- "Let's sing the multiplication tables to the tune of 'Old MacDonald Had a Farm.'"

- Active, hands-on learning experiences can be a real boost for students who find it taxing to remember what they read. When possible, offer options to students that allow for diverse learning styles. For example, rather than requiring everyone to write a report about dinosaurs, perhaps children could be given options such as creating a model of two dinosaurs to illustrate how they are alike and how they are different, creating a poster, or even writing and performing a play.

Strategies to Help a Child Who Has Trouble Taking Notes in Class

1. Accommodate working memory weaknesses by providing reasonable support. For students with weak working memories, it can be very difficult to process information presented orally while also taking notes. For these students, taking notes may impede learning, and the notes that they do take are likely to be incomplete.

    - Set up a system for getting the day's notes from a peer buddy or from the teacher. This should be set up as a daily routine, rather than expecting the student to make the choice each day and then to arrange to get the notes.

    - Allow the student to use a voice recorder to record the day's lecture, and then they can review it later and take notes at home. Note that this requires a lot of extra time at home to review the day's learning. Not all students are willing or able to put in that much extra time.

    - Make the note-taking process easier and more productive by providing an outline at the beginning of the class with space for the student to fill in the details. This serves as a preview of the new material and also highlights the important information that the teacher is expecting the student to take away from the lesson. Looking at that outline later also allows the student and the adults to determine whether or not the student has taken adequate notes.

    - Minimize copying from the board. This seems like such a straightforward task but can be very difficult for some students. Copying from the board requires students to keep information in their heads as they transfer it from the board to the paper. Students have to keep track of what they last wrote, keep that in mind as they look back up at the board, find where they left off, look at the next few letters or words, carry the information back to the paper, and keep it in their heads long enough to finish writing it down.

o   Request that your child be paired with a "note buddy," a child in the class who takes complete notes and makes them available for your child to photocopy.

o   Ask the teacher to provide a copy of their own notes for the day's lesson.

o   Ask the teacher if a "study guide" outlining the main points will be a part of the end-of-unit study packet. Study guides allow the student to review what the teacher feels is the most important information from the unit.

Case Study: Putting It All Together

Sarah is a bright, delightful young teen who has significant trouble keeping track of directions. Her parents and teachers are quite frustrated because she doesn't seem able to remember more than one thing at a time. At home, her parents may assign a few chores and find, hours later, that she has done only one or two of them and says she forgot about the others. Although she learned to read easily and understands what she reads at a high level, she sometimes reads a chapter or two in a book and can barely recall what she just read. She asks people to repeat things so often that it becomes tiresome. At school, Sarah often starts assignments but then strays from the directions. Before she knows it, her written work is far off the mark from what the teacher requested. At other times, she expresses creative and interesting comments during classroom discussions, but when it comes time to write down her ideas, the product is overly simplistic. What can be done to help Sarah?

Her behavior is confusing to her parents and teachers, as well as herself. A psycho-educational evaluation reveals that a weak working memory is the source of many of Sarah's difficulties. Now that they understand the nature of the problem, the diverse set of challenges she presents starts to make more sense.

Sarah's parents are learning to give directions in a much more intentional manner, making the specific directions much clearer and double-checking to be certain that Sarah is processing the information. When several steps are involved, they prompt her to write them down. They know that Sarah is making progress when her mom asks her to complete a few chores while she goes to do some errands. With a smile, Sarah responds, "Mom, if you really want me to do them, write them down. You know that's the only way I'll get it all done." Sarah keeps a small notebook in her purse, so that she always has scratch paper for notes and a place to keep random bits of information that she might otherwise forget, such as hastily offered information like the time and location for the movie outing with her friends. Although the school does not allow students to use cell phones during the school day in class, Sarah is experimenting with the voice memo function at home and finds it useful when she has a brief shopping list or wants to take down directions.

Sarah's mom is experimenting, too. On a few occasions, in her more relaxed and playful moments, she created rap verses that incorporated the information Sarah needed to remember. Sarah and her mom had fun, and the rap format was quite a success. Of course, she can't always make mundane tasks that entertaining!

When it comes to schoolwork, Sarah is gradually learning to highlight the directions on worksheets and other assignments, and to recheck her highlighting as she works to stay on the right track. She and her teachers have found ways for her to get copies of the class notes when there is new or important material presented.

Sarah also finds that the computer really makes her life easier. She uses it for taking notes as she reads, first creating an outline from the chapter headings and subheadings. Typing the information into her computer seems to lock the information more firmly in her mind. Sarah also uses the computer for brainstorming her ideas as she starts papers or projects. The habit of brainstorming first, rather than just jumping in to writing, has been slow to develop. Sarah now works with a tutor who incorporates these recommendations into their sessions. Although she initially balked at what she saw as extra work, as she began to get better grades on her papers and she became used to the routine, her attitude slowly changed.

Sarah still sometimes needs reminders to use the strategies and tools that she has learned. Her parents sometimes get frustrated with her forgetfulness, but they are all relieved at her progress and much more hopeful about her ability to deal with the demands of her life.

Transitioning from Short-Term to Long-Term Goals

As with other areas of executive functioning, the key to building independence is to gradually transfer responsibility for self-management to the child. Kids with weak working memories need to understand just what that means, at an age-appropriate level, so that they can understand how it affects them and what to do about it.

At first, you initiate the strategies, all the while teaching your child about their own cognitive processing profile. ("Elly, I'm going to write down the things that you need to do because you tend to forget stuff when there is a lot on your list." "Amanda, you need to do a web to plan what you will include in your paragraph. That way you can remember all your good ideas when it is time to write.")

The next step is to prompt your child to use the strategies that they have learned. ("Janelle, that's a lot of information to remember. How are you going to keep track of it all?")

Collaborate with your child to think through the rough spots. ("Kwai, do you think it will help you learn your lines if we make an audio recording of the scenes you will be in? Then you could listen to your lines while you read them. If you'd like, you can listen in the car when we're driving to and from soccer practice. Can you think of anything else that might help?")

When your child starts using strategies on their own, your job shifts to monitoring and troubleshooting as problems arise. Sometimes you will be the voice of reality as your child tries to do things the "easy way" rather than taking the extra steps involved in actively, systematically initiating strategies to compensate for weak working memory.

This is not a short-term project! Expect this to be a process that occurs over the years as your child grows and matures.

Educate Others and Advocate for Your Child

It is easy to misinterpret signs of working memory deficits as attempts to willfully ignore directions. Teach family, sports coaches, school staff, and others working with your child about working memory and how challenges in this foundation skill affect learning and performance. Give them information to read. If your child has been tested, consider sharing your child's evaluation report or giving specific examples of their working memory capacity (e.g., "She could only repeat four digits; most kids her age can easily manage six or seven"). Many schools are familiar with the challenges posed by deficits in working memory. If not, you could offer to arrange an in-service presentation for a staff day or through your school's parent organization.

You may need to request special accommodation for your child at school and in other settings, as well. Ask others to write down important information. ("Ms. Baker, could you please write down those directions for Jack's clarinet practice? I'm not sure that he will remember which scales to practice and which pieces to work on. Also, you said something about how many times to run through each song. Please write that down, too.") If your child has an I.E.P. or 504 plan at school, request that they incorporate the types of strategies reviewed in this chapter.

Final Thoughts

Providing the necessary support for a child with weak working memory requires conscious effort on the part of the adults. We are used to giving directives orally, and we presume that listeners can remember our instructions. As therapists, we have had to learn to move out of talking mode and provide written backup regarding agreed-on goals and strategies for individuals who come to us with weak working memories. As one seven-year-old told us, "We talk about stuff in here and it all makes sense, but then I go home, and I can't remember what I agreed to do. Maybe we should write it on a sticky note, and I could put it up on my wall." That is a young girl who is learning to compensate for her own weaknesses!

Helping Children to Plan and Organize

Planning and organization = *The ability to create a structure that brings order to information, materials and tasks, including determining the action steps needed to reach a goal.*

People with weaknesses in planning and organization have trouble independently imposing structure and order on their environment, on information, and on tasks. So, they may have difficulty organizing their "stuff," organizing information in their heads, or planning out a long-term project. When faced with a multi-step project, they may have difficulty systematically thinking through the steps required, and they tend to underestimate the complexity and the time needed to successfully manage demands. While they may be able to complete single tasks well, they struggle when they must juggle multiple demands that compete for their time and attention.

These folks also tend to have trouble seeing the natural organizational framework within a body of information. Not surprisingly, then, they may falter when called upon to prioritize bits of information in order to focus on the most important points. For example, they may read a chapter of a book but then struggle to outline what they have read. Their summaries tend to be a recounting of details, rather than an orderly synopsis of the main themes bolstered by supporting details.

Strategies reviewed in this chapter help children who:

DOI: 10.4324/9781003403517-17

- Have difficulty organizing and tracking multiple tasks over time;
- Underestimate the effort involved in a project;
- Do homework but forget to turn it in;
- Struggle when prioritizing bits of information;
- Arrive at events unprepared; and
- Have trouble organizing their materials and their space.

Below, we've listed general intervention strategies that you'll want to employ with your child or student who finds planning and organizing difficult. Further down, we've provided advice for dealing with more specific scenarios that you're likely to experience with your child or teen. Note that depending on the issue you are addressing with your child, you will typically use only a subset of the strategies discussed in this chapter.

Summary: General Strategies to Help Your Child Plan and Organize

- **Introduce behavioral routines that create order and efficiency.**
- **Teach children and teens to use a tracking system** to plan what and when assigned tasks need to be completed.
- **Highlight the planning process** as the first step of any task.
- **Break down large tasks into component parts.**
- **Provide a clear organizational framework** for new information and teach cognitive routines that help kids to organize what they read and hear.
- **Teach the use of tricks and technology** that help to compensate for organizational weaknesses.
- **Develop templates** for repetitive procedures.
- **Provide accommodations** at home and at school.

Strategies to Help a Child Organize and Track Multiple Tasks over Time

1. Introduce behavioral routines that create order and efficiency.

- Plan a specific time to review tasks with your child each day. If you or another caretaker is available right after school, that's a good time for a review. Or the review can occur in the evening to plan for the next day. If it is just not possible to do this daily, schedule a weekly meeting. However you manage the scheduling, a consistent time is the ideal. This is a time to consider together what things need to be accomplished. Include the various areas of responsibility: schoolwork, chores, activities, and whatever else needs your child's attention.

- Many schools use digital platforms, and the teachers post assignments as well as grades. Check the platform together as part of the review.

Tip:

■ Digital platforms can be very useful, but they are deceptive. First, teachers are pressed for time, and not all teachers post assignments and grades in a timely manner. So, it's not always clear whether a zero is an accurate reflection of a missing assignment or whether the zero will disappear when the teacher posts the grades.

Checking the digital platforms can also be confusing, because in many schools different teachers use different platforms. Students often need to check multiple locations online to gather the information for all of their classes. Disorganized kids may lack a routine for getting all the information. You might need to teach your child to use the tool consistently by checking the platform(s) together as part of the daily routine.

Also, many parents use the digital platform as a way to check up on their kids, and it becomes a punitive process. Try to think of the online platform as a source of information for you and your child, not as a "gotcha."

Finally, teachers often post only the due date for multi-step assignments, so the digital platform is not always helpful for tracking progress.

It's important to know that sometimes the platforms have more features than the school is using. For example, they often have features that can help with planning and tracking the steps required for a multi-step project. Get to know the platform that your child's school is using and learn the capabilities; consider asking the I.T. professionals in your child's school for a tutorial. In some cases, when requested, the school may be able to turn on more features or subscribe to a broader package to enable more options. Think of digital platforms as a tool, but perhaps one that is not as straightforward as it may seem.

- Request a school meeting to consider how the school day can be tweaked to offer a brief time to review and organize tasks with the teacher or a designee who can help the student track school demands. Sometimes this occurs daily and sometimes a weekly meeting is best. One master educator, Margaret Foster, recommends that weekly check-ins in person or via email occur on Thursdays. Then, the student can use Friday to gather materials needed for missing or upcoming assignments to be completed over the weekend. (See Cooper-Kahn and Foster 2013.)

2. Teach children and teens to use a tracking system to plan what and when assigned tasks need to be completed.

- Use an agenda book, a.k.a. a planner, to teach planning! A simple paper-and-pencil planner or a good digital app allows children and teens to keep track of assignments and to plan for both daily and longer-term tasks. Here again, some recommendations from Ms. Foster provide good guidance. There should be room for a daily entry for every class, even if there is no homework. Writing in "none" ensures that the student has thought about the class. Long-term projects are entered on the due date, but they should also be written into the planner on the date assigned. The entry on the date it's assigned indicates that the student must include creating a plan for completion of the project as a current homework task.

- Successful planning includes specific "do-dates," not just due dates. Teach your child to think about long-term projects or other multi-step assignments as a series of steps. Each of the steps should be assigned a "do-date," and those dates should be mapped onto a timeline by entering them into the planner or other calendar system.

3. Highlight the planning process as the first step of any task.

- Teach the importance of executive thinking by considering together what needs to be done and when. "Grandma will arrive on Sunday morning, and we each have a few extra things to do to get the house in order. Sally, you need to clean your stuff off the extra bed in your room so Grandma can sleep there. How long do you think that will take? What's the best time for you to do that?"

- "Sam, you said that you want to take a few kids to the movies for your birthday. We can take three of your friends. Do you know who you want to invite? You should probably contact them this week. Are you going to send a text? When do you think you can do that?"

- "The band performance is coming up. Do you know what you're supposed to wear? How can you find out? I think we need the information by Wednesday so we have time to get what you need if you don't already have it. Do you need to enter a reminder in your planner or add an alert on your phone?"

Tip:

- When complex projects or long-term papers are first assigned, it is helpful to emphasize the importance of planning by starting with a "planning day." Creating a plan can make the project seem less overwhelming, and it is often a relief for kids to have a roadmap (though not always done without some pushback!). Kids and teens often appreciate the fact that they are not expected to do any other work on the project that day. Instead, on the planning day, the child's only task is to lay out the steps, determine needed materials, and develop the timeline for completing the project. This applies to studying for cumulative tests

as well. Creating a study plan is the first day's work. Celebrate
the work done on that first day, because it is the foundation for
independent task management!

4. Break down large tasks into component parts.
    - On planning days for large projects, help your child
      to determine what steps will need to be completed
      in order to successfully meet demands. Consider
      together how much time will be needed for each
      step. Teachers often offer rubrics that define the
      components of school projects, and these can help
      your child with planning.
    - A variety of systems can be used to break down
      large projects and create a concrete tracker for the
      steps. A simple version uses paper or a whiteboard
      with three columns listing tasks: To Do, In Process,
      and Done. Include end dates for deadline-driven
      assignments. Crossing items off the To Do list and
      moving them to the In Process or Done column is
      the best! (Wilkins and Burmeister 2015).
    - Two innovative and dynamic speech/language pathol-
      ogists focus on the use of visual images for planning
      (Ward and Jacobsen 2014). Their model includes
      envisioning the completed project by making a draw-
      ing or using a photograph of the clean room, success-
      ful poster, or written essay. Working back from the
      endpoint, students create images of what they need to
      do to get ready and to do the work.
5. Teach the use of tricks and technology that help to
    compensate for organizational weaknesses. For example:
    - Visual organizers, apps, and mind-mapping soft-
      ware help students to organize a paper or project, as
      well as to track progress on several projects at once.
      Commonly used programs include MindMeister,
      iHomework2, Inspiration, Kidspiration, and
      MindManager. By mapping out the task, the
      student is pushed to consider what is required to
      successfully complete school assignments. Kids can

learn to use the tools by applying them to more than academics. Scouting projects, extracurricular film projects, and graduation parties are just a few of the uses we've seen. (See Figure 15.1.)

Tip:

■ Technology provides great prospects for helping those who are poorly organized. These tools contain the seeds of independence, but children must use them repeatedly before they become habits. Short-term interventions involve teaching your child to use the tool and working with them as they practice. Once they are able to use the technology, your role is to monitor its use and to prompt your child until it becomes a habit. Be flexible in adapting the use of technology and considering new tools as they come on the market. As with so many interventions, this is a trial-and-error process. If it works or has good potential to work, keep at it. If it does not meet your child's needs or suit their style, perhaps something else may work better.

6. Develop templates for repetitive procedures.

● Create a reusable checklist for repetitive multi-step tasks, such as room cleaning or other chores. Older children and teens can participate in thinking through what needs to be done. It's important to be very specific, or you might end up with a clean-looking space with everything shoved under the bed! Store the list on a digital device or laminate a hard copy so that you and your child can access the information, as needed. Consider together when the job needs to be completed and whether or not all steps should be done at one time or if they can be spread out over a couple of days.

● You can use a paper-and-pencil approach, such as an index card, to create a chore card that you hand to your child when it's time to do it, as Dr. Russell Barkley has suggested. A "kitchen clean-up" template might list the following tasks:
1. Clear table of food and dishes.

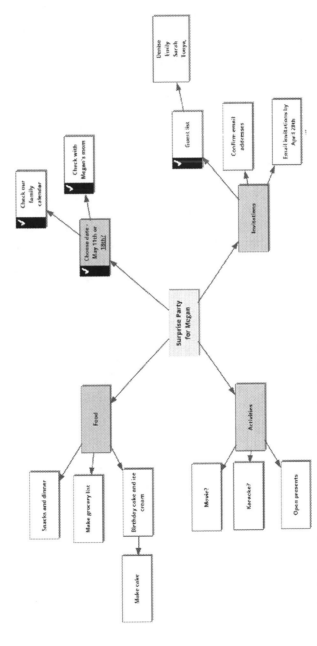

Figure 15.1 Mind map for party plan. Created with Inspiration®

2. Store leftovers in the refrigerator.

3. Load dirty dishes into dishwasher.

4. Wipe down table and countertops.

- Create lists for young children and nonreaders by drawing each step, cutting out pictures from magazines, or creating a picture list on their digital tablet. For children that need a lot of support, particularly in the early stages of learning how to complete a task, such as toothbrushing, consider breaking the task into very small steps using systematic task analysis. Using photographs of the child doing the task can also be helpful.

- Create a template to guide the planning process for multi-step assignments. The template can include the following:

  o Determine how many days there are until the assignment is due. For large projects, plan to finish at least two days in advance to account for unanticipated delays.

  o Highlight the various parts of the assignment on the rubric if there is one. If not, make a list of the sub-tasks.

  o Add hidden tasks to the list, such as time to purchase materials, go to the library, read the information sources, and take notes. In addition to writing time, include an entry for proofreading.

  o How long will each task take? How many days will you need?

  o Finally, map the do-dates onto a calendar.

7. Provide accommodations at home and at school. For example:

- Simplify your child's schedule at home. Consider reducing the number of extracurricular activities, allowing your child to focus on things that are most important and enjoyable to them.

- Bright students with executive weaknesses often find that they can ace just about any class if they take only one class at a time. It is the juggling of many classes at once that is difficult. For high school and college students, sometimes it makes sense to reduce the course load and plan to take one or two courses during the summer or adopt the five- or six-year plan.

- Teach your child to consider the relative importance of the various demands they face. For example, if community service is important to your family, then you and your child may decide that they will put in less homework time over the weekend and accept the risk of a lower grade on Monday's test in order to spend time on a Habitat for Humanity project over the weekend.

- Ask for a syllabus or advance notice of upcoming assignments. This allows you and your child to identify the most demanding times of the week or semester so that appropriate adjustments can be made in the homework/study schedule.

- Ask the teacher to provide a sample of successfully completed projects or papers. (They will likely need to redact the former student's name first.) This concrete example can be a starting point for envisioning the desired endpoint.

- Ask teachers to check in early and often in the marking period if your child tends to fall behind on work. It's so much easier for kids to get back on track if they're only a little behind rather than being so far behind the pack that they can't see how to catch up!

Strategies to Help a Child Who Underestimates the Effort Involved in a Project

1. Highlight the planning process as the first step of any task.
   - When you sit down with your child to model and guide initial planning for a multi-step project, the process also helps them to better understand the time and effort required. Mapping the steps onto a timeline makes this even more concrete.

2. Break down tasks into component parts. For example:

   - For those who repeatedly underestimate the time and effort needed, use the planning time to think more explicitly about how long each step will take and to offer a reality check. ("Do you think 20 minutes will be enough? Remember the last time you went to the library to pick out some resources for that history project? How long did it take? I'm thinking you might need to plan for more library time." "I don't think you can mow the front and the back yards in 15 minutes. Why don't you time yourself today so we can both have a better idea of how long it takes.")

3. Develop templates for repetitive procedures.

   - When you work with older children or teens to create a template for a repetitive school assignment (e.g., weekly current event summary or a lab report) or a multi-step task at home (e.g., cleaning the bathroom, doing yard chores), add a time estimate to the template.

4. Provide accommodations at home and at school. For example:

   - Some teachers provide a packet of information about each upcoming project. These often include a checklist of the steps and when each step is due. If this is not done as part of the normal classroom routine, request it as an accommodation on your child's formal or informal school plan.

   - Ask your child's teachers for very specific instructions for your child, including exactly what is expected and when it is due. Ask for a list of all steps to be done to complete the project, specific expectations for each phase of the work, and due dates for each task. Students who underestimate what's expected sometimes benefit from surprisingly detailed instructions. ("Each section should be approximately one typewritten page long." "The poster should include photos with captions. I expect the poster to be visually appealing in its layout and content. You should use at least two colors." "The essay should be at least three paragraphs long, and each paragraph should include at least five sentences.") Also, if asked, many teachers are willing to review the work along the way, as each step is due, to be sure that the student is on track.

- For older students, a first step in the planning process might be for them to meet with the teacher to clarify expectations and timelines. Learning to ask for appropriate support is a critical skill that can make the difference between success and failure.

Strategies to Help a Child Who Does Homework But Doesn't Turn It In

1. Introduce behavioral routines that create order and efficiency. For example:
   - Getting homework to the teacher involves more steps than one often thinks about unless it repeatedly goes missing. There are many different stops along the way where someone can get off-track. Is the homework getting lost at home? Is the homework getting lost in the backpack or locker? Is it in the proper notebook but forgotten in the process of settling into the classroom? Once you have identified the sticking point, then consider what needs to be added to the routine to get past it.
   - For students who lose track of homework at home, consider instituting the following routine: "Homework is not done until your homework is in its proper folder or notebook, the folders and notebooks are packed into your backpack, and your backpack is on its launching pad." (Stevens 1987)
   - Try different ways of organizing homework to find the one that best suits your child. Some students do best with one folder for all homework so that everything that needs to be turned in is stored in

one place. Others do better when they organize the homework by subject and keep it in the folder for that class.

2. Teach children and teens to use a tracking system to plan what and when assigned tasks need to be completed.

   ● Help your child to expand their homework assignment tracking system to include turning in assignments. When they complete an assignment, they can cross it off of their paper-and-pencil or digital list. Then, when they turn it in, they can put a check mark next to that item. The tricky part, as always, is developing the habit! The goal is to check their list at the beginning or end of each class to stay on track.

   ● Another way to accomplish this is for the student to enter a note to turn in homework into the next day's assignment block for that subject. Then, at the end of class, when they enter their new homework assignment, they will see the reminder to turn in what is due that day.

3. Teach the use of tricks and technology that help compensate for organizational weaknesses. For example:

   ● Several versions of watches are available that can be set to vibrate and show a reminder phrase at the programmed time. "Turn in homework" can be a programmed reminder set to go off at the beginning or end of the class period. If your child is allowed a cell phone in class, it can be set for reminder alarms.

   ● When your child prints out an assignment at home, prompt them to also email it to the teacher and to their own email account or upload it to a cloud-based document storage system. Then, if the hard copy is misplaced, your child can produce it on demand.

4. Develop templates for repetitive procedures. For example:

- Teachers can create a checklist of things to be done upon entering or leaving the classroom.

- Parents can work with their child to create a form that is completed at the end of homework time each day. The form is a simple list of items to be turned in the next day, and the child attaches it to their notebook as a reminder on the next day.

5. Provide accommodations. For example:

- If the teachers have set up a notebook system that does not work for your child, talk with them about allowing alternatives. This can be done informally or as part of a formal individualized plan.

- Involve your child's teacher(s) in building in reminders until the desired pattern of behavior (e.g., turning in homework as soon as the student walks into the classroom) becomes a habit. Teachers understandably balk at the idea of taking on responsibility for your child's job of turning in their work. However, repeated performance of a behavior is what makes it a habit; once the behavior is automatic, then the burden is lifted from the executive system. If you can help the teacher to see this as a step in the process of building independent skills, with the prospect of fading out the teacher's prompting, then the teacher may be more inclined to get on board. If your child's 504 plan or I.E.P. includes teacher reminders as an accommodation, then teachers *must* implement this strategy.

Try This!

Few problems are as frustrating for parents and kids as not receiving credit for homework that was actually completed on time but never turned in. One tried and true behavioral strategy to remedy this is to link an already established habit to one that your child needs help acquiring. To illustrate, Ivan is a seventh-grader who forgets almost everything – except his peanut butter and jelly sandwich! – when he leaves home in the morning to catch the school bus. With daily reminders from his parents, he puts his homework folder on top of his lunch in the refrigerator before going to bed each school night. Then, putting the folder in his backpack, along with his PB&J, is a no-brainer. Ivan not only gets credit for his completed work but also learns how to creatively generate ways to manage his weaknesses.

Strategies to Help a Child Who Struggles When Prioritizing Bits of Information

1. Provide a clear organizational framework for new information and teach cognitive routines that help kids to organize what they read and hear. For example:

   - Discuss the most important points to be learned before the child starts an independent reading task. In educational language, this is known as previewing the lesson. ("You are going to read about the Civil War. This chapter focuses on the personal side of what it was like during that time. I want you to notice what people wore and what they ate on the farms and in the cities, how families managed at home when most of the able men were away, and what daily life was like for the men fighting the war.")

   - Provide an outline of the major topics and subtopics from the text with space for the student to fill in specific information as they listen or read.

   - Offer study questions in advance so that the student understands the learning objectives before beginning to read.

   - Teach kids to ask themselves orienting questions before starting to work. "Why do I need to read this? What is the purpose of the lesson?"

   - Before reading textbook chapters, children and teens can skim the headings to preview the information. If there are study questions at the end of the chapter, reading those is the next step. Then, the reading is layered onto a general idea of what the chapter is about and students can more easily recognize the most important information as they read.

Try This!

Teach the student to build a framework for new material by using the headings and sub-headings chosen by the textbook author. To do this, students sit at their computers with their textbooks open to the chapter and type in all the chapter headings and subheadings before starting their reading. "Teaching students to create an outline of the material by previewing it in this manner is like offering a road map to someone setting out on a journey." (Cooper-Kahn and Foster 2013, p. 97) Some students fill in details from each section as they are reading, while others do better if they go back and take more specific notes after reading through the whole chapter.

2. Provide accommodations at home and at school.

    ● All of the techniques described above can be requested as school accommodations on formal or informal educational plans.

    ● Preview important discussions with your child or teen. For example, when you initiate a family meeting, preview and categorize the information you need to discuss. ("Sammy, we need to sit down together this evening to plan the things you need to get done before we go on vacation. We talked about some chores and also one summer reading project that you need to get done over the next two months. You may have some other things to add to the list. Let's review and plan after dinner tonight.")

Strategies to Help a Child Who Arrives at Events Unprepared

1. Introduce behavioral routines that create order and efficiency. For example:

    ● Think aloud with your child when there is an event or activity that requires gathering gear or materials. Go through the steps involved in ensuring that all the materials are ready to go at the necessary time. "What will you need to have with you for soccer practice? When you come home from soccer practice, where will you put your soccer bag? What will you need to take out of the bag? Where does your dirty soccer uniform go? How and when will the clean uniform get back into the soccer bag? If there is mud on your cleats, where will they go and how will they get back into the soccer bag? How will the soccer bag get to the car?" Develop a consistent routine and provide support until the process becomes automatic and independent.

- Create a launching pad for all items that will be needed the next day. For many kids it works best to have a spot by the door, and part of the evening routine is to think about the next day and then take the needed stuff to the launching pad. If you drive them to school or camp or work, it may work best for them to load their things into the car the night before.

2. Develop templates of repetitive procedures.

- Work with your child to create a checklist of everything they will need when they arrive at an activity. For example, you can print out or keep a copy of the equipment checklist in the soccer bag for a last-minute check before the bag goes into the car.

Strategies to Help a Child Organize Their Materials and Their Space (Locker, Desk, Bedroom)

1. Introduce behavioral routines that create order and efficiency.

- It is generally easier to put a few things away than it is to wait until the chaos is out of control. Build in times for organizing on a regular basis. It may help to do this together, but don't do it for your child without their participation. Define what the organized space should look like. Where does each thing go? What belongs in a backpack or desk? Where do the other things belong? Create categories that help your child think in a systematic way. For example, room categories might include clothes (clean or dirty?), papers (trash or papers to save?), toys, or things for hobbies. The backpack might have current notebooks or folders, supplies that go back and forth each day, loose papers to be saved or trashed, permission slips, and so on. Consider together how to sort the materials and create a place for each.

- Sometimes providing your child with a photograph of an organized desk or all the items that typically belong in their backpack can help them get a better grasp of what it means to be organized.

- Offer to buy supplies to help with organization. Bins or shelves might be useful for storing items in the bedroom. Folders or pouches help some folks to manage the stuff in their backpacks. Remember, though, that different things work for different individuals. Remember, too, that often it is not the supplies or the organizational system that is problematic, but the follow-through when it comes time to use the system. Continue to work with your child to build the routines and habits needed to use the system.

2. Provide accommodations at home and at school. For example:

- Provide frequent monitoring and help with organizing materials. Hands-on help is often needed for younger children. For older children and for those who show that they are capable of more independent functioning, back off of direct help but provide frequent checks to ensure that the space is not getting out of control.

- If keeping things orderly at school is a problem, ask if the teacher or a designee can help by creating a consistent organizing time. For example, some children need prompting to clean their desks or lockers every Friday. Then they can use some weekend time to sort all the papers and items they clear out. A daily or weekly backpack cleaning at home is often helpful, as well.

- Remember to discourage school staff from managing your child's desk clutter via a "desk angel." This is a teacher or other staff member that cleans the child's desk for them. It is much better to set this up so that someone works with your child so that they build the foundation for organizing their materials on their own.

Tips:

- Remember to prioritize the goals for organization. Although a messy room may drive you crazy, there are times when it may serve your child better if you focus on developing a system to get long-term projects done on time.
- Don't assume that your child knows how to organize a backpack, notebook, or locker. Talk to them about organizational methods that might work for them and let them watch you clean out your kitchen junk drawer!

Case Study: Putting It All Together

*L*et us introduce you to Jim. He tends to wait until the last minute to start papers and projects, generally stating (and believing!) that the work will be "no big deal" and won't take long. Although Jim managed to do okay in elementary school, he is having significant difficulty in middle school. He seems genuinely surprised each time he discovers anew that starting work the night before an assignment is due does not allow enough time to get all the work done. Like many students, Jim has become more discouraged over the years. Now in eighth grade, he tends to respond to his difficulties by giving up or pretending *that he doesn't care. His parents are very worried about what's in store for all of them when Jim gets to high school.*

Jim's new Language Arts teacher has helped his parents see that Jim has developmental delays in his ability to independently plan and organize his assignments, belongings, and even his thoughts.

Jim's planning and organizational deficits are complicated by his feelings of demoralization and his tendency to give up when he gets frustrated. With their new insight into what they had previously assumed was a lack of motivation, Jim's parents and the school have recently initiated interventions to help Jim learn to organize and plan his work. Even though Jim is in the eighth grade and, in theory, should be able to do this on his own, his parents have gone back to providing a higher level of external structure and organizational support, as they did for him when he was younger. They review his assignments with him and help break them down into component parts with checklists for him to follow. They are using a computer program for mapping out tasks, and they have found that Jim is taking more initiative now on setting up new assignments.

At school, teachers provide specific timelines for completing the components of long-term projects to help guide Jim in his planning. They set interim due dates to keep him on track. Jim is starting to understand his own difficulty, so he is feeling more hopeful about being able to do well at school. His parents are trying to carefully balance out their roles as they offer help, assisting in a developmentally appropriate way that does not promote learned helplessness or overdependence. Now there's a challenge!

Transitioning from Short-Term to Long-Term Goals

The goal of your interventions as you help your child with planning and organizing is to create systems that become habitual and to give your child a repertoire of ways to approach a task. Short-term interventions create the structure for your child. You are providing this support so that your child can meet expectations while you use the tasks of daily life to teach them how to plan and organize. As they mature and their proficiency increases, you ease up on the support. However, the objective is clear from the outset: you are teaching them ways to independently manage demands.

Teachers will recognize an important teaching approach here known as *scaffolding*. While the content is not social studies or language arts, the process of teaching planning and organizational skills at school or at home is the same. Just as with any other content area, the student will need instruction, practice, and feedback until they accumulate sufficient knowledge and experience to build up some momentum and take off on their own. One experience builds on another over time, and the skills they have learned work together in such a way that the scaffolding can be removed and the building stands on its own. However, with disorganized kids, you should expect that there will be a tendency to revert back to disorganized mode, at times. Your monitoring, or perhaps monitoring by a tutor or coach, will be important for a long time.

Educate Others and Advocate for Your Child

Planning and organization are necessary for efficient task completion and self-management. When kids struggle with these skills, they need direct, intensive help to develop successful habits.

Remember, the goal is not to promote overdependence or learned helplessness. Such problems may occur when parents and other important adults complete tasks *for* rather than *with* the child and when they continue to provide more support than needed. Children and adolescents develop more effective planning and organizational skills through practice plus maturation. No amount of wishing, lecturing, prodding, or punishing leads to skill development. If your child is generally putting forth adequate effort, one of the most useful ways you can help is to promote better understanding and remind others that disorganization is not due to a moral flaw or lack of interest in performing well.

Help for your child can take a variety of forms. Some schools, public and private, focus a great deal of effort on teaching organizational skills. Find out what your child's school can offer. Be sure to look at the ways that your child will be taught the skills for independence, not just how their weaknesses will be accommodated.

Most schools use some version of a digital learning management system to post assignments and grades. Check out the system for yourself and help your child learn to navigate it, as needed. If the system is not being used effectively and efficiently, discuss this with school administrators.

While many well-organized parents do a remarkable job of supporting and teaching their own children and adolescents, you may need to seek a tutor or coach if you have difficulty with organizing yourself.

Final Thoughts

Kids are not always thrilled about putting in the time that is required to develop improved planning and organization skills. How much and how far you can coax, push, or lead a child is not something that is clearly defined. Hopefully, the general principles offered in the first half of the book give you some guidelines.

Remember, these skills can be learned in a variety of arenas, not just schoolwork. Some parents cut off all outside activities with the intention of pushing their child to focus on school and so perform better. Instead, we recommend that you work with your child to pick the one or two extracurricular activities that put a spring in their step, and then use these as training grounds for planning and organization skills, too. In fact, like most students, disorganized kids do best when their days include a reasonable balance between school and outside activities.

16

Helping Children Monitor Their Behavior

Self-monitoring = *The ability to observe our own behavior and to measure our progress against expectations. We use the term self-monitoring here as a broad term that includes oversight of both academic and social-emotional behavior.*

Self-monitoring can be viewed as the brain's quality control system. The ability to step back and observe one's own behavior is essential to both school success and to social competence. Kids with weak ability to monitor themselves tend to be oblivious regarding their own efforts and whether they are meeting standards. Despite clues along the way, these kids often are completely surprised when they receive negative evaluations of their work or their behavior.

Successful self-monitoring is much like driving a car. It seems effortless when it is going well. Yet when we drive, we are constantly engaged in monitoring our own behavior, assessing surrounding vehicles and environmental conditions, and the interplay between the two. We adjust our driving speed or make minor course corrections without conscious effort. However, if you think back to when you first learned to drive, you may remember how complex and effortful the task seemed. In contrast, experienced drivers automatically complete these monitoring functions and may only need to consciously think about how they are doing when they are fatigued or encounter unexpected events (e.g., a car pulling out in front of them).

DOI: 10.4324/9781003403517-18

In academics, poor self-monitoring is particularly apparent in math and writing. Students with weaknesses in this executive skill tend to make seemingly careless computation errors and have trouble proofreading their written work.

Children and teens who find it a challenge to monitor their own social-emotional behavior may not easily learn from previous experiences. Simply put, if a child doesn't know what they did to irritate their peers, how can they avoid doing it again next time?

Interventions for children with self-monitoring weaknesses are designed to help them develop routines for comparing their own behavior to a standard, develop intentional goals, and tune in to environmental feedback. With repetition over time, these activities can become automatic, even though they will require self-conscious effort at the start.

You may notice that there are fewer examples of interventions in this chapter than in the previous intervention chapters. The problems arising from weak self-monitoring and the solutions for dealing with them overlap a great deal with the interventions for problems with other executive skills. After all, the long-term goal of intervention for all executive weaknesses is to help children understand their own behavior and know what to do to help navigate the problems. So, building self-awareness and self-observation is built into the interventions presented in earlier chapters. We offer some interventions specific to self-monitoring in this chapter. However, if your child has difficulties with self-monitoring, you might want to read through the recommendations for other executive skills to get more ideas of how to help.

Strategies reviewed in this chapter help children who:

- Get upset with the outcome of situations but lack a realistic, systematic approach to making things go better;
- Drift off target and don't notice that they have moved away from the goal;
- Make seemingly "careless" errors;
- Fail to adjust behavior based on feedback;
- Don't notice when peers are no longer interested in the topic of conversation; and
- Are genuinely surprised when they get in trouble for misbehavior ("What did I do?").

Below, we've listed general intervention strategies that you'll want to employ with your child who has difficulty monitoring their behavior. Further down, we've provided advice for dealing with more specific scenarios that you're likely to experience with your child or teen. Note that depending on the issue you are addressing with your child, you will typically use only a subset of the strategies discussed in this chapter.

Summary: General Strategies to Help Your Child Learn How to Self-Monitor

- **Highlight the process of self-review and analysis of behavior.** Many children with these weaknesses don't engage in the crucial step of analyzing their past successes and failures in order to improve future performance.
- **Encourage your child to set an intentional goal and to systematically monitor their efforts.** Engaging in the effort to self-monitor is more important, at first, than the outcome, because we're trying to build the habit of self-monitoring. Still, a positive outcome is very reinforcing!
- **Provide external structure and feedback.** This needs to be done in a sensitive, developmentally appropriate manner.
- **Teach the use of tools and techniques to improve monitoring,** including checklists for repetitive tasks.
- **Teach the use of technology** to help the child monitor their performance.

Strategies to Help a Child Who Gets Upset with the Outcome in a Situation but Lacks a Realistic, Systematic Approach to Making Things Go Better

1. Highlight the process of self-review and analysis of behavior.
    - "Billy let's look at the teacher's comments on this assignment together. It looks like you lost credit on your essay because you didn't answer all the questions in the assignment. Did the teacher say

anything else that would help you figure out what she was looking for?"

- "Samantha, I'm sorry that you weren't invited to go to the movies with the other kids. Do you think there's something that you did that upset them? I don't know if it's relevant or not, but Sarah's mom mentioned that she heard that you were mean to Sarah for hanging out with her other friends. Do you think that might be the issue?"

2. Encourage your child to set an intentional goal and to systemically monitor their efforts. For example:

- "Jackie, last time you had a math test you lost points for calculation errors even though you knew how to do the problems. What's your goal for this test? Great. Review your answer and do a quick check of your calculations before moving on to the next problem. I like that goal. I hope it goes well!" And later: "How did that strategy of checking your calculations work out for you? Did you feel like it was helpful? Were you able to do the review and still get through all the problems?"

- "I know how upsetting it was when your brother was allowed to go to the pool yesterday and you missed out. Let's try again. If you'd like to go to the pool this afternoon, you need to get your chores done in the morning. How will you stay on track? Would you like to use a checklist? Okay, the goal for this morning is to check off each task as you do it and then use the checklist to see what else needs to be done." And later: "Whew, I'm impressed. You checked off four of the five chores, and it looks like you did a good job on them. So, just for this afternoon, I'm going to give you a pass on the last chore, because you really stuck with the strategy. You can do the last chore before dinner."

Strategies to Help a Child Who Doesn't Notice When They Have Gone Off on a Tangent

1. Encourage your child to set an intentional goal and to systematically monitor their efforts.

   - "Carey, I know you got mad at Jillian for telling you that you get lost in the weeds when you tell a story. Is that something that you'd like to work on? We could help you by working on that at home. We could come up with a few strategies to try. It would be like having weed whackers for your brain! Let's think about what you could do and how I could help you."

2. Provide external structure and feedback. For example:

   - Monitor the child's performance along the way and prompt them to go back to the topic and refocus.

     o "Stop for a minute, Carey. Do you remember my question? You didn't finish answering it. What happened after band practice?"

     o "Remember, the goal of this paper is to present one side of a controversial argument. Do these points support your position?"

     o "You certainly know a lot about the Civil War. Let's focus on this specific question, though. Can you tell us the most important three events of the Battle of Gettysburg?"

     o "Brenda, I'm so glad you enjoyed the new video game. I know you have a lot you would like to say about it. But we need to focus now on the plans for today and who you would like to invite to go to the pool with us."

     o "You were talking about what happened on the playground today, but now I'm having trouble following you. Can you get back to how Joe hurt himself?"

3. Teach the use of tools and techniques to improve monitoring. For example:

- Teach the student to highlight key words in the directions and to review them to be certain they are on topic.
- Work with the student to develop an outline before they begin writing, and to use the outline as a template as they write. If the writing is done on a tablet or computer, they can create the outline and then fill in details and add information to create full sentences.

Strategies to Help a Child Who Doesn't Notice "Careless" Errors

1. Provide external structure and feedback. For example:

- Make the evaluation criteria explicit.
  - o "You will lose points if you have not put your name on the paper or have skipped any questions. Remember, name on the paper and all questions answered."
  - o "The assignment sheet says that you will be graded on the presentation of the material, including the design and appearance of the cover. That means that the cover page should be clean, neat, and have an interesting design that reflects what your paper is about. I do not want to see erasures and handwritten corrections. If you have made corrections, you should print out a new, corrected copy of the cover page."
  - o "When you clean up after you make yourself a snack, I should not be able to tell what you had to eat or even that you made a snack at all. Make sure that you have cleaned up your trail. That includes using a sponge to wipe up little spills near the microwave and crumbs on the counter."

- Prompt the child to check their work against the standard. For example:

    o About ten minutes before the exam or in-class assignment is due, the teacher can make a quick announcement: "Please go to the first page, make sure your name is on your paper, and then check to make sure you haven't skipped any questions." If your child has an I.E.P. or 504 plan, you may want to consider adding this accommodation, which does not adversely affect classmates and may, in fact, be helpful to some of them, too.

    o Help children recheck their own performance on papers and projects assigned as homework. "Deanna, let's take a look at the checklist to see if you have all the pieces that your teacher is expecting."

    o Give your child feedback that helps them learn when a chore is complete: "Tina, you did a great job loading the dishwasher. Now, I see one more thing you need to do. Do you see it? Just wipe off the counter above the dishwasher, and then your work is done and you can have some free time."

    o Help your child evaluate completion of chores on their own: "Before I come upstairs to look at your room, I want you to go back up and check it yourself. I want you to stand at the door, and this time pretend you are the parent. See if you think the work is all done."

2. Teach the use of tools and techniques to improve monitoring. For example:

   - For math computation, teach the student to high-light or circle math operation signs (plus, minus, times, divided by).

   - Teach the student to say each math calculation problem aloud so that they are less likely to miss the operation sign.

   - Direct the student to use a specific copy-editing procedure (e.g., circle misspellings, underline punc-tuation/capitalization errors).

- Develop a work routine and have your child practice it until it becomes automatic. For example, Sierra's grandmother practiced the following with her:

    o Read the directions out loud.

    o Underline key words (e.g., *not, all, if*).

    o Reread the directions after completing your answer, and ask yourself, "Did I answer the question?"

- Walk through a "guesstimate" procedure for math problems. Ask the student to estimate the answer and to make an educated guess about whether the answer is likely to be correct. ("Do you think the answer will be less than or greater than ten?" "Let's see, the problem talks about how many cookies the girl ate for her snack. Your answer is 3,500. That's a lot of cookies for one person! Does that sound reasonable?")

- If the assignment packet includes a rubric to help the students determine how they will be graded, coach children to refer back to it at each step of the project and then to grade themselves before pronouncing the work complete.

- Ask your child to estimate how long it takes to complete a task. For example, ask them to guess how long it will take to pack their lunch and backpack. Write down their estimate and then time them.

4. Teach the use of technology to help a student self-monitor. For example:

    - Coach students to use the editing features built into their word processing app.

    - Coach students on how to enable the word prediction feature on word processing apps.

    - Allow the student to use a calculator, calculator app, or math facts table.

    - Encourage the use of writing apps and software to generate outlines and review written work. Some writing programs provide templates for different types of writing.

Tip:

■ When prompting children to monitor their behavior, it is important to stick to observations of the behavior and to avoid "riders" – added-on comments that exact an emotional price. Riders carry a negative tone that overrides any other content in the message. Below is an example of two different parental responses to the same behavior, the first includes riders and the second doesn't. Which response do you think is likely to be most effective?

"Ellen, you left your dishes on the table again. I don't know how many times I've told you not to do that! Why are you such a slob? Don't you care about how this place looks?"

"Ellen, you left your dishes on the table. This seems to be a recurring problem. Can you think of anything we might be able to do to help you remember to tidy up the kitchen when you make yourself a snack?"

If you can keep the negative tone out of your messages, you will likely find that your child is more receptive to your feedback and suggestions.

Strategies to Help a Child Who Doesn't Adjust Behavior Based on Feedback

1. Highlight the process of self-review and analysis of behavior. For example:

   • Encourage your child to analyze past incidents in order to improve their ability to think about behavior. ("Kenya, the last time we were at the playground, you pushed a little girl down the slide. I realize you thought she would enjoy it, but she didn't. She seemed really scared. Did you see her face because that was a scared face. What's another way that you would know that she wants you to back off?")

   • When your child is calm, ask them to generate other ways to handle a problem or specific situation. Ask them about the possible consequences of each option. ("I know that your sleepover with

223

Tracy didn't turn out like you wanted. Let's talk about what you could've done differently to prevent the argument. Interesting idea. How do you think that would go over?")

- When possible, stop the action and help your child analyze their behavior. Then do a replay including more effective behaviors. Remember to incorporate a brief discussion of what they *should* do, not just what they did wrong. ("Serena, hold on here for just a minute. I heard Mary say that she didn't want you sitting so close to her. What do you think you should do? Yes. Arm's length. That's a good idea. Let's see how that works.")

Tip:

■ Teaching social skills to children is more complex than you might think. A full overview of how to approach social skills problems is outside the scope of this book, but research in this area suggests that the best outcomes occur when social behavior is taught in natural settings, when behaviors are carefully assessed in advance, when each child's specific deficits are targeted, and when transfer from the teaching environment to real life is part of the work. If your child does not make progress despite your best efforts, consider seeking consultation from a professional who is well versed in interventions for social skills deficits.

Strategies to Help a Child Notice When Peers Lose Interest in the Topic of Conversation

1. Provide external structure and feedback. For example:
   - "When you talk about your favorite movie, you sometimes say more than the other kids want to hear. So, I want you to keep your talk about that

to three sentences. No more than three sentences about the movie. Got it?"

- "When I walked in the room, I saw you over there with two other girls. It looked to me like they turned away when you said something to them. Did you notice that? That probably means that they did not want to talk with you."

- "Let's talk about what happened on the school trip. James apparently got tired of you talking about your previous trip to the zoo. He tried to change the subject a few times. Do you remember what he said?"

- "Cindy kept trying to talk with you about the prom while you kept talking about math class. I think her facial expression and trying to change the subject were clues that she was no longer interested in hearing about math class."

2. Teach the use of tools and techniques to improve monitoring, including checklists for repetitive tasks. For example:

- Teach and practice reading body language in social interactions. "How can you tell, even without words, whether someone is bored or interested in what you are saying?"

- Make a list together of ways someone might indicate boredom and review it when you are "replaying" where things go wrong in social interchanges.

- Sarah's school counselor has worked with her teachers to help her slow down and read the facial expression of the person to whom she is talking. When that doesn't give her enough information about whether or not she is being clear in her conversation, Sarah has learned to directly ask trustworthy friends if she has been talking too long or if she is making sense.

Strategies to Help a Child Who Is Genuinely Surprised When They Get in Trouble for Misbehavior ("What Did I Do?")

1. Highlight the process of self-review and analysis of behavior.

    - "Jon, I know you were surprised when your Sunday school teacher asked you to leave the class because you were talking. Sometimes it's hard to remember to listen quietly to the teacher when you have so much that you'd like to say. Maybe we can think about clues that would help you to notice when the teacher is getting upset. Here are some possibilities: think about how the teacher looks at you, what she says, and what other kids are doing. I know you don't want to get in trouble, and it is important to be able to figure out how to prevent this from happening in the future."

2. Provide external support and feedback. For example:

    - Offer in-the-moment prompts. For instance, Pat is a bright 12-year-old who has trouble anticipating the consequences of her behavior. Even though her P.E. teacher blew the warning whistle three times, she was surprised when she got pulled from the soccer game for being too rough. Once she calmed down, her teacher agreed to stay close to her on the side-lines and to use her name with a brief reminder, since the whistle didn't seem to register with her. Now, the teacher uses a brief, targeted phrase, like "Hands, Pat!" to remind her to keep her hands to herself.

Case Study: Putting It All Together

*L*uis *is a fifth-grader who struggles with self-monitoring. Although he is bright and wants to do well, he often skips test questions, not noticing that he has blanks on the answer sheet. He only sees his errors when the test is returned with vivid red Xs marking the overlooked test questions.*

Luis tends to spend a long time completing homework, but he doesn't catch mistakes, particularly when he perceives the task as easy. When completing a chore such as taking out the trash, he may not notice that he has dropped items or that the top of the garbage can is not latched. It is only when his father tells him the next morning that the squirrels helped themselves to leftovers (and made quite a mess) that he becomes aware that his performance was not quite up to standard.

Luis's parents and teachers have become quite frustrated with his inconsistent performance and frequent missteps. They have tried punishing Luis, lecturing him, and reminding him to be more careful. Nothing seems to help. Luis is as frustrated as the adults. He is also quite discouraged. He sometimes talks about feeling stupid, most recently when he mistakenly thought that he did great on a project and then got a low grade due to overlooking part of the assignment.

Luis' parents have become increasingly concerned about his loss of self-confidence and waning self-esteem. They've decided to take him to a psychologist for a few sessions to learn more about self-monitoring and other executive skills so that he will understand that his difficulties are not due to poor motivation or a lack of intelligence.

Luis and his parents learned to create a system where they edit and check his work much like a copy editor does for a professional writer. Instead of standing over him while making corrections as they used to do, Luis's parents review his homework and mark omissions and errors while he works on other tasks. They highlight the portions that need editing, and they make a quick note in the margin to indicate the type of mistake (spelling, punctuation, capitalization, lack of clarity, math error). Twice a week, Luis also works with a tutor who has both an educational background and specializes in executive functioning. The tutor is helping Luis experiment with ways to improve his self-monitoring. So far, he has learned that proofreading aloud works best for him (he is a strong reader), and he is learning how to use the spelling and grammar check features more effectively on his tablet. Luis and his tutor are also experimenting with a checklist to help him consistently reread directions to ensure that he has done what he was asked to do.

Luis and his parents have met with all of his teachers, and they have agreed to check in with him 15 minutes before the end of any quiz or test. If there are blank sections or questions, they point this out in a sensitive manner to give him time to complete the work. Some of his teachers have found that taking 30 seconds to make this double-check announcement to the whole class benefits other students as well. In addition, Luis's math teacher allows him to use a calculator to double-check his computations on tests.

At home, Luis's parents remind him to do a visual inspection after completing a chore, and when appropriate, they do this with him. If a part of the job is not completed, they acknowledge his good effort and gently prompt him to finish what needs to be done.

Transitioning from Short-Term to Long-Term Goals

It is important for parents and teachers to help kids learn how to keep better track of how they are doing. Providing external cues, prompts, and feedback helps children learn what to watch out for and to check how they are doing. We begin by staying physically close to the child and providing frequent verbal and nonverbal cues. For example, a parent might ensure that the child is brushing their teeth adequately by standing next to them and watching while they brush. Next, the parent leaves the room briefly while they brush and offers verbal reinforcement when they check back. Then, the child may brush independently and use a plaque-detecting rinse once a week that shows any missed areas by turning the plaque a bright color. When the child is consistently doing a good job, the weekly rinse may be dropped entirely, reviving it only occasionally if parents think they're slipping.

As with other areas of executive function, we need to teach the child or teen about their own profile in a straightforward, nonjudgmental manner and make self-observation an explicit goal. Then we teach the tricks and systems that will help them to monitor their own work more accurately. We back away from active involvement as the child's or teen's own self-monitoring system improves and move to just prompting the use of strategies that they have learned. When we see them begin to initiate strategies on their own, we support their independence by offering praise for using what they have learned.

Our long-term goal is to help children develop a sufficient internal quality control system so that external monitoring is greatly reduced or no longer needed. We are looking for evidence that the process of self-monitoring is becoming more automatic and less effortful over time. For a small group of kids, the self-monitoring system is slow to develop and yet we want to encourage independence. When this is the case, independence involves learning to enlist the help of others to provide feedback and support.

Educate Others and Advocate for Your Child

Kids who struggle with self-monitoring often demonstrate inconsistent performance and are prone to "careless" errors. Parents should talk with teachers to help them understand that such mistakes are not related to a lack of motivation but, instead, to developmental weaknesses in quality control. Since kids with certain temperaments attempt to manage self-monitoring problems by pretending not to care about their performance, parents sometimes need to help teachers, coaches, and other important adults understand the need to look beyond a child's "surface" presentation to provide an appropriate level of assistance. And although it is tempting, no amount of lecturing has ever been an effective intervention.

Weak self-monitoring often occurs in combination with impulsiveness and poor regulation of attention. Teachers often encounter this cluster of behaviors and may have some good ideas to share. Both at home and at school, it is essential to provide these supports in a noncritical manner. Every best-selling author has a great editor, and kids with limited self-monitoring skills may also need to have their work reviewed by a trusted adult.

Final Thoughts

As noted above, children who have trouble with self-monitoring are generally impulsive as well. For a child to determine how they are doing, they must first slow down enough to think and review their performance. Many of the interventions to reduce impulsive behavior are also useful for improving self-monitoring. Efficient self-monitoring also requires paying adequate attention and developing habits and routines for regularly checking how one is doing. It is a complex, but important behavior. Helping children and adolescents to develop better self-monitoring can reduce their risk of academic underachievement, inconsistent school performance, and social problems.

17

Special Topic

Helping Children with Emotional Regulation

Emotional regulation = *The ability to be thoughtful, flexible, and intentional about how we respond to our own feelings.*

Emotional regulation is a process that allows us to take our own "emotional temperature" and make choices about how we want to respond. Good emotional regulation allows us to keep our behavior within an acceptable range so that we can meet the expectations and goals that are important to us.

In contrast, when emotional regulation is a challenge, kids' feelings and behavior often seem out of control. When the child hears that they cannot have cookies before lunch, that they have to clean their room, that they can't go to a party with their friends, or that they have to do their homework, it can trigger a meltdown that hijacks the day for all those in their wake. When kids or teens regularly respond to everyday difficulties of life with emotional meltdowns or out-of-control behavior, we say that they are "dysregulated."

We know that children and teens who struggle with executive functioning are at risk for problems with emotional regulation. It's not hard to see how these might be connected. When something happens that triggers strong feelings, we have to press the pause button before we respond. This allows for a small cushion of time to think about what sets us off and to consider expectations, rules, and personal goals. We scroll through options for how to proceed and consider the likely outcome of

DOI: 10.4324/9781003403517-19

each one. Finally, we choose the option that is most likely to meet our needs, and we decide how and when to carry through with it. All of this requires good impulse control, flexibility, adequate working memory, the ability to monitor our own feelings and behavior, and well-developed planning and organization skills.

Even so, executive functioning is not the only important consideration when we look at how to build better emotional regulation. It also helps to understand two other crucial ingredients: managing physiological arousal and emotional literacy. Let's look at each of these briefly.

Physiological arousal is a term for what happens when our bodies become stimulated and we are on alert. Research shows that some people are more easily stimulated than others. Stimulation can come from our emotions ("I'm mad!" or "I'm worried"), from our sensory system ("They're making too much noise!"), or from our physical state ("I'm tired and hungry!"). All of these go into the same "arousal bucket," adding to the risk of having our feelings overflow their container and getting out of control. For example, if we are tired, then we are more likely to lose control when something happens that is emotionally challenging. Those who tend to be easily stimulated can quickly fill their buckets, and they are prone to difficulties with emotional regulation.

There's yet another critical link between physiological arousal and children's emotional regulation. We have compelling evidence that when parents' arousal level is high during interactions with their child, then the child's level of arousal increases, too. The challenges of raising a child with executive functioning weaknesses can lead even the calmest of parents to lose their cool on occasion. When this happens repeatedly, our kids' development suffers. One researcher summarized the results of studies on family interactions and long-term development of children with ADHD.

> Harsh, critical, and highly emotional parenting causes strong physiological (physical) reactions in the bodies of both parents and children. These reactions can be measured in a number of ways, including rapid heart rate responses during parent–child interactions. When parents are harsh, highly emotional, and critical, their children's bodies react as if a major threat has occurred.
>
> *(Beauchaine 2020)*

In other words, parents can contribute to overfilling their children's arousal buckets when their own reactions are not well-regulated.

But there is hope here, too. The same researcher studied treatment aimed at increasing positive interactions within the family and helping parents to regulate their own emotions in response to their children. The good news? He found that when parents reduced their own "negative parenting behaviors," their children were calmer, and their behavior improved. These findings are in line with what many researchers have found, and the takeaway message is clear. When adults can calm themselves before dealing with their child's strong emotions, everybody benefits!

Finally, the other element of emotional regulation that is important for you to know about is emotional literacy. Emotional literacy is simply the ability to use words to label our feelings. Brain imaging studies show that when children (and adults!) label their feelings, activity in the parts of the brain responsible for automatic emotional reactions quiets down (see Lieberman et al. 2011 for a summary of the research). We experience less distress over difficult situations, so we are better able to keep our feelings and behavior within an acceptable range. It's important to know that naming our feelings is different from reimagining and rehashing a situation endlessly. In fact, that can be a problem for self-regulation. However, labeling our feelings helps us to better control our behavior. You may have heard the phrase, "Name it to tame it." It applies here.

Strategies reviewed in this chapter address children who need help to:

- Build basic skills for self-regulation;
- Need a little extra support to manage their feelings;
- Need a lot more support to manage their feelings and to recover once they lose control.

In this chapter, you will find general intervention strategies that you'll want to employ with your child or student with difficulty regulating emotions. You'll notice that the chapter is organized just a bit differently than the previous chapters on ways to help. The strategies are organized into broad categories of intervention rather than specific situations. As with the other chapters on ways to help, within those categories you will find examples of scenarios and scripts to guide you. Choose the strategies that best target the difficulties you're dealing with.

Summary: General Strategies to Help Your Child with Emotional Regulation

- **Focus on calm interactions** and teach children ways to calm themselves.
- **Teach emotional literacy,** the ability to identify and label the full variety of feelings.
- **Use proactive strategies** to build positive behaviors.
- **Intervene** before the problem gets overwhelming.
- **Introduce strategies** that help children to monitor their feelings and to put them into perspective.
- **Give children time and space** to process strong feelings.

Strategies to Help Children and Teens Build Foundation Skills for Self-Regulation

1. Focus on calm interactions and teach children ways to calm themselves.

   - Practice responding to strong emotion with a quieter voice than your child. Loud voices increase our own and others' arousal level. Speaking softly calms things down. If you're thinking, "But my child won't hear me when he's shouting!" then try this. When your child is yelling, say softly "There is candy in the top drawer of my desk if you'd like some." You might be surprised to find that your child heads right over to your desk! Be sure you've added a favorite candy in advance.

   - Walk away if you're too upset to interact thoughtfully. Take time to calm yourself. When you do, you take the heat out of your own interactions, and you teach the importance of taking some time away by modeling it for your child. ("I'm too upset right now to think clearly. I need to cool down before we talk any more about this.")

   - Find productive strategies that work for you when you need to calm down. Deep breathing is a quick and easily learned tool that creates physical and mental calm. For a low-tech way to get started, practice this: close your eyes and take a few deep breaths. Breathe from your diaphragm, taking air in through your nose and releasing it slowly through your mouth. Breathe slowly and rhythmically. Count your breaths until you reach ten. Feel calmer? Most people do. *Four-seven-eight* breathing is another way to bring the arousal level down. Breathe in for four counts, hold for seven counts, then breathe out for eight counts. There are also many free smartphone apps and smartwatch features that offer visual imagery to guide your breathing. The better able you are to use strategies to calm yourself, the easier it will be to teach them to your child, too.

- Particularly with young children, soothing is most often an interactive process. When things go well, parents of infants learn what helps their child to calm down. For some it's a soft tune or a gentle dance in the arms of an adult. Some kids respond best to a gentle hug, while others are irritated by touch. Dysregulated kids often need a regulation partner well past their early years. Find what works for your child and do it together. ("Hey, buddy. Let's go outside and look for lightning bugs." "Breathe with me. Let's go for ten deep breaths.")

- At a quiet time, help your child to come up with a list of strategies for self-calming. Here are just a few of the ones that have helped children we've worked with: retreating to a dark, quiet place (a long, fabric play tunnel, free-standing tent, or a makeshift fort made with a sheet and some chairs), a warm bath, a long shower, headphones and a curated playlist, cuddling with a beloved dog or cat, reading, reading with a parent, walking around the block. Prompt your child to choose a strategy, as needed.

- Getting outdoors to look at the trees or to take a short walk is a calming activity that works for many. When it's possible, aim for walking in a park or on a tree-lined street rather than in a built-up, urban area. Nature is a proven strategy for calming (and for restoring executive functioning).

- Exercise is another proven strategy that suits many kids and teens (and adults). Some folks rely on a hard run to help themselves calm down. One child we knew balked at breathing exercises and instead ran up and down the steps of her three-story home when she was upset.

- Allow access to strategies that work, even though they might not make sense to others. One child we heard about found comfort near the warmth and the rhythmic sound of the clothes dryer in her laundry room. In the classroom, design a small space that can serve as a calm-down corner. In one school where the space was unusually tight, the teacher allowed a young, dysregulated student to crawl under his desk with a book when he was feeling out of control.

- For better emotional regulation over the long haul, try introducing activities or training that teach mindfulness. Mindfulness is the ability to observe one's own feelings and sensations without judgment or external action. Be aware that traditional mindfulness approaches do not work for everyone. Adaptations may be needed to engage those with ADHD so that they can benefit from mindfulness training. When it goes well, mindfulness training improves self-regulation. Learning mindfulness teaches us to bring awareness to our internal experience and to momentarily detach from the flow of the world around us. There are many mindfulness exercises readily available online. Additionally, yoga, tai chi, and meditation classes all promote mindfulness.

2. Teach emotional literacy, the ability to identify and label the full variety of feelings.
    - Be a mirror for what you see.
        - "Whoa! That's an angry looking face. What happened?" "I saw you crumple up your paper. You must be really frustrated with that

drawing!" "You look ready to do a happy
dance! What's making you so happy-wiggly?"

o   When you reflect your child's feelings back to
them, try to match the intensity too. You don't
want to scream and shout just because your
child does but do give your words some oomph
so that they resonate with the experience. If
you say "You seem mad" in a sweet voice, then
"mad" feels totally disconnected from the internal experience of anger.

● Model that all feelings are acceptable, though not
all behaviors are okay. We sometimes fall into the
trap of rejecting our kids' feelings because they
make us uncomfortable or because we take them
personally. For example, dysregulated kids often
shout things like, "You're a terrible mom. I hate
you!" In response, we might say, "After all I've done
for you, you have no right to be angry!" Instead,
re-focus yourself and your child on the feeling
and the source of the problem. "I get it that you're
upset because I said that you can't go to Sam's
house now. I need you to stop shouting and then
we can talk about a better time to go."

● Simple books that label feelings and offer brief
examples of emotionally laden situations are particularly helpful for young children. They can serve
as a good jumping-off point for conversation. "Tell
me something that makes you feel worried/happy/
upset/angry?" For an interesting and creative
take on talking about feelings that also introduces
mindfulness, try the book *Invisible Things* (Pizza and
Miller 2023). It's just quirky enough that kids who
say that they're too old for picture books might
enjoy it.

● Feelings posters are another good tool to teach
vocabulary for emotions. They show photos of
facial expressions paired with the label for the emotion shown. Hang one in your child's bedroom and
use it as a conversation starter.

- Talk about your own emotions. "I'm having a lousy day today. I don't agree with some things going on at work, and I didn't sleep well last night. I'm angry and I'm tired. This is just not a good day." "I'm really disappointed because I planned to go out to lunch with some friends, but now they're all backing out. I was looking forward to it, and now I'm really bummed."

- Talk about the emotions of others. "She sounded angry! Does she usually yell like that?" "Paul was so quiet today, and he looked a little sad."

- When your child is silent, you can use your own experience to help them put the emotions into words. For example, "I heard what Jeremy said to you. If someone said that to me, I think I would be really sad and maybe mad, too. How are you doing?" "Wow! You put so much work into that project! I would be really frustrated if I did all that work, and my project wasn't chosen for the science fair." It is okay if your child says nothing in response. You are still teaching that it's helpful to label feelings and you are providing words that they can use in the future.

Strategies to Help Children and Teens Who Need a Little Extra Support to Manage Their Feelings

1. Use proactive strategies to build positive behaviors.
   - Set up clear rules and expectations regarding behavior, focusing on what you want them to do rather than what not to do. ("Use words when upset.") Post a list. Be generous with your praise when your child demonstrates any of these behaviors.
   - Create a systematic behavior management system that identifies goal behaviors in very specific and measurable terms. For example, "Start homework at 4:00." "Set table for dinner by 5:50 pm." "Play

quietly during sister's nap time." "Use gentle hands with brother." Track daily success. Offer a menu of rewards for points earned for each goal. (For step-by-step guidelines for building a good behavior management system, see Barkley and Benton 2013.)

- Plan ahead for possible trouble spots.

  o Preview the situation and be clear about your expectations. "We're leaving soon to go visit with Grandma. I expect you to stay right next to me while we walk up to Grandma's apartment. We will each say hello to Grandma, and we'll see how she is feeling today. Then you can take out your drawing things and your snack, and you can sit at the kitchen table while I help Grandma with a few things around the apartment. We will probably be there for an hour and a half. No fussing or asking how much longer. If you can follow all the rules, then we can stop and get an ice cream cone on the way home. Got it? Four rules: Stay with me. Greet Grandma. Draw. No fussing." "Mallory, this dance recital is going to be all about your sister. I know that the performances can run long, but I expect you to sit with us for the whole time. You can listen to your own music if you use your earbuds, so you don't disturb anybody."

  o Change the nature of the task. For example, give the child a specific task to help with transitions. "Jack, I'd like you to stand next to me by the door at the end of recess. Your job will be to hold the bin to collect all the outdoor play equipment as everyone heads inside."

2. Intervene before the problem gets overwhelming.

- Learn the signs of escalating arousal levels in your child and initiate calming strategies. We all have tells that show we're having trouble managing our emotions. For some, it's a tone of voice. For others, it's a facial expression or the hissing sound we make as we harshly blow air out through billowed cheeks.

We may feel hot or notice our hearts racing. What are your tells? What are your child's?

- At a calm time, teach your child about their tells. ("Jackie, when you were upset today, I noticed that your voice changed to a whisper and you scrunched up your forehead. Did you notice? Maybe when that happens it's a good time to find a quiet spot to calm yourself down.")

- Help your child to put their feelings into context by linking them to the trigger. ("You seemed to get upset when I said it was time to clean your room. How can I help?")

- Help your child to think flexibly about difficult situations.

  - Make suggestions if your child is unable to come up with ideas. ("I know that your brother can be a pain when he gets into your stuff. I'm sorry that he ruined your Lego boat, and I'll deal with him. Still, we both know that it's going to happen again if we don't change some things. What could we do to protect your Lego creations? Here's one idea. Maybe we could get a big tray that you could build on. Then it would be easy to move your building without breaking it, and we could put the tray up on top of your bookcase before you leave your room.")

  - Accept all suggestions but set limits on the behaviors. ("That's true. You could hit him. What would happen if you do that? You would end up being the one who gets in trouble. So, what are some other ideas?")

- For a straightforward model, follow our five-step plan when your child seems at risk of losing control.

  - Give words to the child's feelings. ("You seem really upset/angry/worried.")

- o Ask brief questions to understand, and then listen. ("What's going on? What happened?")
- o Offer understanding and put the feelings into context. ("Yeah. I don't like it when people tell me what to do either.")
- o Set a clear limit. Don't use a lot of words here. ("But sometimes, there are rules to follow. And in our house, electronics go off at 8:00.")
- o FYI: You can negotiate if the child makes a reasonable request. ("Okay. Maybe we can change the cut-off time to 8:30 now that you're older. I'll think about it and get back to you tomorrow.")

Strategies to Help Children and Teens Who Need a Lot More Support to Manage Their Feelings and to Recover Once They Lose Control

1. Introduce strategies that help children to monitor their feelings and to put them into perspective. There are good resources that offer systems for teaching children and teens to monitor their arousal level. These can be used at home or in a classroom. In fact, many schools are already familiar with these systems.
   - "The Incredible Five Point Scale" offers guidelines and visual supports to teach kids about self-regulation. The five-point scale can be adapted to a variety of situations at home and at school and can be individualized for different kids. (Buron and Curtis 2021)
   - "Zones of Regulation" is designed to help children learn to recognize their own feelings, assess their level of arousal, and adjust their arousal to what's needed for the situation. (Kuypers 2011)
2. Give children time and space to process their feelings. (Credit goes to the Child Welfare Training Institute Publication 2007 for some of these suggestions.)

- If your child's emotional outburst is on the less intense end of the spectrum, you will notice that they are able to respond to your nonjudgmental observation about their feelings. While your child may need to vent, their actions are non-threatening.

  o Be firm but gentle as you work your way through the five-step model we've included in the previous section.

  o Help your child to think about their current behavior, their choices, and consequences.

- When your child's meltdown is more intense, you will need to allow more time for their arousal level to diminish. A full-on, intense fight-or-flight episode triggers a complex cascade of changes in the body. During this time, the body is primed for action rather than reflection.

  o Back away to give your child physical space. Focus on using a calm voice and helping your child to access their ability to reason. Set expectations and limits. Offer choices. Wait quietly.

  o Maintain a restful and soothing environment.

- Help your child to make restitution by doing something for the person or people hurt by the behavior. This helps to teach the connection between behavior and consequences, creates the opportunity for positive feedback, and offers hope. ("Jamie, when you were so upset with your brother, I lost the time that I was going to use to make that special cake that Grandma likes. What do you think you could do to make that up? Maybe you could help me to make the cake after dinner, and then it will still be done before she gets here tomorrow.")

If your child continues to be dysregulated despite these strategies or if there are frequent episodes of threatening or dangerous behavior, then it is time to seek the help of a mental health clinician or behavioral specialist. These professionals can help you to assess the factors that can lead a child to be dysregulated, create a plan for how to help, and design a crisis plan, if needed.

Seek out specific information on treatment for kids with significant physical aggression. (For example, see the Child Welfare Training Institute Publication 2007 and McDonnell 2019.)

If the problem situations extend to the school environment, then you can request a meeting to consider the need for a formal plan to help with the behavior. (There is more information about formal school plans in Chapter 6: Assessment). If your child has an Individualized Education Plan (I.E.P.), then a Functional Behavioral Assessment (F.B.A.) is federally mandated if the I.E.P. team determines that a student's behavior interferes their own learning or the learning of others and the team needs more information to provide appropriate educational programming. The team will use the information gathered from the F.B.A. to develop a Behavioral Intervention Plan, or B.I.P. While most often provided for those who have I.E.P.s, an F.B.A. and a B.I.P. can be completed for students who are not on a formal plan.

Case Study: Putting It All Together

Samuel is a six-year-old boy with ADHD whose exuberant smile and enthusiastic interest in the world charm most adults. He has the good fortune of having parents whose energetic style fits their son well. They cherish his wild moments and enjoy his high energy. Nonetheless, they became concerned about his frequent tantrums when he did not get his way. At the suggestion of his pediatrician, Samuel's parents sought a consultation with a psychologist.

From the very first session, Samuel demonstrated his tendency to lose control when faced with limits. He asked his mother repeatedly for another snack after she told him that he could pick just one from the basket in the office. When his mother continued to deny his request, Samuel whined and cried. In the waiting room, he took out more and more toys, playing with each one for just a few minutes. Samuel ignored his father's directions to put some of the toys away. In fact, the more his dad pressed, the more boisterous and less organized his play became. In response, Samuel's father explained the importance of cleaning up after himself, of listening to his parents and generally being "good." When Samuel continued to take out toys, Samuel's father seemed increasingly agitated and became loud and stern.

Samuel's parents and the psychologist collaborated to create a four-step plan to help Samuel develop better emotional regulation. First, they learned and practiced some simple calm-down strategies. They learned these in the psychologist's office, and everyone participated, including Samuel's favorite stuffed animal. Second, they read kids' books about emotions with Samuel, and they made a point of using naturally occurring situations to briefly talk about their own and others' feelings. They also learned to respond to whining and tantrums by first labeling Samuel's feelings and then re-stating expectations in a firm but gentle tone using a minimum of words. Finally, they created a simple behavior plan that laid out family rules and incorporated small rewards for successfully performing the target behaviors.

It took only two months for Samuel's behavior to turn around. His parents knew that they were on the right track when Samuel started to respond to limits with words like, "It makes me so mad when you say that!" His tantrums were less frequent, and he often complied with limits without making a fuss. It was a short course of treatment because Samuel's issues were relatively mild, and his parents were consistent in their efforts.

On the other hand, Max's dysregulated behavior is more intense and longstanding. At 13 years of age, he still has emotional meltdowns at home and at school. Max often complains that he is too hot or too hungry to concentrate. He becomes upset when his parents ask him to do something that he considers to be a waste of time, like doing homework or cleaning his room. At school, he sometimes challenges his teacher when asked to do an assignment or when things don't go according to his expectations. Max's meltdowns at school are less frequent than at home but can be more problematic because they are upsetting to some of the other students and raise safety issues. In the past, Max has thrown his notebook and stormed out of the classroom in frustration on a few occasions.

Max's behavior, while still difficult at times, has improved over the years. His parents have learned that he needs more preparation and more consistent routines than their two other children. They understand his sensory and emotional triggers, and they have learned what helps Max to calm himself. At home, when Max is upset and losing control, they initiate a preset series of steps. Using simple language, they label his feelings, put them in context by stating what likely led to being upset, and then suggest that he draw quietly in his room or find something to do in the backyard for a while. His parents have also learned to take breaks for themselves when they need it. While they used to stay on him when Max was having a meltdown, his parents instead direct him toward calming activities and then give him time to regain control. Max and his parents also developed a list of preferred activities that motivate him to stay on track. He earns points toward his favorite activities for staying in control and for meeting other behavioral goals.

Over time, Max has learned to take a break when he notices his own signs that he's losing it. He sometimes has loud and angry outbursts, but these are much less frequent, and he recovers more quickly. Importantly, Max can often independently calm himself now.

The course of Max's progress at school has been a bit rockier. He is aware that the other kids keep their distance, so he has an added level of emotion caused by embarrassment and by his anger at being left out of many social activities. His teachers are sometimes frightened by Max's strong feelings, and they understandably worry for the safety of the other students. At times, this leads some of the school staff to try to exert control in heavy-handed ways.

Max has an individualized education plan (I.E.P.) at school that includes meetings with the school psychologist, specific accommodations for when he is at risk of losing control, and consultation for the teachers. Max's I.E.P. has changed over time to reflect his progress with emotional and behavioral regulation. When Max was younger, the school psychologist was often called to the classroom when Max became upset. While the teacher ensured that the other students were safe, the psychologist went through the same steps that worked for Max at home. As soon as he was able, they went back to her office while he recovered. As Max's behavior and self-awareness improved, the school team created a new plan for what to do when he started to become upset in the classroom. Max was allowed to move to a separate space in the room or to give the teacher a "quick exit pass" if he needed to go to the psychologist's office to calm himself. The plan was not foolproof, and Max's hardest times occurred in the year that he had a teacher who did not really "get" him. He still has difficulty, at times, when there is a substitute teacher who does not know him well.

The intensity and pervasiveness of Max's dysregulation are such that his progress is occurring slowly and over the years. However, all members of his home and school team are quick to point out how much Max has matured. Max, too, is proud of the progress.

Transitioning from Short-Term to Long-Term Goals

Like all areas of development associated with executive functioning, we start by providing external supports and build awareness that leads to independent self-regulation over time. In the initial stages of helping dysregulated children, adults serve as "regulation partners." At the same time, we teach the basic skills of self-calming and labeling emotions. As children and teens make progress in their ability to manage their emotions with our help, we explicitly teach them to recognize their own signs that they are at risk of losing control. In time, they will learn to deliberately interrupt the rising tide of their own escalating arousal and to respond in ways that allow them to successfully manage the ups and downs of life.

Sometimes these changes take longer than we would wish. Since strong feelings interfere with our ability to use our thinking brains, learning to manage emotions can be a slow process. For parents, it requires perseverance and, perhaps, a leap of faith to trust the process that leads to improvements. The hidden benefit is that helping our children and teens with emotional regulation involves getting better at managing our own emotional reactions, too!

Educate Others and Advocate for Your Child

Issues with emotional regulation seem to generate more concern in families than any other problem related to executive functioning. The disruption to family life and the worries for the child's future can lead to angst and urgency. It's important to know that we have seen real and significant changes in kids' emotional regulation when they experience the magical combination of ingredients: understanding, informed intervention, and time to mature.

Often adults get stuck thinking of dysregulation in narrow ways, such as "It's just bad behavior." When the issue is defined in this way, then the interventions tend to be similarly narrow. Rules and limits are important, but they are not all that is needed.

Help others to consider the various factors that might contribute to your child's delays in the development of good emotional regulation. What executive functioning delays might be a factor? Are there difficulties managing physiological arousal or delays in emotional literacy that need intervention? How can school staff and other adults help your child to build these skills?

Classroom teachers must maintain order and ensure that one child's behavior does not repeatedly interfere with the learning or safety of other students. Teachers may fall back on a punitive approach to your child's missteps when they worry about the effect of one child's behavior on the overall well-being of the class. If this is the case, consider asking for help from the school psychologist or a school-based behavioral specialist.

Remember, too, that not all adults are good at maintaining calm in the presence of dysregulated students. Be open and clear about ways you are working on this at home, and perhaps that will encourage others in your child's life to do so, too.

If your child's issues persist, it may be time to initiate an assessment of their behavior at school and consider the need for an Individualized Education Plan (I.E.P.) if your child does not have one already.

Final Thoughts

When our kids struggle with emotional regulation, it is disruptive to our own lives as well as theirs. As parents, we must reflect on our own emotional regulation to consider whether we are responding intentionally and thoughtfully when we interact with our children. If an honest self-appraisal leads you to feel that this is a challenge for you as well as your child, we hope that you will proceed without self-blame or shame. Instead, adopt the non-judgmental approach to change so well voiced by proponents of a type of therapy called dialectical behavioral therapy (Linehan 2015). To paraphrase: "You are doing the best you can right now. And we know you can do better."

Learning to calm yourself and to find moments when you can step back from the challenges brings renewal into your own life and helps you to bring your best self to all the roles that matter to you. In turn, that will benefit your child, too.

18

Concluding Thoughts

Raising a child with executive weaknesses requires patience, flex-ibility, humor, and creativity. Out of sync with developmental expectations, your child faces situations wherein routine demands put them at risk for inconsistent performance at best, or failure at worst. We hope the knowledge you have acquired from this book about the nature of executive skills and possible interventions gives direction to your efforts to help your child succeed.

The Zen of Intervention Planning

The goal of interventions is to help our children extend their abilities, one small step at a time, by working right at the edge of what they can do now and helping them move on to the next step. This requires an ongoing evaluation process as maturation occurs, as learning and experience move our children forward, and as expecta-tions change.

So, we must continually reevaluate our own efforts. Are we doing too much? Are we doing enough? Do we need to experiment with dif-ferent ways of providing support?

Maintaining the delicate balance between support and skill build-ing is essential to promoting healthy development. If we only accom-modate executive weaknesses without attempting to strengthen them, we may be promoting dependency and helplessness. However, if we

DOI: 10.4324/9781003403517-20

expect our children to develop these skills without appropriate accommodations, it is unlikely that they will succeed. In the face of repeated inability to meet expectations, children get overwhelmed and become demoralized. So, we want to offer appropriate levels of support and accommodation.

However, just to make adults' jobs even more complex, we need to reiterate here that one of the most challenging aspects of raising a child with executive dysfunction is dealing with inconsistencies in performance. On some days, in some situations, on some tasks, your child may perform beautifully. However, even on a similar task, on a different day, your child may struggle. In our clinical work, we have developed an appreciation for how this variability confounds children and adults alike.

Now for some good news! As complex as this all sounds, this is a job that we have seen done well over and over again. Parents with whom we have worked have demonstrated remarkable grace and wisdom, even as they fly by the seat of their pants. It is our goal to ground you in specific knowledge to use as guideposts, so perhaps you are flying in a more determined direction.

However, there is no standard formula for parenting. Between the extremes of doing too much and not doing enough, you find lots of variability. It is essential to regularly test the waters by fading support and accommodations to see if your child has gained sufficient skills to manage tasks independently.

The "No Victims" Approach

We hope we have made it clear that kids who must operate in the world without the benefit of strong executive skills deserve our understanding and compassion. They got a bum deal on this one! However, it is the ability to accept and master one's own challenges in life that constitutes strong character. Understanding executive weaknesses provides an explanation for difficulties, not an excuse. By balancing support with skill building, we promote development in our children without giving them a free pass on expectations.

When we actively involve kids in determining what is getting in their way and thinking about how to get around their weaknesses, we promote an active, engaged approach to building success. We expect kids to get weary of the effort, at times, and we offer empathy as we listen to their inevitable frustration, anger, and sadness.

We also offer straightforward guidance, making it clear that they may have to work harder than other kids in their areas of weakness, because these particular skills do not come naturally to them like they do for some others. Parents and professionals must also help children identify and build on those things that *do* come naturally to them so that they can move forward with confidence and competence.

Building a Life

School is such an important focus of kids' lives and occupies such a large percentage of their time and efforts in the first two decades of life that adults sometimes lose perspective and focus exclusively on academic success. We do not mean to dismiss its importance in any way. At the same time, however, school does not constitute a whole life.

We do not want the child's cumulative grade-point average to be the sole measure of their success. We encourage you to think more broadly about what it means to be well adjusted and create a life. In this way, you encourage your child to have a more balanced view as well.

Kids must be supported in their strengths, whatever those are. Is your child interested in drama? An enthusiastic dog lover? A natural at baseball? Provide opportunities for expanding these interests and experiencing real pleasure in the world by helping your child do what they do best. A child who is very compassionate might be just the person to make sandwiches for the homeless shelter. A teen with great people skills might benefit from the skills and sense of competence they can build by working part-time at a local retail store.

Dr. Robert Brooks, a psychologist and author who has written about building resilience in children and adults with learning disabilities, describes the importance of helping people discover their *islands of competence*:

> Many of these children and adults seem to be drowning in an ocean of self-perceived inadequacy... If there is an ocean of inadequacy, then there must be islands of competence – areas that have been or have the potential to be sources of pride and accomplishment.
>
> He goes on to explain the potential that lives on these islands. "If we can find and reinforce these areas of strength, we can create a powerful 'ripple effect' in which children and adults

may be more willing to venture forth and confront situations that have been problematic."

(Brooks 2005)

Like Dr. Brooks, we believe that our children's best hope for the future may lie in the discovery of some strength that blossoms into an island of competence, and perhaps even becomes a continent of possibilities for personal satisfaction and job success. After all, people thrive when they build a life around their strengths. There are many different paths to success, even though this is sometimes hard to keep in perspective during the school years.

Who Can Help?

Teachers, sports coaches, and scout leaders all can have a role in helping your child develop better executive skills. Remember to pool all available informal resources. Whether or not the person has specific professional training, some folks have a marvelous intuitive sense of what a particular child needs in order to build competence and to be successful. However, in some cases, you may wish to seek the help of professionals.

Tutors can be very helpful for kids struggling to meet academic demands. When you enlist a tutor, seek one who uses the specific course content as an opportunity to work on the broader issues of task management, as well as working on the class material.

Executive functioning coaches specialize in helping people learn how to approach tasks and to meet well-defined goals.

Mental health professionals who specialize in working with children and families struggling with learning disabilities and ADHD can be an invaluable resource as well. They can counsel parents to help them understand and facilitate their child's development. At times, it can be helpful to have the therapist work individually with a child to help them understand their own strengths and weaknesses. Additionally, a mental health professional can help if your child is suffering from some of the secondary or co-occurring problems associated with executive issues, including frustration, anxiety, and depression.

A Field in Progress

The study of brain functioning, in general, and executive skills, specifically, is an active and exciting arena. Our understanding of both typical and atypical brain development is growing through basic research and advances in technology that allow scientists to watch the brain at work. Research approaches that combine data across global networks have opened new avenues for scientific advancement. In addition to these research advances, in the last decade there has been increased focus on the study of interventions, leading to a better understanding of how to help children and teens who are struggling.

Those of us who work directly with children with executive weaknesses in clinical settings benefit from an additional source of learning. On an almost daily basis, we hear from children, parents, and teachers about what works for them and what does not. We know that there is no "one size fits all" approach and that we need to consider each child's personality, environment, and cognitive profile in order to design the most effective interventions. We look forward to hearing from those of you who are on the front lines, and hope that you will contact us with your ideas so that we can learn from you.

May you find strength, good humor, grace, and joy in your parenting. We hope this book will help you in your efforts.

Appendix

Below are some examples of tests that tap various aspects of executive functioning in children and adolescents. Remember that no single test can stand alone as a complete measure of executive functioning skills. Assessment is most useful when different measures are used to look at executive skills in several ways and across multiple settings – for example, behaviors a parent observes, behaviors a teacher observes, and performance on formal test measures. So, an evaluator may choose one or more of these tests in combination with other measures. Keep in mind that the results of any tests of executive skills must be put into a meaningful context by looking at how your child performs in daily life and how your child performs in other areas of development (such as IQ, motor skills, and social–emotional functioning).

Parents sometimes ask how to prepare their child for assessment, whether they should practice certain skills or otherwise help their child "get ready." It's important to know that the interpretation of your child's performance on tests given during a psychoeducational assessment is based on the expectation that the test questions and the format of some types of testing tasks are unfamiliar. For this reason, practice or preparation can "muddy the waters" and invalidate the test results. The only preparation needed for assessment is a good night's sleep, a good breakfast, and encouragement to do their best.

Functional Assessments

These are tests that evaluators administer to children and adolescents during the assessment session to directly engage executive skills and the ability to manage attention. Some of the tests are narrow measures of one or a few related skills (e.g., verbal memory) and others are broad measures that look at many different skills.

- Behavioral Assessment of the Dysexecutive Syndrome for Children
- California Verbal Learning Test – Children's Version (C.V.L.T.-C.)
- California Verbal Learning Test – Third Edition (C.V.L.T.-III)
- Category Test (Halstead-Reitan)
- Children's Category Test
- Controlled Oral Word Association
- Das-Naglieri Cognitive Assessment System
- Delis-Kaplan Executive Function System (D.-K.E.F.S.)
- Naglieri Cognitive Assessment System – Second Edition (C.A.S.2)
- N.E.P.S.Y. Second Edition (N.E.P.S.Y.-II)
- Neuropsychological Assessment Battery
- Rey-Osterrieth Complex Figure Test
- Stroop Color and Word Test
- Tower of London D.X. 2nd Edition
- Test of Everyday Attention for Children – Second Edition (T.E.A.-Ch. 2)
- Trail Making Test (Halstead-Reitan)
- Wisconsin Card Sorting Test

Continuous Performance Tasks

These measures typically involve a period of sustained attention to a relatively simple task (e.g., tapping a button when a certain letter is presented on a screen or a sound is heard). They measure the ability to sustain focus at a consistent level over time, as well as other areas such as impulse control and response speed.

- Conners' Continuous Performance Test – 3rd Edition (Conners C.P.T.-3)
- Integrated Visual and Auditory Continuous Performance Test – 2 (I.V.A.-2)
- Test of Variables of Attention (T.O.V.A.)

Behavior Rating Scales

These measures provide an opportunity for individuals who observe a child or adolescent in different settings (e.g., at home, or at school) to describe some of the behaviors they have noted, and to what degree those behaviors are affecting the child or adolescent in that setting. Most scales have similar forms for parents and teachers, and some also have self-report forms to gather the child or adolescent's own observations.

- The Barkley Deficits in Executive Functioning Scale – Children and Adolescents
- Behavior Rating Inventory of Executive Function – Second Edition (B.R.I.E.F.-II)
- Behavior Assessment System for Children and Adolescents – Third Edition (B.A.S.C.-3)
- Brown A.D.D. Scales
- Conners 3rd Edition

Bibliography

Alfimova, M.V., Korovaitseva, G. I., Lezheiko, T.V., & Golimbet, V. E. (2012). Effect of BDNF Val66Met polymorphism on normal variability of executive functions. *Bulletin of Experimental Biology and Medicine, 152*(5), 606–609. https://doi.org/ 10.1007/s10517-012-1587-x

American Psychiatric Association. (2022). *Diagnostic and statistical manual of mental disorders* (5th ed., text rev.). https://doi.org/10.1176/appi.books .9780890425787

American Psychological Association. (2020, May 1). *Guidance on psychological tele-assessment during the COVID-19 crisis.* https://www.apaservices .org/practice/reimbursement/health-codes/testing/tele-assessment -covid-19

Anderson, P. (2002). Assessment and development of executive function during childhood. *Child Neuropsychology, 8*(2), 71–823.

Anderson, S. (2007). *Self-help skills for people with autism: A systematic teaching approach.* Woodbine House.

Anderson, V. (1998). Assessing executive functions in children: Biological, psychological, and developmental considerations. *Neuropsychological Rehabilitation, 8*(3), 319–349.

Barkley, R. A. (2005). *ADHD and the nature of self-control.* Guilford Press.

Barkley, R. A. (2006). *Attention-deficit hyperactivity disorder: A handbook for diagnosis and treatment* (3rd ed.). Guilford Press.

Barkley, R. A. (2012). *Executive functions: What they are, how they work, and why they evolved.* Guilford Press.

Barkley, R. A. (2020). *Taking charge of ADHD: The complete, authoritative guide for parents* (4th ed.). Guilford Press.

Barkley, R. A., & Benton, C. M. (2013). *Your defiant child: Eight steps to better behavior* (2nd ed.). Guilford Press.

Baron, I. S. (2004). *Neuropsychological evaluation of the child.* Oxford University Press.

Bashe, P. R., Kirby, B. L., Baron-Cohen, S., & Attwood, T. (2005). *The OASIS guide to Asperger syndrome: Advice, support, insight, and inspiration.* Random House.

Beauchaine, T. P. (2020, August). Parenting skills and behavior challenges in children with ADHD. *Attention Magazine*, 16–17.

Beauchaine, T. P., & Crowell, S. E. (2020). *The oxford handbook of emotion dysregulation.* Oxford University Press.

Best, J. R., & Miller, P. H. (2010). A developmental perspective on executive function. *Child Development, 81*(6), 1641–1660. https//:doi.org/10.1111/j.1467-8624.2010.01499.x

Biederman, J., Fried, R., Tarko, L., Surman, C., Spencer, T., Pope, A., Grossman, R., McDermott, K., Woodworth, K. Y., & Faraone, S. V. (2017). Memantine in the treatment of executive function deficits in adults with ADHD: A pilot-randomized double-blind controlled clinical trial. *Journal of Attention Disorders, 21*(4), 343–352. https//:doi.org/10.1177/1087054714538656

Biederman, J., Monuteaux, M. C., Doyle, A. E., Seidman, L. J., Wilens, T. E., Ferrero, F., Morgan, C. L., & Faraone, S. V. (2004). Impact of executive function deficits and attention-deficit/hyperactivity disorder (ADHD) on academic outcomes in children. *Journal of Consulting and Clinical Psychology, 72*(5), 757–766. https//doi: 10.1037/0022-006X.72.5.757

Bor, D., & Owen, A. M. (2007). A common prefrontal–parietal network for mnemonic and mathematical recoding strategies within working memory. *Cerebral Cortex, 17*(4), 778–786. https://doi.org/10.1093/cercor/bhk035

Breaux, R., Dvorsky, M. R., & Becker, S. P. (2021). ADHD in COVID-19: Risk, resilience, and the rapid transition to telehealth. *ADHD Report, 29*(2), 1–9.

Brooks, R. (2005). *The search for islands of competence: A metaphor of hope and strength.* http://www.drrobertbrooks.com/writings/articles/0506.html

Brown, T. E. (2013). *A new understanding of ADHD in children and adults: Executive function impairments.* Routledge.

Buron, K. D., & Curtis, M. (2021). *The incredible 5 point scale* (2nd ed., rev.). 5 Point Scale Publishing.

Channon, S., Pratt, P., & Robertson, M. M. (2003). Executive function, memory, and learning in Tourette's syndrome. *Neuropsychology, 17*(2), 247–254.

Child Welfare Training Institute, Institute for Public Sector Innovation Muskie School of Public Service, University of Southern Maine. (2007). *Parenting physically aggressive children and youth.* Participants Guide. http://depts.washington.edu/allcwe/sites/default/files/sites/default/files/caregiver/parentingpayguide.pdf

Cooper-Kahn, J. A., & Foster, M. (2013). *Boosting executive skills in the classroom: A practical guide for educators.* Jossey-Bass.

Cortés Pascual, A., Moyano, N., & Quílez-Robres, A. (2019). The relationship between executive functions and academic performance in primary education: Review and meta-analysis. *Frontiers in Psychology*. https://doi.org/10.3389/fpsyg.2019.01582

Cowan, N. (2014). Working memory underpins cognitive development, learning, and education. *Educational Psychology Review, 26*(2), 197–223. http://www.jstor.org/stable/43549792

Cragg, L., & Gilmore, C. (2014). Skills underlying mathematics: The role of executive function in the development of mathematics proficiency. *Trends in Neuroscience and Education, 3*(2), 63–68. https://doi.org/10.1016/j.tine.2013.12.001

Culhane-Shelburne, K., Chapieski, L., Hiscock, M., & Daniel Glaze, D. (2002). Executive functions in children with frontal and temporal lobe epilepsy. *Journal of the International Neuropsychological Society, 8*(5), 623–632.

Dawson, P., & Guare, R. (2018). *Executive skills in children and adolescents: A practical guide to assessment and intervention.* Guilford Press.

Denckla, M. B. (1989). Executive function, the overlap zone between attention deficit hyperactivity disorder and learning disabilities. *International Pediatrics, 4*(2), 155–160.

Denckla, M. B. (2007). Binding together the definitions of Attention-Deficit/Hyperactivity Disorder and learning disabilities. In L. Meltzer (Ed.), *Executive function in education: From theory to practice* (pp. 5–18). Guilford Press.

Denckla, M. B. (2019). *Understanding learning and related disabilities: Inconvenient brains.* Routledge.

Dendy, C. (2008, February). Understanding the link between executive functions and school success. *Attention Magazine,* 18–21.

Dendy, C. (2017). *Teenagers with ADD, ADHD and executive function deficits: A guide for parents and professionals* (3rd ed.). Woodbine House.

Di Santo, S., De Luca, V., Isaja, A., & Andreetta, S. (2020). Working memory training: Assessing the efficiency of mnemonic strategies. *Entropy, 22*(5), 577. https://doi.org/10.3390/e22050577

Dolan, A. (2014, February 4). *Procrastination: Strategies to get kids started.* http://ectutoring.c om/procrastination-strategies-get-kids-started

Doyle, C., Smeaton, A. F., Roche, R. A. P., & Boran, L. (2018, May 28). Inhibition and updating, but not switching, predict developmental dyslexia and individual variation in reading ability. *Frontiers in Psychology, 9.* https://doi.org/10.3389/fpsyg.2018.00795

Duff, C. T., & Sulla, E. M. (2015). Measuring executive function in the differential diagnosis of attention-deficit/hyperactivity disorder: Does it really tell us anything? *Applied Neuropsychology: Child, 4*(3), 188–196. https://doi.org/10.1080/21622965.2013.848329

Elosúa, M. R., Del Olmo, S., & Contreras, M. J. (2017). Differences in executive functioning in children with Attention Deficit and Hyperactivity Disorder. *Frontiers in Psychology, 8,* 976. https://doi.org/10.3389/fpsyg.2017.00976

Frender, G. (2004). *Learning to learn: Strengthening study skills and brain power* (Rev ed.). Incentive.

Frick, M. A., Darling, R. P., & Brocki, K. C. (2022). Can attachment predict core and comorbid symptoms of attention-deficit/hyperactivity disorder beyond executive functions and emotion regulation? *British Journal of Clinical Psychology, 61*(1), 93–111. https://doi.org/10.1111/bjc.12317

Gathercole, S. E., Dunning, D. L., Holmes, J., & Norris, D. (2019). Working memory training involves learning new skills. *Journal of Memory and Language, 105*, 19–42. https://doi.org/10.1016/j.jml.2018.10.003.

Giedd, J. N. (2004). Structural magnetic resonance imaging of the adolescent brain. *Annals of the New York Academy of Science, 1021*, 77–85.

Gioia, G. A., & Isquith, P. K. (2002). New perspectives on educating children with ADHD: Contributions of the executive functions. *Journal of Health Care Law and Policy, 5*, 124–163.

Gioia, G. A., Isquith, P. K., Guy, S. C., & Kenworthy, L. (2000). *Behavior rating inventory of executive function, professional manual*. Psychological Assessment Resources.

Gioia, G. A., Isquith, P. K., Kenworthy, L., & Barton, R. M. (2002). Profiles of everyday executive function in acquired and developmental disorders. *Child Neuropsychology, 8*(2), 121–137.

Gnanavel, S., Sharma, P., Kaushal, P., & Hussain, S. (2019). Attention deficit hyperactivity disorder and comorbidity: A review of literature. *World Journal of Clinical Cases, 7*(17), 2420–2426. https://doi.org/10.12998/wjcc.v7.i17.2420

Goldberg, D., & Zweibel, J. (2005). *The organized student: Teaching children the skills for success in school and beyond*. Simon & Schuster.

Goldberg, E. (2001). *The executive brain: Frontal lobes and the civilized mind*. Oxford University Press.

Greene, R. W. (2021). *The explosive child: A new approach for understanding and parenting easily frustrated, chronically inflexible children* (6th ed.). Harper.

Hale, L. K., Kirschen, G. W., LeBourgeois, M. K., Gradisar, M., Garrison, M. M., Montgomery-Downs, H., Kirschen, H., McHale, S. M., Chang, A. M., & Buxton, O. M. (2018). Youth screen media habits and sleep: Sleep-friendly recommendation for clinicians, educators and parents. *Child and Adolescent Clinics of North America, 27*(2), 229–245. https://doi.org/10.1016/j.chc.2017.11.014

Hasslinger, J., Jonsson, J., & Bolte, S. (2022). Immediate and sustained effects of neurofeedback and working memory training on cognitive functions in children and adolescents with ADHD: A multi-arm pragmatic randomized controlled trial. *Journal of Attention Disorders, 26*(11), 1492–1506.

Healy, J. (2004). *Your child's growing mind: Brain development and learning from birth to adolescence* (3rd ed.). Broadway Books.

Hill, E. L. (2004). Executive dysfunction in autism. *Trends in Cognitive Sciences, 8*(1), 26–32.

Kelley, M. L. (1990). *School-home notes: Promoting children's classroom success.* Guilford Press.

Klass, P., & Costello, E. (2003). *Quirky kids: Understanding and helping your child who doesn't fit in - when to worry and when not to worry.* Random House.

Kleinhans, N., Akshoomoff, N., & Delis, D. C. (2005). Executive functions in autism and Asperger's disorder: Flexibility, fluency, and inhibition. *Developmental Neuropsychology, 27*(3), 379–401.

Kuypers, L. (2011). *The zones of regulation.* Social Thinking Publishing.

Lester, B. M., & Lagasse, L. L. (2010). Children of addicted women. *Journal of Addictive Diseases, 29*(2), 259–276. https://doi.org/10.1080/10550881003684921

Lieberman, M. D., Eisenberger, N. I., Crockett, M. J., Tom, S. M., Pfeifer, J. H., & Way, B. M. (2007). Putting feelings into words: Affect labeling disrupts amygdala activity in response to affective stimuli. *Psychological Science, 18*(5), 421–428. https://doi.org/10.1111/j.1467-9280.2007.01916.x

Lieberman, M. D., Inagaki, T. K., Tabibnia, G., & Crockett, M. J. (2011). Subjective responses to emotional stimuli during labeling, reappraisal, and distraction. *Emotion, 11*(3), 468–480.

Linehan, M. (2015). *DBT skills training manual* (2nd ed.). Guilford Press.

Lyon, G. R., & Krasgenor, N. A. (Eds.). (1996). *Attention, memory, and executive function.* Paul H. Brookes Publishing.

Mahan, B. (2016). *5 ways to overcome the wall of awful.* https://www.adhdessentials.com/wp-content/uploads/5-Ways-to-Overcome-The-Wall-of-Awful.pdf

McDonnell, A. (2019). The reflective journey: A practitioner's guide to the low arousal approach. *Studio, 3.*

Meltzer, L. (Ed.). (2007). *Executive function in education: From theory to practice.* Guilford Press.

MTA Cooperative Group. (1999). A fourteen-month randomized clinical trial of treatment strategies for attention-deficit/hyperactivity disorder. *Archives of General Psychiatry, 56*(12), 1073–1086.

Murphy, L. (2020, May 15). Supporting high school student's executive function while teaching the writing process. *Landmark School Outreach Blog.* https://www.landmarkoutreach.org/blog-post/ef-and-writing/

Nadeau, K. G., Littman, E. B., & Quinn, P. O. (2000). *Understanding girls with AD/HD.* Advantage Books.

Naglieri, J. A., & Pickering, E. B. (2003). *Helping children learn: Intervention handouts for use in school and at home.* Paul H. Brookes Publishing.

Nigg, J. T. (2006). *What causes ADHD?: Understanding what goes wrong and why.* Guilford Press.

Nigg, J. T. (2017a). Annual research review: On the relations among self-regulation, self-control, executive functioning, effortful control, cognitive control, impulsivity, risk-taking, and inhibition for developmental psychopathology. *Journal of Child Psychology and Psychiatry, 58*(4), 361–383. https//:doi.org/10.1111/jcpp.12675

Nigg, J. T. (2017b). *Getting ahead of ADHD*. Guilford Press.

Pauli-Pott, U., Mann, C., & Becker, K. (2021). Do cognitive interventions for preschoolers improve executive functions and reduce ADHD and externalizing symptoms? A meta-analysis of randomized controlled trials. *European Child and Adolescent Psychiatry, 30*(10), 1503–1521. https://doi.org/10.1007/s00787-020-01627-z

Pavuluri, M. N., Schenkel, L. S., Aryal, S., Harral, E. M., Hill, S. K., Herbener, E. S., & Sweeney, J. A. (2006). Neurocognitive function in unmedicated manic and medicated euthymic pediatric bipolar patients. *American Journal of Psychiatry, 163*(2), 286–293.

Petrovic, P., & Castellanos, F. X. (2016). Top-down dysregulation: From ADHD to emotional instability. *Frontiers in Behavioral Neuroscience, 10.* https://doi.org/10.3389/fnbeh.2016.00070

Pizza, A., & Miller, S. (2023). *Invisible things*. Chronicle Books.

Pychyl, T. A., & Sirois, F. M. (2016). Procrastination, emotion regulation, and well-being. In F. M. Sirois & T. A. Pychyl (Eds.), *Procrastination, health, and well-being* (pp. 163–188). Elsevier Academic Press.

Quinn, P. O., & Stern, J. M. (2001). *Putting on the brakes: Young people's guide to understanding attention deficit hyperactivity disorder.* Magination Press.

Redick, T. S. (2019). The hype cycle of working memory training. *Current Directions in Psychological Science, 28*(5), 423–429. https://doi.org/10.1177/0963721419848668

Reiter, A., Tucha, O., & Lange, K. W. (2005). Executive functions in children with dyslexia. *Dyslexia, 11*(2), 116–131.

Rich, B. A., Schmajuk, M., Perez-Edgar, K. E., Fox, N. A., Pine, D. S., & Leibenluft, E. (2007). Different psychophysiological and behavioral responses elicited by frustration in pediatric bipolar disorder and severe mood dysregulation. *American Journal of Psychiatry, 164*(2), 309–317.

Roberts, B. A., Martel, M. M., & Nigg, J. T. (2017). Are there executive dysfunction subtypes within ADHD? *Journal of Attention Disorders, 21*(4), 284–293. https://doi.org/10.1177/1087054713510349

Rooney, K. (1990). *Independent strategies for efficient study.* J.R. Enterprises.

Rosenau, P. T., Openneer, T. J. C., Matthijssen, A. M., van de Loo-Neus, G. H. H., Buitelaar, J. K., van den Hoofdakker, B. J., Hoekstra, P. J., & Dietrich, A. (2021). Effects of methylphenidate on executive functioning in children and adolescents with ADHD after long-term use: A randomized, placebo-controlled discontinuation study. *Journal of Child Psychology and Psychiatry, 62*(12), 1444–1452. https://doi.org/10.1111/jcpp.13419

Shallice, T., Marzocchi, G. M., Coser, S., Del Savio, M., Meuter, R. F., & Rumiati, R. I. (2002). Executive function profile of children with attention deficit hyperactivity disorder. *Developmental Neuropsychology, 21*(1), 43–71. https://doi.org/ 10.1207/S15326942DN2101_3

Shaw, P., Stringaris, A., Nigg, J., & Leibenluft, E. (2014). Emotion dysregulation in attention deficit hyperactivity disorder. *American Journal of Psychiatry*, *171*(3), 276–293.

Shipstead, Z., Redick, T. S., & Engle, R. W. (2012). Is working memory training effective? *Psychological Bulletin*, *138*(4), 628–654. https://doi .org/ 10.1037/a0027473.

Sibley, M. H. (2017). *Parent-teen therapy for executive function deficits and ADHD: Building skills and motivation*. Guilford Press.

Sibley, M. H., Coxe, S. J., Zulauf-McCurdy, C., & Zhao, X. (2022). Mediators of psychosocial treatment for adolescent ADHD. *Journal of Consulting and Clinical Psychology*, *90*(7), 545–558. https://doi.org/10.1037/ ccp0000743

Siegel, D. J. (2001). *The developing mind: How relationships and the brain interact to shape who we are*. Guilford Press.

Silverman, S., & Weinfeld, R. (2007). *School success for kids with Asperger's syndrome: A practical guide for parents and teachers*. Prufrock Press.

Snyder, H. R., Miyake, A., & Hankin, B. L. (2015). Advancing understanding of executive function impairments and psychopathology: Bridging the gap between clinical and cognitive approaches. *Frontiers in Psychology*, *26*. https://doi.org/10.3389/fpsyg.2015.00328

Snyder, J. M. (2001). *AD/HD & driving: A guide for parents of teens with AD/ HD*. Whitefish Consultants.

Sparks, S. D. (2023, May 10). Dyscalculia and dyslexia: Reading disabilities offer insights for math support. *Education Week*. https://www.edweek .org/teaching-learning/dyscalculia-and-dyslexia-reading-disabilities -offer-insights-for-math-support/2023/05

Stevens, S. (1987). *Enabling disorganized students to succeed*. The Learning Development Network.

Stien, P. T., & Kendall, J. C. (2004). *Psychological trauma and the developing brain*. Haworth Press.

Strauch, B. (2003). *The primal teen: What the new discoveries about the teenage brain tell us about our kids*. Random House.

Suchy, Y. (2009). Executive functioning: Overview, assessment, and research issues for non-neuropsychologists. *Annals of Behavioral Medicine*, *37*(2), 106–116.

Tanguay, P. E., & Rourke, B. P. (2001). *Nonverbal learning disabilities at home: A parent's guide*. Jessica Kingsley Publishers.

Taylor, S. J., Barker, L. A., Heavey, L., & McHale, S. (2015). The longitudinal development of social and executive functions in late adolescence and early adulthood. *Frontiers in Behavioral Neuroscience*, *9*, Article 252.

Torre, J. B., & Lieberman, M. D. (2018). Putting feelings into words: Affect labeling as implicit emotion regulation. *Emotion Review*, *10*(2), 116–124. https://doi.org/10.1177/1754073917742706

van Stralen, J. P. M. (2020). A controlled trial of extended-release guanfacine and psychostimulants on executive function and ADHD. *Journal of Attention Disorder, 24*(2), 318–325. https://doi.org/10.1177/1087054717751197

Vink, M., Gladwin, T. E., Geeraets, S., Pas, P., Boss, D., Hofstee, M., Durston, S., & Vollebergh, W. (2020). Towards an integrated account of the development of self-regulation from a neurocognitive perspective: A framework for current and future longitudinal multi-modal investigations. *Developmental Cognitive Neuroscience, 45*. https://doi.org/0.1016/j.dcn.2020.100829

Ward, S., & Jacobsen, K. (2014, August). Staying a beat ahead. *Attention Magazine*, 12–15.

Webster-Stratton, C., Reid, J., & Beauchaine, T. P. (2013). One-year follow-up of combined parent and child intervention for young children with ADHD. *Journal of Clinical Child and Adolescent Psychology, 42*(2), 251–261. https://doi.org/ 10.1080/15374416.2012.723263

Weinfeld, R., Jeweler, S., Barnes-Robinson, L., & Shevitz, B. (2006). *Smart kids with learning difficulties: Overcoming obstacles and realizing potential.* Prufrock Press.

Willcutt, E. G., Chhabildas, N., Kinnear, M., DeFries, J. C., Olson, R. K., Leopold, D. R., Keenan, J. M., & Pennington, B. F. (2014). The internal and external validity of sluggish cognitive tempo and its relation with DSM-IV ADHD. *Journal of Abnormal Child Psychology, 42*(1), 21–35.

Williams, P. G., Suchy, Y., & Rau, H. K. (2009, April). Individual differences in executive functioning: Implications for stress regulation. *Annals of Behavioral Medicine, 37*(2), 126–140. https://doi.org/10.1007/s12160-009-9100-0

Winner, M. G. (2016). *Social thinking and me.* Think Social Publishing.

Wright, P. W. D., & Wright, P. D. (2023). *Wrightslaw: Special education law* (3rd ed.). Harbor House Law Press.

Zelazo, P. D., & Carlson, S. M. (2020). The neurodevelopment of executive function skills: Implications for academic achievement gaps. *Psychology and Neuroscience, 13*(3), 273–298. http://doi.org/10.1037/pne0000208

Zelazo, P. D., & Müeller, U. (2002). Executive function in typical and atypical development. In U. Goswami (Ed.), *Handbook of childhood cognitive development* (pp. 445–469). Blackwell Publishing.

Zink, N., Markett, S., & Lenartowicz, A. (2020, August 18). *A new era for executive function research: On the transition from centralized to distributed executive functioning.* https://doi.org/10.31234/osf.io/be7nm

Zondervan-Zwijnenburg, M. A. J., Richards, J. S., Kevenaar, S. T., Becht, A. I., Hoijtink, H. J. A., Oldehinkel, A. J., Branje, S., Meeus, W., & Boomsma, D. I. (2020). Robust longitudinal multi-cohort results: The development of self-control during adolescence. *Developmental Cognitive Neuroscience, 45*. https://doi.org/10.1016/j.dcn.2020.100817

Index

Printed in the United States
by Baker & Taylor Publisher Services